I0125988

Well-Intentioned Whiteness

GEOGRAPHIES OF JUSTICE AND SOCIAL TRANSFORMATION

SERIES EDITORS

Mathew Coleman, *Ohio State University*
Sapana Doshi, *University of California, Merced*

FOUNDING EDITOR

Nik Heynen, *University of Georgia*

ADVISORY BOARD

Deborah Cowen, *University of Toronto*
Zeynep Gambetti, *Boğaziçi University*
Geoff Mann, *Simon Fraser University*
James McCarthy, *Clark University*
Beverley Mullings, *Queen's University*
Harvey Neo, *Singapore University of Technology and Design*
Geraldine Pratt, *University of British Columbia*
Ananya Roy, *University of California, Los Angeles*
Michael Watts, *University of California, Berkeley*
Ruth Wilson Gilmore, *CUNY Graduate Center*
Jamie Winders, *Syracuse University*
Melissa W. Wright, *Pennsylvania State University*
Brenda S. A. Yeoh, *National University of Singapore*

Well-Intentioned Whiteness

GREEN URBAN DEVELOPMENT AND
BLACK RESISTANCE IN KANSAS CITY

CHHAYA KOLAVALLI

THE UNIVERSITY OF GEORGIA PRESS
Athens

© 2023 by the University of Georgia Press
Athens, Georgia 30602
www.ugapress.org
All rights reserved

Set in 10.25/13.5 Minion 3 Regular

Most University of Georgia Press titles are available from popular e-book vendors.

Printed digitally

Library of Congress Cataloging-in-Publication Data

Names: Kolavalli, Chhaya, author.
Title: Well-intentioned whiteness : green urban development and Black resistance
    in Kansas City / Chhaya Kolavalli.
Description: Athens : University of Georgia Press, [2023] | Series: Geographies of
    justice and social transformation | Includes bibliographical references and index.
Identifiers: LCCN 2022040117 (print) | LCCN 2022040118 (ebook) |
    ISBN 9780820364087 (hardback) | ISBN 9780820364094 (paperback) |
    ISBN 9780820364100 (epub) | ISBN 9780820364117 (pdf)
Subjects: LCSH: Sustainable urban development—Missouri—Kansas City. |
    Sustainable urban development—Kansas—Kansas City. | White people—Race
    identity—Missouri—Kansas City. | White people—Race identity—Kansas—
    Kansas City. | Green movement—Missouri—Kansas City. | Green movement—
    Kansas—Kansas City. | Minorities—Missouri—Kansas City. | Minorities—
    Kansas—Kansas City. | Marginality, Social—Missouri—Kansas City. |
    Marginality, Social—Kansas—Kansas City. | Social stratification—Missouri—
    Kansas City. | Social stratification—Kansas—Kansas City.
Classification: LCC HT243.U62 K365 2023 (print) | LCC HT243.U62 (ebook) |
    DDC 307.1/41609778411—dc23/eng/20230103
LC record available at https://lccn.loc.gov/2022040117
LC ebook record available at https://lccn.loc.gov/2022040118

CONTENTS

ACKNOWLEDGMENTS

I owe a lot of people thanks, for the luck and privilege I've experienced. To my advisors: Ann Kingsolver—I'm so grateful to have been able to learn from you; Don Stull—thank you for trying your best to teach your students how *not* to write like an academic (please don't send this book back to me marked up in red ink—I did my best!).

I'm grateful to the National Science Foundation, the University of Kentucky Women's Club, the Food Connection at the University of Kentucky, and the anthropology departments at both the University of Kentucky and the University of Kansas for giving me the resources and time to engage in this work. And to Sarah Lyon, who gave me the opportunity to learn alongside her and other writers at Human Organization, a position that made this work financially feasible. Thank you.

I owe a great deal to my parents: the most thoughtful, intelligent, and funny people I know. Thanks, Mom, for the discount archival services—you deserved more than the hourly rate you asked for. Thanks, Dad, for making sure I could afford toilet paper during fieldwork, since the NSF says that isn't an allowable expense. You both deserve more thanks than that, but this is what's going in print.

Heather, Jenna, Lauren, Dayton—for debating, discussing, and digesting all of these ideas with me over the past decade. I love learning with, and from, you. We should've just made a podcast—a sponsorship from HelloFresh would've been more lucrative. Jameson: thank you for showing up to that ridiculous pallet gardening class; it changed everything.

Finally, to the folks in Kansas City who spoke with me over the course of my work on this book: I'm so grateful you allowed me to listen and to share my perspective—I know it is one of many. Thank you for letting me into this conversation.

Well-Intentioned Whiteness

INTRODUCTION

Gardeners dread blight. Caused by a fungus, its first symptoms are found on foliage—large black splotches that cause leaves to wither and that eventually spreads to the plant's stem, which rots and collapses from the inside out. When blight affects a vegetable garden, the contaminated plants must be pulled out and burned and the soil must be covered with mulch or tarp and left for months until the blight spores are killed. "Blight" is also a common term within urban planning, ubiquitous among people engaged in green urban development and in discourse justifying urban food production. Urban food projects are often heralded as "fighting blight," eliminating urban eyesores, "beautifying" cities in the battle against blight. These projects are incentivized with tax breaks and through "blight elimination" programs. This discourse is not neutral or apolitical—it is deeply racialized. In Kansas City and other U.S. cities, neighborhoods most often referred to as "blighted" are primarily occupied by Black urban residents. Furthermore, while today "blight" is a technical term used by urban planners and financiers, its original use was deeply and transparently violent. "Blight" circulated within American discourse starting in the early twentieth century, as the Great Migration brought African Americans and other immigrants and people of color to northern cities (Herscher 2020), an influx that was portrayed as a direct threat to property values, to economic development, and to formerly white cities and neighborhoods (Herscher 2020). Today, "blight" still functions as a proxy for race—often, specifically, for the presence of African Americans—and the threat to white space in U.S. cities. This book explores one city's attempt to eradicate "blight" through green urban development and considers the question: what does it feel like to have your neighborhood called blighted? To be considered a blight on the urban landscape?

Kansas City's metropolitan region is home to an abundance of urban food projects. Over twenty farmers markets operate throughout the week in the metropolitan area, a food hub is currently under development in the industrial West Bottoms neighborhood, nearly every grade school includes a garden program, and over 150 urban orchards dot the city, planted by a nonprofit and tended by neighbors. Over three hundred community gardens are spread throughout Kansas City—operated not only by community members but also by grocery stores, hospitals, and corporate offices. And in the city's thriving farm-to-table dining scene, you will often find a kitchen garden incorporated into restaurant design. Restaurants prominently list the urban farmers they have sourced from, as a growing number of high-production small-scale urban farm business have developed in the city, aided by extremely low land prices and high rates of vacancy in Kansas City's urban core.

Most of these projects have sprung up since 2010. As the city government and nonprofit sector have begun heavily promoting and funding such initiatives as part of green urban development, urban food production has become a norm in discussions of the city's growth. Policy makers in Kansas City purport that these projects will address urban hunger, crime, unemployment, vacancy, and "blight" while simultaneously beautifying the urban core. They draw on significant federal funding streams such as EPA grants for the remediation of brownfields sites and federal stimulus dollars—funds which are further leveraged, locally, to secure support from myriad public and private stakeholders. Municipal promotion of green urban infrastructure is extensive. For example, Kansas City, Missouri, policy makers are currently developing their Municipal Farm project—nearly five hundred acres of city-owned urban property that will house several large-scale urban farm projects, including one aimed at reforming "at risk" Black and brown youth.

But even as policy makers are increasingly vocal about their support for urban food projects, there are many in Kansas City who voice concerns about this development agenda's potential to address serious urban problems. In fact, many low-income Kansas Citians of color worry that urban food projects will *exacerbate* problems like gentrification, racial inequality, and poverty. This tension is encapsulated in an argument that took place at a public forum on urban food projects between a wealthy white urban developer and a low-income Black home gardener, which is worth pausing on in some detail.

The May 2015 Grow & Tell forum in May was co-hosted by the City of Kansas City, Missouri, and the Missouri Department of Conservation, with the aim of helping formalize municipal support for urban food projects as a key mechanism of KC's green urbanism plans. The event invitation, which was sent to local urban growers, institutional food purchasers, community garden organizers, schoolyard garden practitioners, nonprofit leaders, former mayors, and representatives from philanthropic foundations, announced the forum as a manifestation of the city's intent to "promote access to healthy foods, productive use of surplus land, creation of local jobs and economic activity, and [to] help foster public/private efforts to capitalize on opportunities created by the current momentum in urban agriculture." Through presentations, breakout sessions, and networking, city officials hoped to strengthen their partnerships with supportive organizations and formalize the metro-wide approach to urban food production.

The argument took place during a roundtable discussion on regulatory and policy barriers in urban agriculture that was attended by twenty-five of the two hundred Grow & Tell guests. For the first thirty minutes, the white, upper-middle class, local food advocates in the room dominated the discussion, tossing back and forth ideas about how to better match growers to institutional markets. During this discussion, Neferet—a Black farmer who grows food on the East (understood by those in Kansas City as predominantly low income, African American) Side of the city—had been growing increasingly, visibly frustrated. Both she and the only other grower of color in the room, fidgeted, sighed, and shook their heads. Suddenly, as a local business mogul discussed strategies for large-scale land acquisition, Neferet interrupted the conversation and stated emphatically:

> But growing food is related to *greater issues* for me. Access to food is a *human right*. I live in 64127 [a Kansas City zip code]. That is the most desolate area in Kansas City. These [farming] projects you're talking about, the neighborhoods that do those projects get a lot of attention, because of that urban agriculture. They get a lot of resources. But 64127 has a lot of seniors and renters who live at poverty level. They don't want to, and can't, grow food like I do. So no one wants to fund projects in my particular area ... What do we do? I was living in 64127 since before the highway was built, and I remember when they stenciled those lines in and cut us out of the city. What are we supposed to do to get support?

In her interjection Neferet sought to bring up several questions important to her and to other East Side residents: How can we talk about urban food production and not discuss food as a human right? How can we discuss land access and urban farms in the city and not discuss the racialized policies such as highway placement and disinvestment that created vacant lots of land? Why do Kansas City neighborhoods with a high concentration of urban farms get more resources and praise than other neighborhoods? What can low-income communities do to receive the attention of local policy makers, when they lack the interest or means to engage in urban farming? Her interjection was followed by uncomfortable silence. Finally, when Danny—a white investor in a food hub project located in an area of Kansas City he refers to as blighted—spoke up, his response didn't engage with any of the points Neferet was trying to make:

> Agriculture can show people how to grow. It can give them hope. How are people [in your neighborhood] gonna know how or want to grow food if you don't show them? I remember when my neighborhood, Manheim, was a lot like your neighborhood. I was broke. I remember being worried that the repo man was gonna come for me that day. And one day I drove past an empty lot, and I stopped. I took a trowel and dug up weeds around this bench on that lot. And to this day that bench is clear. So even if you don't have control over your economy, or your social situation, you have control of your body and your time and your garden. You can do that.

Danny's response reframed Neferet's pressing concerns and questions about race, space, and justice, into matters of individualized action—if you're upset about the economic conditions in your neighborhood, he suggests, start a garden. Moreover, their interaction highlights the complex, divergent understandings of race, space, and history at play in Kansas City. Locally, discourse around "blight" is emblematic of these divergent understandings. It's a discourse that features frequently, carrying a number of different connotations. For example, the city's 2015 Urban Agriculture Zone Ordinance (Article VI) facilitated the creation of numerous urban food projects; it was crafted with the input of an advisory team made up of several prominent, white, local food advocates. The ordinance offers significant tax incentives to qualifying small businesses that grow produce or livestock on urban property designated as "blighted" (Missouri 2015). Blight is loosely defined in this ordinance as a space of "economic and social liability" (Missouri 2015)—colloquially, it is used as a way for white Kansas City residents to refer to Black neighborhoods. Policy makers involved in green infrastructure development use "blight" obliquely, using it to refer to any "undesirable" area that can be "eliminated" or turned into an "oasis." Conversely, for some Black East Side residents, the original racialized usage of the word is clear: blight references purposeful city disinvestment and violence toward Black lives. "Blight" references white Americans' concerns about the "economic disturbance" people of color will create in formerly all-white cities (Herscher 2020). An African American friend of mine once asserted, "*Blight* is a word of white supremacy." Thus, many people of color in KC use blight as a verb, to signify America's historical legacy of legalized racism, actualized in urban spaces through restrictive covenants and racially prejudicial zoning (Gordon 2008; Sugrue 1996). Neferet, in reference to preferential city government investment in a neighboring community over her own, said "we are being blighted . . . they are leaving us to blight."

While a lot has been written about green development and how it intersects with racialized urban inequality, this story has most often been told in numbers, statistics, and with a bird's-eye view. We know little about how the urban poor—those who are often most acutely affected by this development—feel about green urbanism. And yet, it's very important to understand the impacts of these development agendas. As our climate changes, it's likely that more leaders and policy makers will seek out models of sustainable urban growth. Green urban development—and within that sphere, urban food projects and the local food movement—is often commonly considered to be an inherently equitable model of development, by virtue of its "greenness"—meaning policy makers are less likely to investigate the racialized impacts of this type of investment.

An analysis of green urban development in Kansas City—a mid-size midwestern city—can tell us a lot. Much of the scholarship on green urbanism has focused on major cosmopolitan cities, where global financial interests often guide urban development. In contrast, nonprofits, philanthropic foundations, and other third-sector organizations—everyday people and actors—play a much more significant role in urban development in mid-size U.S. cities. In these cities (and especially in postindustrial cities), affordable land is abundant and often located near valuable downtown areas—meaning that speculative developers can sometimes more easily, and swiftly, change the city landscape. There is an urgent need to understand how green urbanism manifests in these contexts—the actors, scale, and implications are unique. By understanding this process, and engaging in conversation within our communities we can better meet the pressing opportunity, in the Midwest, to (re)develop our cities in *new* ways—ways that are racially equitable, green, and affordable.

This book offers a "peopled," contextualized story about how exactly green urban development—specifically, in this case, development primarily via promotion of urban food projects—can affect racially segregated U.S. cities. In Kansas City, green urban development is guided by a primarily white set of actors in local government, the third sector, and philanthropic organizations;

the policies they enact are informed by narratives of urban sustainability, agriculture, and history constructed solely by white voices. I draw on the narratives of low-income Black Kansas City residents to explore the impacts of this phenomenon and find that the promotion of urban food projects has furthered racialized inequality spatially, within food charity programming, and within the urban local food economy. In targeting "blight," urban policy makers disrupt and displace Black communities. Further, in this book I expand the historical lens we use to look at green urbanism, by examining the processes playing out in today's Kansas City in relation to global racial projects such as settler colonialism and urbicide. I argue that white structural privilege is spatialized through green urban development and illustrate how urban residents of color encounter, and contest, urban spaces built to exclude them.

In arguing the above, I contribute to interdisciplinary scholarship on whiteness, green urban development, and urban agriculture and food movements. Scholarship at the intersection of these topics has greatly expanded in recent years—it's well established, now, that urban agriculture is intertwined with gentrification, and that the local food movement can be unbearably white. But, even with increased public discussion of white privilege post-2020, I argue that the way whiteness operates—how it takes up space in our cities, our policy, and our institutions—is still an amorphous process. White privilege can either feel like an insidious personally held ideology, or a massive behemoth—such as in the criminal justice system—too institutionalized to disrupt. But whiteness takes up space—in our cities and institutions—in much more mundane ways, often unconsciously, and even through well-intentioned progressive policy like green urbanism.

I lay forth this rationale to explain the format of the book: *Well-Intentioned Whiteness* is an in-depth ethnographic case study of how white structural privilege is developed in green urban planning. Green urbanism involves creating more sustainable systems in all aspects of city life; I document how, in Kansas City, the white ideology upholding green urbanism understandings of food access, food aid, urban planning, and green business development. I go into minute detail in each of these sectors—naming and following individuals, organizations, and policy process—in order to make a clear case for *how* individually held ideology becomes policy and ultimately affects urban governance. As I noted earlier, whiteness is now oft-publicly discussed in the United States. This makes holistic, fine-grained analysis of how whiteness takes up space in our cities even more important. This book examines this process intimately through Kansas City's green urbanism, and in doing so, fleshes out our understandings of how racial inequities can be (re)created by everyday urban actors.

Urban Greening Initiatives as a Lens into
Racialized City Space and Policy

Kansas City's adoption of green urbanism, beginning around 2010, has not been an isolated process—a growing number of U.S. cities are incorporating green urban development initiatives into their planning repertoires. Green urbanism (alternatively called green urban development or infrastructure) is a multipurpose strategy that "promises to produce healthy ecosystems while mitigating urban woes from crime to depressed real estate markets" (Safransky 2014, 238); it can involve myriad different infrastructural projects, including (but not limited to) the creation of urban parks and greenspace, walk- and bike-ability improvements, the promotion of urban food production, and the use of biodiversity to address urban pollution. It would be incorrect, however, to think of green urban development as an ecological justice initiative—it is a growing, multibillion-dollar industry that capitalizes on urban decline (cf. Safransky 2017b; Goodling et al. 2015). Urban greenspace and walk-ability improvements can be marketed as indices of "quality of life" and "well-being"— valuable currency in the competition between cities for economic investment (cf. Florida 2005; Herrick 2008; Smart 2003; Sassen 2004). Cities use green urbanism as part of "competitive place marketing" strategies, which are used to attract young, white, upwardly mobile tech-industry millennials—the highly sought after "creative class" that is thought of, by many urban planners, as a major economic driver of city wealth (cf. Lloyd 2006; Wilson and Kiel 2008). While the implementation of green urbanism differs widely in various geographic contexts, in Kansas City, it is primarily enacted via the promotion of urban food production—in this case, urban farms and community gardens are key in the city's branding of itself as hip and environmentally friendly (see also Walker 2016; Alkon 2018b).

Urban food production as part of green urbanism is quite distinct from historical socioecological justice movements, such as urban environmentalism and the environmental justice movement, which might, at first, seem to be informed by similar ideologies of ecological stewardship. These movements, however, are rooted in, and led by, low-income activists of color, who call attention to and contest the disproportionate placement of environmental hazards in their communities (cf. Alkon et al. 2013; Gioielli 2015; Hamilton and Curran 2013). Similarly, activists within the food sovereignty and food justice movements view food production through the lens of racial equity and prioritize worker ownership of means of production (cf. Horst et al. 2017; Sbicca and Myers 2017; Alkon 2018). In contrast, urban food production as part of green urbanism both attracts the creative class and serves as a means for municipalities to pass responsibility for food and income assistance from the public domain on to the private sector and the poor themselves, a process known as neoliberal governance (cf. Ghose and Pettygrove 2014; 2018). For example, when cities promote community gardens as a way for the poor to supplement meager grocery budgets, they're encouraging low-income urban residents to conceive of poverty and health inequity as a result of their individual choices, rather than an outcome of economic policy (see also Poppendieck 1999; Bedore 2014; Guthman 2013). Danny's recommendation to Neferet—growing one's own garden instead of complaining about economic precarity and spatial inequality—is emblematic of this "self-subjectification" ideology, which individualizes and pathologies inherently racialized and structural problems.

Furthermore, these green urban improvements often play a role in gentrification—a racialized process that uniquely and acutely affects communities of color. Gentrification occurs when public agencies and private developers identify neighborhoods for (re)development. The development of new housing, the attraction of new business, and the in-migration of wealthier residents contributes to a raise in cost of living—extant neighborhood residents often can't afford increased rent and property taxes and are forced to move (cf. Alkon 2018b). In the process of "green gentrification" or "environmental gentrification," the creation of "green" goods drives up property values and physically displaces indigenous residents (Gould and Lewis 2013). This displacement can occur even when urban food projects are organized by local activists, with the participation and benefit of neighborhood residents explicitly in mind. For example, green amenities such as farmers markets and community gardens are often co-opted by rentiers and financiers to rebrand and market a neighborhood as higher value; this in turn allows these same actors to raise rents and generate surplus profit (cf. Alkon et al. 2020; Alkon and Cadji 2015; 2018; McClintock 2018a). Unsurprisingly, many scholars have argued that without focused public policy interventions, these sorts of environmental improvements tend to increase racial inequality (Gould and Lewis 2013; Curran and Hamilton 2018).

The enumerated issues highlight the inherently racialized ways that capital circulates in neoliberal U.S. cities. While green urbanism signals an embrace of progressive values such as environmentalism, it is nevertheless still imbricated in racialized processes of uneven development as urban elites profit from both environmental problems and their solutions (cf. Goodling et al 2015). Uneven development (i.e., the way profiteers ensure continued accumulation of capital by investing, and moving, money within a city) shapes cities differentially and without regard for its impact on urban residents; the process actively devalues the lives of some residents in order to create value in other residents and neighborhoods (cf. Smith 1996; Harvey 1989; McClintock et al 2018). More specifically, the devaluation of Black spaces is central to capital accumulation and the production of white space (Seamster and Purifoy 2020; Purifoy and Seamster 2020). The creation of "green" urban amenities depends just as much on these cycles of capital accumulation and devaluation as any other urban profit-making venture; actors involved in urban (re)development use green urbanism to generate profits from previously devalued, non–income generating inner-city neighborhoods (Pettygrove and Ghose 2018). In this context, it is unsurprising that many low-income urban residents of color see "green" improvements in their neighborhood (such as the construction of bike lanes) as a sign that they will soon be pushed out (cf. McClintock et al. 2018a).

Foodies and Third-Sector Urban Governance

Third-sector actors—those who work within nongovernmental or nonprofit organizations—increasingly play an important role in urban governance, and often, in green urban development. This is because neoliberal capitalism and resultant federal policy changes over the past fifty years have profoundly altered the relationship between the state and NGOs, drastically changed the structure of public welfare programs in the United States, and fundamentally transformed the governance structures of local municipalities (Lyon-Callo 2004; Kingsolver 2002; Maskovsky and Kingfisher 2001). Beginning in the 1970s, U.S. domestic neoliberalism increasingly dismantled New Deal social services such as welfare, public health care, and public education (Goode and Maskovsky 2001). Concurrently, policy makers have tended to redefine their purviews away from providing for citizens and toward "empowering" people to provide for themselves (Russell and Edgar 1998). This shift has been facilitated by the redirection of public revenues to private enterprises, such as third-sector organizations, whose contracts with the state for delivery of social services are not well monitored (Edgar and Russell 1998). In the process, as public policies move away from universal access and toward privatized forms of assistance, new urban policy mediators have been created.

Today, a diverse mixture of public and private actors—not just those in local government—are involved in designing and implementing urban policy. Globally, as well, governmental bodies are no longer solely responsible for shaping social policy—agencies such as the World Bank, IMF, multinational corporations, and third-sector organizations have been invested with increasing power to govern national and local communities (Okongqu and Mencher 2000; Wedel 2004; Stryker and Gonzalez 2014). Within neoliberal governance, we see the retreat of state-sponsored social support and the advance of what Ruben (2001, 435) terms the FIRE sector: finance, insurance, and real estate. As cities face shrinking tax bases, the FIRE sector ends up playing a strong role in shaping urban geography through measures such as empowerment zones, tax increment financing, and other privatization measures that benefit white, urban elites (Ruben 2001, 446). Marginalized citizens who fail to thrive in this economic system are blamed for personal failure and cultural deficiency, as the economic winners justify increasingly privatized governance structures with ideologies of neoliberal personal responsibility—the concept that individuals alone are responsible for their socioeconomic success.

In Kansas City, one third-sector group—local food movement advocates, "foodies"—holds an outsize level of involvement and influence in urban politics. Foodies, as an identity and a social movement, arose in the U.S. at the beginning of the twenty-first century as national discourse and prominent media personalities popularized and valorized the production and consumption of "local," "healthy" food (Kato 2013; McClintock 2017). Concurrently, a whole host of alternative agrifood movements such as the anti-GMO movement, the Slow Food Movement, and the concept of the hundred-mile diet all furthered national focus on our food and how it is grown. These movements often invoke a privileged sense of white agrarian "tradition" and encourage the development of preindustrial, artisan products. As Michael Pollan's *The Omnivore's Dilemma* was published in 2006, and Kingsolver, Hopp, and Kingsolver's *Animal, Vegetable, Miracle* in 2007—to name several influential food movement texts—local foodies embarked on a sort of institutionalization, tapping into popular and academic readings to shape the associated discourse. In contrast to global agrarian movements, such as the Food Sovereignty movement, the local food movement in the United States is largely made up of whites with economic privilege and focuses on market-based modes of food system change rather than larger scale critique of neoliberal privatization and demands for landed independence (Aistara 2011; Clendenning, Dressler, and Richards 2015).

As these politics of "good" artisanal food have risen to a national scale, activists and policy makers have adopted the discourse and promotion of local food within their own different social movement contexts—and have opened numerous new streams of funding to support urban food projects (Reynolds 2014; Miewald and McCann 2014). Food thus becomes not only a means of addressing urban disinvestment in U.S. cities within urban greening initiatives but also a way of narrating and enacting alternative visions for schoolchildren (Bonilla 2014), spreading political beliefs such as Black Nationalism (McCutcheon 2011), evangelizing (Bielo 2013), and addressing a number of other issues (cf. Sbicca 2018). The economic disinvestment affecting many postindustrial U.S. cities dovetails with these new funding streams to provide ample space for urban greening schemes and community food security programs. Accordingly, we often see green urban development via urban food projects take hold in postindustrial cities that have lost jobs, seen population declines, and have been affected by the housing crisis (Meenar 2012). For example, foodies are responsible for most urban food charity in Kansas City and have played significant roles in the development and implementation of green infrastructure projects—with the result that their input has been incorporated into many urban land use policies. Yet, as in the case of other third-sector entities now fulfilling state responsibilities, the ideologies and policy activities of Kansas City foodies are neither well understood nor monitored.

While NGO s or nonprofits are idealized as spaces in which "people help others for reasons other than profit or politics," in practice this is far from true: third-sector actors are neither disinterested nor apolitical (Fischer 1997, 442; Schuller 2012). Nonprofit actors play a huge role not just in the circulation of welfare capital in cities but also in shaping hegemonic discourse and social policy agendas concerning the urban poor—their ideologies are not abstracted from this process. For example, other scholars have highlighted that foodies often hold predominant beliefs in neoliberal ideologies of personal accountability. Programmatically, this manifests within foodie-led nonprofits in a focus on "empowerment"—such as farming entrepreneurship programs for "underprivileged" Black youth—and programs utilizing the cast-offs of capitalism's inefficiencies, such as farm gleaning programs that redistribute to the food insecure produce deemed by grocery stores and high-end consumers as aesthetically unacceptable. Programmatic foci such as these further the depoliticization of structural problems into technical issues that can be addressed via the capital-based mechanisms of nonprofit programming (cf. Ferguson 1990; Rosol 2012). This latter ignores bigger structural issues, for example, the mass incarceration system that destabilizes the home lives of many Black youth and the inadequate minimum wage and affordable housing crisis that leave many unable to afford fresh produce.

Racialized City Space, Differently Understood

Urban greening initiatives, such as those that foodies develop in Kansas City, do not operate on "clean slates"—race is inscribed geographically in the city and is perceived differently by individuals of varying race, class, and gender positionalities (Brown 2000; Wilson 2012; Kobayashi and Peake 2011; Melly 2013; Drake 2014; Finney 2014). The built environment of the city—streets, houses, neighborhoods—is a powerful reminder of how racially restrictive covenants, zoning, and prejudicial renting and loaning practices have created clear boundaries of race, class, and privilege (Gordon 2008; Sugrue 1996). In turn, this built environment shapes the ways racial and class identities are differently constructed and perceived—the spaces we live in are an important part of our embodied identities (cf. Zhang 2008; Notar 2012; Schein 2012). Thus, it's helpful to think of urban planning as a racial project—a way that "races" are given real-life significance as cities are organized to create and contain racial difference (Omi and Winant 1994; Wilson 2012).

The way we talk about urban space tends to valorize market-based development, which naturalizes racial inequality and unevenly developed U.S. cities—struggling urban neighborhoods are simply discussed as economic underperformers (Logan and Moloch 1987; Low 1996; Kennedy 2000; Caldeira 2005; Rothstein 2017). As noted earlier, "blight" is a development term that dates to the 1920s—at the time, it served as a means for urban planners to identify areas of the urban core (often communities of color) that threatened to drain taxpayers and decrease the value of downtown business centers (Gioielli 2015). Over the course of the 1930s and '40s, "blight" designations and their racialized differential valuations of life were institutionalized at the federal level—a Federal Housing Administration (FHA) publication from that time ranked "races and nationalities with respect to their beneficial effect upon land values" (cited in Herscher 2020). This policy language elides the fact that racialized discrimination has led to economic disparity and discursively links social dysfunction to communities of color (Smith 1996; Susser 1996; Maskovsky 2014; Harvey 2008). This sort of racialized policy—combined with the suburbanization of middle-class whites—has contributed to the decreased tax bases, racial segregation, and urban decline that we see in the urban cores of many U.S. cities (Davis 1986; Kingfisher 2002; Harvey 2008).

"Food deserts"—a key analytic in urban planning and discourse—are an apt example of how urban policy (re)enforces these racialized urban divides. The term food desert—a USDA classification that refers to areas where it is difficult to access "fresh" food—has been critiqued by activists and scholars for abstracting hunger from the political processes that cause it, for painting urban areas as desolate, and for contributing to perceptions of the urban poor as aberrant (cf. Sbicca 2012; Bradley and Galt 2014; Shannon 2014; Reese 2019). Additionally, this analytic might not be the most useful way to understand hunger and health: purely place-based approaches to understanding health and wellness do not accurately account for how individuals interact with their environments—for example, many urban shoppers strategically travel to the grocery stores that best meet their needs, regardless of which stores are most spatially convenient (Pettygrove and Ghose 2016; Kato 2013; Kolavalli 2019). The food desert analytic does, however, serve powerful functions for city planners interested in profit-making—racialized discourse that constructs inner-city communities of color as infrastructurally insufficient provides justification for redevelopment and capital extraction in these spaces (Pettygrove and Ghose 2018). It is imperative to closely examine who exactly benefits from spatial narratives and analytics such as "food desert" and "blight" that (re)enforce racialized power hierarchies (cf. Pettygrove and Ghose 2016; Anderson 1987; Simpson and Bagelman 2018).

Scholars in Black geographies have provided cogent explanations for the racialized nature of urban development—cities are organized to contain and compartmentalize racialized difference in order to support and maintain hegemonic white privilege (McKittrick 2006:xii; Rutland 2018; Shabazz 2015; McKittrick and Woods 2007; Woods 1998; Robinson 1983). McKittrick has argued that market-based models of urban planning—such as those that target economically underperforming, "blighted," space—are better seen as acts of "spatial colonization," in which profit is made from "erasure and objectification of subaltern subjectivities, stories, and lands" (McKittrick 2006, x). More explicitly, scholars argue that urban planning is inherently anti-Black (cf. Rutland 2018). This scholarship builds on the concept of "racial capitalism"—a framework that emphasizes how capitalism *requires* human difference and, in the process of exploiting it, enacts sociospatial, racialized violence (cf. Rutland 2018; McClintock 2018b; Pulido 2017; Robinson 1983). This hierarchical valuation—monetization—of some lives and communities is foundational to the way capital operates in U.S. cities and, more broadly, has been central to the colonial spatial imagination (cf. King 2016; 2018). Green urban development, similarly, exploits racialized urban devaluation for profit (cf. Pulido 2017; McClintock 2018b): neighborhoods that have been victims of environmental racism—those labeled food deserts, blighted, or "vacant"—are redeveloped in ways that allow white elites to profit, while original community members are displaced.

Throughout this book, I use the term "urbicide" to refer to this process of racialized devaluation in urban development. The theory has most often been used by scholars of the Mideast (cf. Crane 2017; Bayat 2012) in reference to the use of the city as an apparatus of warfare (cf. Abujidi 2014), or "deliberate violence against the urban environment" (Crane 2017, 188). I find, however, that it's a helpful way to look at the displacement of Black bodies, and the erasure of Black contributions, to Kansas City. Urbicide refers to the destruction, or removal, of homes, lives, and communities that urban elites want to control; it functions to render some human lives as waste (Berman 1987; Graham 2004; McKittrick 2011). I've adopted this theory because many Black East Side residents who shared their narratives for this book used it to describe urban (re) development to me—acts of disinvestment and displacement in their neighborhoods were discussed as acts of genocide and warfare, enacted by the city government, with the purpose of driving Black residents out. Thus, urbicide is useful as a lens here, bringing into focus how Black lives are often devalued in order to create city space that supports whiteness.

Conceptualizing Whiteness in Green Urban Development

By referencing "whiteness," I'm not referencing "race" or phenotypic difference. Rather, "whiteness" here refers to an institutionalized system of power that benefits whites in myriad ways—a system that is central to the development of the United States. Whiteness is an unacknowledged and pervasive system of laws, ideologies, and normative cultural expectations that enforce a racial hierarchy (Harrison 1995; Alexander 2012; Burton 2015; De Genova 2002); individual ideologies of those who benefit from white privilege are analyzed not as moments of individual bias but in service of understanding the narratives and images that support this systemic racism (Bush 2011, 3; Feagin 2009; Frankenberg 1993). The framework of "white public space," in particular, is useful for understanding how structural whiteness is created and enforced (cf. Brodkin et al. 2011; Price 1998). This framework posits that a key way hegemonic structural whiteness maintains power is through its refusal to be seen, which is accomplished through discourse denying the existence of racism, through color-blind language, and the refusal to acknowledge racialized inequality (Bonilla-Silva 2006; Mueller 2017). As one example, white nurses uphold white public space in their profession by ignoring clinical studies on Black health and focusing on individual rather than systemic causes of poor health (Page and Thomas 1994; see also Bush 2011).

Whiteness is implicated in city spaces in ways that regulate and patrol people of color (Davis 1990; Fiske 1998; Low 2009) in a variety of ways, such as surveillance, the increasing "militarization" of the city, and discriminatory housing practices. It "takes up space" through the creation of urban spaces that privilege Euro-Americans over nonwhites (Kobayashi and Peake 2000). It is implicated in our spatial laws and legal structure that valorize and reward private property and capital accumulation, while at the same time constraining racialized groups to urban space where homes cost more, appreciate less, and where zoning, investment practices, and policing control the exchange values of their property (cf. Lipsitz 2007). Some scholars have argued that discursive valorization of profit-driven urban renewal centers whiteness, positioning it as a savior in the midst of urban decay (cf. Stovall and Hill 2016). At the same time, Black-owned businesses, industries, urban histories, contributions, and even residencies themselves are often overlooked and disregarded in dominant city (re)development narratives (Safransky 2014; Stovall and Hill 2016).

Urban policy has long been used to create and enforce spatialized white privilege. For example, zoning in the United States has always been racially informed—these land use policies emerged in the first several decades of the twentieth century as a means of protecting property values and policing the spread of Black and immigrant communities into white neighborhoods (Silver 1997; Fischler 1998a; Fischler 1998b). In southern cities, zoning has historically been explicitly used as a means of enforcing racial segregation (Silver 1997). These policies that shape urban space both reflect and shape our societal ideologies (cf. Hirt 2014; Rutland 2018). Urban development agendas, such as zoning and red lining, impose what Hirt (2014, 3) calls a "moral geography" on our cities. The ubiquity of these agendas makes them invisible; through this invisibility they exercise the power to shape movement, ideology, and urban citizenship. While very often no longer explicitly racist, urban land use policy today nonetheless still reflects and enacts racial ideology—and race-based violence—in U.S. cities.

Much of the racialized nature of urban planning is rooted in dominant (whitened) ideology about what a "good" life looks like, and which urban citizens deserve to flourish (cf. Rutland 2018). Urban planners' (broadly conceived to include anyone involved in city [re]development) main agenda is to remake physical spaces in a way that protects and improves people's lives "according to period-specific conceptions of human flourishing" (Rutland 2018, 3). This agenda is built on a bedrock of assumptions about what a "good" life looks like and what constitutes as a hazard to human welfare; these ideas, of course, are inherently racialized. Often, a better life for some people (often white) is imagined and built at the expense and devaluation of others (often people of color) (cf. Rutland 2018).

None of this is new—during European colonization, slavery, Jim Crow, and now in the present political landscape, racial control in the United States has been predicated upon spatial control (Lipsitz 2007; Razack 2002; Kobayashi and Peake 2000). Thinking about green urban development through the lens of "settler colonialism" helps center this spatial violence. Through settler colonialism, best understood as a process rather than a singular event, colonizers work to eliminate or displace indigenous inhabitants and appropriate their land (cf. Pulido 2018; McClintock 2018b; Simpson and Bagelman 2018). The United States, Canada, and Australia are all examples of white settler colonial societies; in all three cases, settlers acted on the belief that lands could be legally deemed uninhabited if the people who lived there were "not Christian, not agricultural, not commercial, not 'sufficiently evolved,'" (Razack 2002, 3). In colonial Latin America, claims that Indians had "no activity of the soul," that they were "degraded men" not to be regarded as fellow humans, supported Spanish acquisition, exploitation, and murder of the land and its indigenous residents (Galeano 1971). Likewise, eighteenth-century Europeans who arrived in present-day Australia claimed *terra nullius*—nobody's land—as discursive and legal support for colonization, though an estimated seven hundred fifty thousand aboriginal inhabitants inhabited the continent, as their ancestors had for likely more than fifty thousand years (Connor 2005).

Current green development discourse in the United States draws on white settler ideology as well. Settler colonialism is an ecological project as much as it is a political one—key to settler colonialism has been colonizer assertion that "natives" are unfit ecological stewards of the land (cf. Simpson and Bagelman 2018; McClintock 2018b). This idea of *terra nullius* often shows up in discourse around "vacancy." In a number of postindustrial cities where "vacant" land is abundant, such as Kansas City, green urban development discourse encourages white urban migration by invoking frontier imagery, heralding the abundant land available for "urban pioneers" to claim (McClintock 2018b; Stoval and Hill 2016). In this context, it's important to problematize what we mean when we highlight "vacancy." In a critical assessment of urban agriculture in Lansing, Michigan, deLind (2014, 4) offers a few poignant questions to consider in light of "vacant" land being given by the Land Bank to a white-led urban farming venture:

What is an empty lot? Empty of what? As I watch and listen to Urbandale residents I am convinced that empty lots do not exist. The neighborhood is full of history and memory and story, all grounded in a real place. At farm markets, residents volunteer, "My father built that house." "We used to cut through the woods to swim in the Red Cedar." "I planted that tree when I was six." To dismiss these attachments . . . is to depoliticize whole communities . . . to dismiss much of what makes a neighborhood a neighborhood.

Like "blight," the concept of vacancy is often deeply racialized. As DeLind prompts, one might question of whom or of what is the land vacant? To whom is the "vacancy" a problem? Who stands to benefit from the proposed solution to that vacancy?

One outcome is that often, false narratives of urban emptiness and abandonment help facilitate white land grabs (cf. Safransky 2014). Alkon and Mc-Cullen (2011) argue that local food movement advocates perpetuate white settler discourse by valorizing a "white farm imaginary,"—a romanticized, spatial, agrarian narrative specific to whites—while ignoring "Native American displacement by white homesteaders, the enslavement of African Americans, the masses of underpaid Asian immigrants who worked California's first factory farms, and the mostly Mexican farm laborers who harvest the majority of food grown in the USA today" (945). These spatial imaginaries grant power and privilege to some and elide the significant contributions and histories of (racialized) others, while supporting whitened narratives of U.S. history and space (Slocum 2007; Alkon and Agyeman 2011; Kato 2013).

A growing number of scholars have explored the ways whiteness is embedded in urban food projects (cf. Hoover 2013; Slocum 2007). Researchers have explored the lack of diversity in food organization leadership (Alkon and Mares 2012; Lyson 2014), the white missionary zeal that animates many urban food projects in the United States (Guthman 2008; Guthman 2011a; Slocum 2007), the whiteness implicated and reproduced in much local food branding (Van Sant 2016), and how discourse surrounding urban food projects is often informed by whitened notions of food, diets, and health (Guthman 2012; Harper 2011; Paddock 2014). Others have theorized how the whiteness of urban food may be (re)created simply through the spatial clustering of white bodies (Slocum 2006; Slocum 2012; Ramirez 2014). In this book, I push us beyond understanding whiteness as creating discrete, uncomfortable moments at local food spaces. With detailed analysis of individual ideology, this case study demonstrates how the whiteness of the urban food movement can and has impacted green urban development ideology. More broadly, I explore green urbanism through the lens of white settler colonialism.

Kansas City

Bifurcated by a state line and encompassing both Kansas and Missouri, Kansas City houses over six hundred thousand residents: 55 percent white, 29 percent African American, and 19 percent Hispanic or Latino. It holds a 22 percent poverty rate, higher than the national average of 14.8 percent (U.S. Census Quick Facts 2015). Kansas City is comprised of both Kansas City, Kansas (KCK) on the west, and Kansas City, Missouri (KCMO), on the east, but for many reasons, it is more useful and appropriate to conceptualize the city as one complete metropolitan unit rather than as a divided entity. The city line has been utilized in industry "bidding wars," as Missouri and Kansas city governments tempt developers with tax incentives (Shortridge 2012, 7); however, among city residents, the state line is rarely spoken of as an important geographic landmark of the metropolitan area.

Like other large American cities, Kansas City has witnessed dramatic growth in income inequality and the sedimentation of city pockets experiencing persistent poverty and hunger (Berube 2014). Food insecurity across the metro area, at 12 percent, is slightly higher than the national average (Kumar et al. 2017). However, in Jackson County, Missouri (the East Side of Kansas City)—the vantage point from which *Well-Intentioned Whiteness* analyzes urban greening initiatives—residents experience some of the highest rates of poverty and food insecurity in the metro area. Almost 15 percent of the population in Jackson County is food insecure (Kumar et al. 2017). An overwhelming majority of Kansas City's green urban development projects are implemented on the East Side, as it experiences high rates of housing vacancy and provides ample vacant space for urban farming initiatives.

Kansas City serves as a uniquely appropriate site to study racialized urban space and green urban infrastructure initiatives. The city has, since 2010, received increasing amounts of public and private investment for its green urban infrastructure initiatives. These latter receive bipartisan support within local urban governments and in hegemonic discourse. But while funding for urban food production has grown via these green infrastructure initiatives, hunger has concurrently risen—particularly within metropolitan areas, such as the East Side of Kansas City, that receive the highest number of urban food projects (Gundersen et al., 2016a). This indicates that such projects may not be operating in the ways policy makers purport they do.

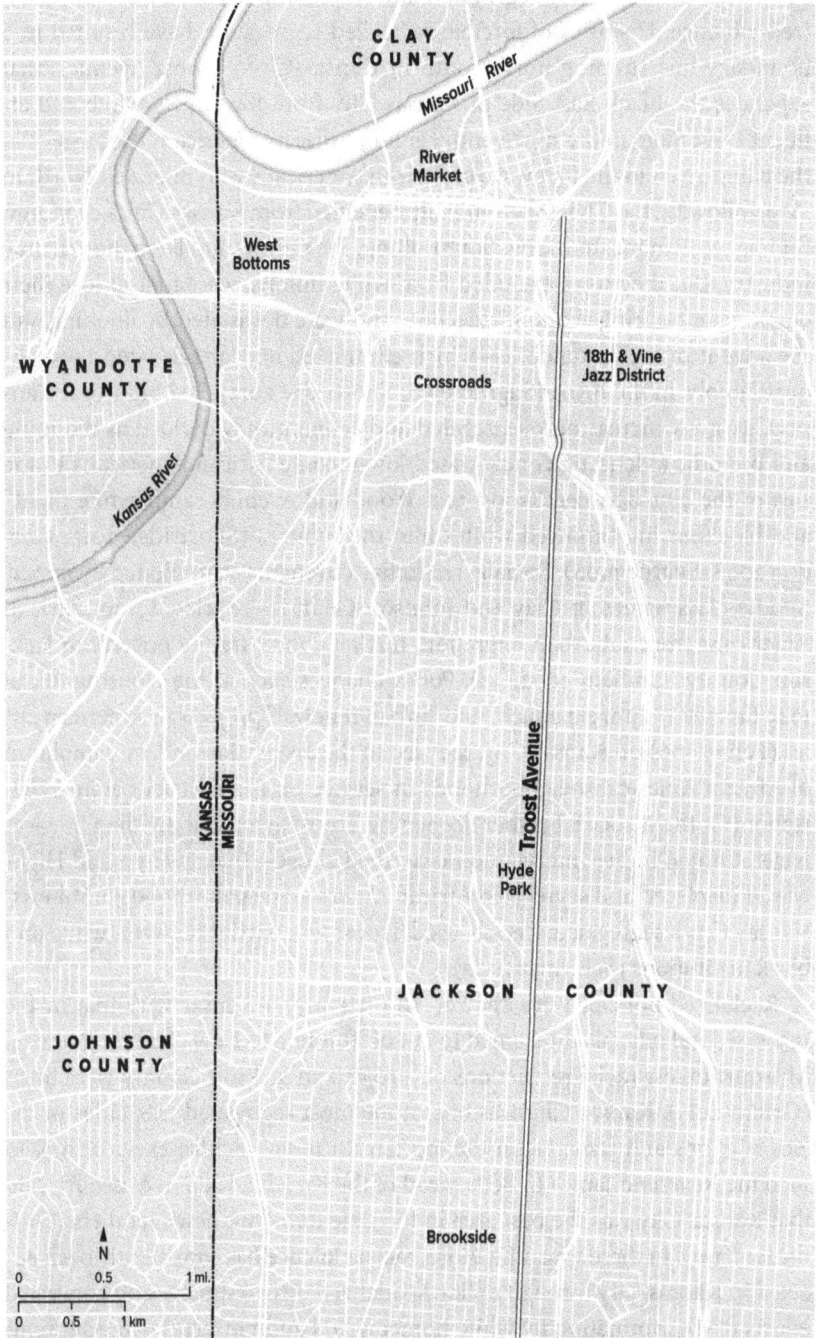

CLAY
COUNTY

Missouri River

River
Market

West
Bottoms

WYANDOTTE
COUNTY

Crossroads

18th & Vine
Jazz District

Kansas River

KANSAS
MISSOURI

Troost Avenue

Hyde
Park

JACKSON   COUNTY

JOHNSON
COUNTY

N

0   0.5   1 mi.

0   0.5   1 km

Brookside

Overview of Kansas City Metropolitan Region

Kansas City is starkly segregated and has a long history of urban racialized violence. Histories of forcible racialized segregation have resulted in a boundary line running north/south in Kansas City—Troost Avenue—that separates the Black East Side of Kansas City from the largely white and affluent West Side. In the nineteenth century, African American "exodusters"—the name given to the first wave of African Americans who migrated North in 1879, following the Civil War—initially benefited from Kansas City's economy, finding work in meatpacking, flour milling, the railway and later, the wartime industry. But they were excluded from white unions, were first to lose their employment during economic decline, and were devastated by flooding and the advent of the automobile—which eliminated and/or relocated these industrial jobs in the 1950s (Sugrue 1996; Shortridge 2012). Postindustrial Kansas City grew increasingly segregated and economically divided as redlining and prejudicial lending concentrated low-income African Americans to the east of the city, between Troost and Woodland Avenues, and "white flight" and blockbusting funneled whites into the suburbs (Shortridge 2012; Gordon 2008; Sugrue 1996). Racially restrictive covenants championed by upper-middle class whites in Clay and Johnson Counties restricted poor African Americans from suburban migration, further concentrating poverty in Jackson County (Gotham 2002, 40). Policy changes such as the Housing Act of 1949 financed "slum clearance" and "urban renewal" projects in American cities (Pena 2006); in Kansas City, they led to the dislocation and/or demolition of African American neighborhoods in service of Jazz District commercialization(Gotham 2002). Further deepening Troost as a racial dividing line—as Neferet noted in her intervention described above—Interstate 70 and Highway 71 displaced and segregated African American neighborhoods; until 1955, Kansas City's segregated schools used Troost as a barrier between white and black institutions (Schirmer 2002).

Racialized policies were enacted so blatantly in Kansas City that in the 1930s, federal officials threatened to cut off funding to New Deal programs in Missouri unless racial restrictions on projects in Jackson County were lifted (Griffin 2015). Kansas City was one of the most segregated U.S. cities in the '60s and '70s and remains on the top ten list today (Schirmer 2002, 97). In 1970 the Reverend James L. Betts, head of the Ku Klux Klan in Missouri, said that Kansas City was the best area in the state to recruit new members (Griffin 2015, 141). In these ways and more, racial violence has consistently been enacted in Kansas City through policy, spatialized disinvestment, and concerted efforts of discrimination by white homeowners and powerful white supremacy groups.

Legend:
- African American or Black majority
- White majority
- Hispanic or Latino majority
- No majority

CLAY COUNTY

Missouri River

WYANDOTTE COUNTY

Kansas River

KANSAS
MISSOURI

Troost Avenue

JACKSON COUNTY

JOHNSON COUNTY

N

0   0.5   1 mi.

0   0.5   1 km

Racial Segregation in Kansas City

At the same time, Kansas City has an important and storied history of Black self-determination and mobilization against racial injustice. One of the oldest historically Black colleges, Western University, was founded in 1865 on the Kansas side of the city, and Wheatley-Provident Hospital has produced more African American medical specialists than any other U.S. city (Griffin 2015). In 1941 a wartime rally sponsored by the NAACP drew five thousand Black Kansas Citians who fought for African American employment in wartime industry (Gillis 2007). Black Kansas City residents rioted against the Kansas City, Missouri, local government in 1968 following the assassination of Dr. Martin Luther King Jr. The city had refused to shut down in honor of Dr. King's funeral on April 9, prompting peaceful protests and a subsequent violent response from the Kansas City Police Department (Griffin 2015). Today, a strong public discourse in Kansas City challenges racial inequality—public protests against issues such as the privatization of downtown area sidewalks, discriminatory policing in neighborhood grocery stores, and housing inequality are frequent and widely attended.

"Insider," Engaged Ethnographic Research

Well-Intentioned Whiteness is a product of "insider," engaged, and collaborative ethnographic research[1]—the questions that sparked this project, and that inform this book, are deeply personal. I have been involved in different roles in the urban food movement in the Kansas City area since 2012, gradually transitioning from participant to researcher during that time. I am part of a family with deep agricultural history; my father's family in Shimoga, India, produces areca nut and coffee on large plantations; and my mother's parents, in El Dorado, Kansas, grew vegetables on vacant lots, foraged for mushrooms and nuts, and sold their goods at farmers markets. When I went to college at the University of Kansas (located in Lawrence, Kansas, just a short drive south of Kansas City), I wanted to be a part of the food movement there, to link into my family's history. Joining in community garden workdays and local foodie potlucks in Lawrence and Kansas City left me feeling isolated—a majority of the folks involved in these circles came from privileged backgrounds and were excited about "getting their hands dirty" and celebrating their new interests in the imperfect beauty of heirloom produce. These sorts of narratives didn't resonate with me—while my family enjoys the act of growing and foraging for food, for us, it doesn't carry any social privilege or capital. Potluck dinners I attended were full of vegan Indian-inspired dishes, and white local foodies explaining to me the myriad health benefits of coconut oil and turmeric—a jarring experience for someone who had been the subject of derision in grade school for eating "ethnic" cuisine. Discussions at these events centered on color-blind narratives about the uplift that gardening programs could offer those experiencing poverty, mental illness, or homelessness, or those who were victims of the mass incarceration system. These experiences of marginalization within the local food movement led me to the questions that informed this project: Why is the production and consumption of food touted as a solution to so many urban problems? Who is shaping this discourse and these policy agendas that draw on urban food production as a tool for economic uplift? How do other folks of color feel when presented with this narrative about food and agriculture that marginalizes or ignores their histories?

This work of mine within the Kansas City area food system provided a research-based social network that I drew upon and expanded during the twenty-six months of research that informs this book. This experience also positioned me in specific ways—as both an "outsider" and an "insider" (Narayan 1993; Chin 2006). In interviews and daily interactions, participants in this project variously indexed me as white, a person of color, upper-middle class, as someone who had experienced poverty, as an immigrant, and as a Kansan. These various indexations of my identity deeply impacted this project and are inextricable from the narratives presented in this book. For example, many white foodies I interviewed assumed I was sympathetic to disparaging comments about people of color because of my light skin and perceived class privilege—and would then highlight my minority status, asking me for advice in recruiting participants of color for their programs. While perceived insider status led to many painful moments, in which I felt I was made complicit in racist discourse, it also granted me access to a narrative that other researchers of color might have been excluded from (May 2014). At the same time, my nonwhite status benefited me in other ways, opening doors into other realms of discourse: for example, several Black interviewees immediately jumped into talking about white supremacy with me, unprompted, one stating "your people are no stranger to colonialism either."

I undertook the research shared in this book as an attempt to trace how everyday ideology, specifically unconscious whiteness, gains power and is spatialized. In tracing this process in Kansas City, I spoke with, and wrote about, Black communities. I find it important to note that I sit uneasily with that tension—as a brown scholar speaking about communities I'm not a part of (see also Vasudevan 2021). I hope this book's readers will supplement the perspectives shared here by reading widely, and diversely, from whiteness and food studies scholars who hold other identities.[2]

Well-Intentioned Whiteness is based on twenty-six months of ethnographic research conducted between 2013 and 2017, ninety in-depth semi-structured interviews, interactive social mapping, six focus groups, and archival research. During this period, I lived in an East Side neighborhood classified as a "food desert" and involved myself in various green urban development projects. I tended plots, daily, at several East Side community garden sites, participated in gardener training programs and classes, worked for a small-scale farm at City Market farmers market, helped manage an East Side farmers market, attended events hosted by various urban food and urban greening organizations in Kansas City, attended monthly neighborhood council and housing meetings for East Side neighborhoods, and participated in district meetings and other events hosted by the city to interact with urban residents. I met and engaged with local foodies (who hold policy-making positions) by participating in working group meetings offered by urban food nonprofits, planning coalitions for food nonprofit fundraisers, and other informal sites—such as happy hours, potluck dinners, and volunteer farm workdays.

In order to protect participant identities, I use pseudonyms for both individuals and organizations. For white foodies, in addition to using pseudonyms, I have altered life histories, ages, and other identifiable characteristics to further anonymize my interviewees. It's helpful to de-identify individuals at this level for several reasons—first, power and violence is enacted on a mass, structural scale. I analyze a lot of individual ideologies in this book, but it's important to remember that ideology becomes powerful when it is adopted structurally. By deemphasizing individuals, I'm hoping to instead draw attention to broader systems of whiteness upheld by many individual voices, combined. Second, my intention is not to vilify specific foodies for their ideologies. Many white foodies in KC are hopeful that urban food projects can positively impact others—their intent, with this work, is often not to further racialized inequality. Deeply anonymizing their voices helps, again, to emphasize structural violence, rather than interpersonal violence—whether it is intentionally enacted or not.

I use the identifiers "Black"[3] and "African American" interchangeably and always follow a research participants' self-identification. Both terms index complex racial, ethnic, class, political, and generational identifications (Thomas-Houston 2005); for example, several young, Black, self-identified "politically radical" research participants found the identity of "African American" offensive, as it implied, like "Irish American," a voluntary migration to the United States. Self-chosen racial and ethnic signifiers are never static; I do my best to represent research participants as they asked to represented in this particular sociopolitical moment. Racialization (cf. Omi and Winant 1994), of course, is about power rather than biological identities (Silverstein 2005). When I refer to black and white I am making reference to power relations rather than any inherent biological reality; furthermore, individuals may identify in multiple ways not captured by these static markers.

Overview of the Book

Well-Intentioned Whiteness examines urban greening projects from the perspective of low-income, predominantly African American residents of Kansas City's East Side—those for whom these projects are intended to provide the most benefit. I explore the development and implementation of green urbanism policy in Kansas City and contrast how these projects actually function, in comparison to the discourse that animates them. Throughout the book I analyze present-day policies by grounding them in historical context—an approach that emerged through conversation with Black East Side residents. I argue that green urban development is best conceptualized in the context of other global racial projects, such as white settler colonialism. Using Kansas City as a case study, *Well-Intentioned Whiteness* dissects how green urban policy agendas supporting spatialized white privilege are conceived, developed, implemented, and contested.

The chapters are arranged loosely in three sections—chapters 1 and 2 focus on elided, and then dominant, understandings of history and space in Kansas City. Chapters 3, 4, and 5 document how dominant whitened understandings of urban space turn into policy and examine the effects of this policy on food charity programming and the local food economy. Chapters 6, 7, and 8 each explore powerful acts of resistance against these dominant narratives and policy agendas.

This introductory chapter has provided an overview of green urban development and governance, racialized urban space, and whiteness. Chapter 1 offers a counterhistory to dominant media and policy representations of Kansas City's history and green economy, which are primarily constructed and informed by white voices. It demonstrates how Kansas City policy makers have, since the city's inception, displaced and exploited Black communities for the benefit of white elites.

Chapter 2 examines how KC's green policy makers come to develop their ideologies about urban disinvestment, hunger, and poverty. The chapter draws on in-depth interviews with white local foodies in Kansas City to better understand how the most dominant and influential ways of knowing vacancy, and blight, are developed. Chapter 3, in turn, demonstrates how this ideology transforms into urban policy and governance strategies—showing that foodies have powerfully shaped local ideas about green land use and zoning in ways that support white public space in Kansas City.

Chapter 4 documents how green urban development, which has led to a proliferation of urban food projects, affects food aid in Kansas City. From 2010 onward, food charity programming in Kansas City has shifted to partner food aid with mandatory nutrition education courses and classes in urban food production; I explore this current day food-aid paradigm within the context of historical state regulation of Black bodies and Black diets in Kansas City.

In chapter 5, I turn to examine the premise, heralded by green urban development advocates, that urban agriculture is an equal opportunity occupation that provides a stable income and involvement for all in the burgeoning green economy in Kansas City. Disrupting this claim, the chapter analyzes the raced and class-based dynamics of the alternative agrifood movement from the perspective of production and distribution.

Chapter 6 argues that green urban urbanism has so powerfully influenced understandings of "productive" urban citizenship that neighborhoods in Kansas City are forced to adopt the movement's goals in order to receive city and private support. I use a case study of one Kansas City neighborhood that strategically leverages green urban development projects to acquire funding for other, more urgent community needs, while simultaneously working to resist outside investment and gentrification.

In chapter 7, I explore the actions of some Black urban farmers in Kansas City, who purposefully use urban agriculture to draw attention to, and contest, how racism has been historically spatialized in the city. The narratives shared in this chapter elucidate how people of color respond to spatially dominant whiteness in U.S. cities.

In the final chapter, I discuss my collaborative efforts to create policy change within Kansas City. I share how attempts to disrupt the dominant whitened narrative surrounding urban sustainability were met with backlash and reveal larger challenges in disrupting white supremacy. The book closes with policy recommendations for equitable green urban development—ideas that were developed by low-income African American residents of Kansas City during focus group interviews.

Well-Intentioned Whiteness was written in hopes of disrupting dominant whitened narratives surrounding racialized urban development and sustainability. In urban policy circles, green urban development and urban food production is increasingly spoken of as an unequivocal boon to cities. My hope is that this book will help disrupt the idea that these projects present an inherently equitable approach to transforming urban space. While often depicted as such, nothing intrinsic to the way green urban development operates is politically progressive or new. Viewed from the perspective of many low-income Black Kansas City residents, green urban development is merely the newest legal mechanism of displacing Black bodies from land valuable to whites.

CHAPTER 1

Green Urbicide

*A History of Displacement and Urban Violence
in Kansas City between the Nineteenth
and Twenty-First Centuries*

At a panel presentation at the Kansas City Public Library, I listened to speakers discuss the economic benefits various shopping centers and entertainment districts have brought to the city. The panel's topic was economic development; facing a crowd of around eighty, local policy makers and investors perched on barstools and highlighted what they called Kansas City's "economic anchors"—the Sprint Center Arena and Power and Light Entertainment District, the up-and-coming Crossroads Entertainment District, and the Country Club Plaza shopping district. Built in the 1920s, the Country Club Plaza was designed with Spanish architectural influences and sported an open-air design—manicured medians and lush parks are interspersed between high-end retail outlets. This local economic anchor was also racially restrictive—people of color were not able to start businesses in, or own homes near, the plaza. One panelist—a prominent, white, investor in the plaza—noted that the shopping district generated over $30 million in revenue last year. As he spoke, he was interrupted—a young woman of color in the audience stood and authoritatively yelled out, "My Grandpa helped build the Plaza."

Why did she feel the need to interject? Exploitation of Black labor and displacement of Black bodies have been key to Kansas City's growth and economic development. These contributions and displacements aren't often highlighted in dominant narratives about Kansas City's history. This erasure of state-sanctioned violence against racialized groups—of urbicide—and an individualization of the inequities it causes is central to the way white privilege operates. For this audience member, and other KC residents of color, it can feel incredibly painful to hear about the economic value whites have generated from your displacement and segregation.

There are myriad other racialized groups marginalized within Kansas City. For one, there's been a significant Latinx community in Kansas City since the

1830s. Railroad companies recruited Mexican low-wage laborers and transported them into the city in boxcars. These laborers were then restricted to living in communities along the rail lines, on the Kansas side of the state line. The city's Latinx population was particularly hard-hit by a flood in 1951; this displacement and labor exploitation—which continues today, as many larger peri-urban farms in Kansas City hire and underpay migrant laborers, Latinx among them—is unacknowledged in dominant discourse about Kansas City's history. At the same time, the violence of urban development in Kansas City (and green urban development) uniquely and acutely affects Black urban residents—much of the discourse used to justify (re)development initiatives pathologizes urban problems as problems with African Americans. Subsequently, the "uplift" promised by green urban (re)development initiatives is often directed at Black bodies and Black spaces.

Both scholars in Black geographies and those researching and writing on settler-colonial cities have emphasized that physical markers of presence on the urban landscape are key linchpins that link to the circulation of power and municipal authority. "Sociocultural erasure" of both indigenous residence and violence enacted by white elites—the creation of a "sanitized landscape of national forgetting"—is central to the maintenance of white settler-colonial society (Razack 2002; McClintock 2018b). The stories we tell about our cities, and the plans we build to organize them, reflect—and create space to enact—racialized subjugation and violence (Rutland 2018). Building on these key theories of space, race, and erasure, this chapter articulates how urban elites in Kansas City have both displaced populations of color in service of economic growth and sanitized and rebranded this violent history via place-based green urbanism branding. The history presented here builds on this work by making a case for how the marketing and promotion of neighborhoods that hold histories of both Black community and white violence are "cleaned from ethnic memories and politics" and utilized as profit-drivers in green urban development (Davila 2004, 11). This tactic is central to Kansas City's green urbanism and will, arguably, be central to the green urban agendas of other municipalities working to generate profit from devalued areas of city space.

Specifically, in this chapter I lay out an abbreviated history of displacement in the Kansas City metropolitan area, from the 1800s to current day, highlighting how displacement of and disinvestment in Black communities has been a central strategy for urban growth. Further, I highlight how this displacement has often disrupted Black-led urban food initiatives. By sharing this history, this chapter counters dominant representations of Kansas City's green economy, which are primarily shared by white voices. This chapter documents how creation of greenspace by displacing Black communities—for the benefit of white Kansas Citians—is not a novel aspect of today's green urbanism and argues that this history is both whitewashed and key to the strategies many profiteers use for urban value creation in the city today.

Early Displacements and Geopolitical Formations in Kansas City

The metropolitan area that today comprises Kansas City, located at the junction of the Kansas and Missouri Rivers, was home to the Kansa, Osage, Otos, Pawnee, and Missouri nations when French fur traders settled the area in 1822 (Gitlin 2010). The Choutou family led this migration and established a trading post on the north bank of the Missouri River, presently Northeast Kansas City (Shortridge 2012, 10). This location facilitated easy contact with the area's primary trappers, the Kansa (Shortridge 2012, 10). This original settlement site became the northern point of today's racially divided Troost Avenue, named after Dutch doctor and slave owner Benoist Troost—the path, at that time, led to the Missouri River and was used by the Osage Indians as a trade route (Griffin 2015, 3). The Choutous brought enslaved Africans with them to their two-hundred-acre working farm in current-day West Bottoms; by the early 1830s, their settlement had attracted hundreds of other French-speaking settlers to the area (Shortridge 2012, 11).

Kansas City grew, housing twenty-five hundred residents by 1853 and then four thousand by 1860, as white settlers and the laborers they enslaved migrated north to the fertile valley along the Missouri and Kaw Rivers (Griffin 2015, 4).[1] Much of the migration in the 1850s into present day Kansas City came from Southern states—Kentucky, Virginia, Tennessee, North Carolina—as farmers left intensively cropped plantations and sought fertile land (Griffin 2015, 4). White settler residents of Kansas City's Westport—a trading hub and gateway to Oregon, Santa Fe, and California trails—grew the settlement's size and wealth with trade profits from Shawnee and other remaining tribal populations in the area (Shortridge 2012, 15). Crucially, white traders took advantage of the federal cash resettlement payouts given to these native groups to trade and accrue capital for their growing city. Forcible removal of Indigenous residents helped facilitate physical expansion of the growing city; the Osage Treaty of 1825 began this violence and pushed Kansa and Osage tribes from along the Missouri River to reservations in Central Kansas, allowing French settlers to expand out of the West Bottoms and into present day Kansas City (Gitlin 2010). The Kansas-Nebraska Act of 1854, a violent displacement that uprooted ten thousand Native inhabitants, freed up even more land for the city's westward growth (Shortridge 2012, 20).

Pawnee Indian Settlement in Platte Valley—Northwest Kansas City, 1868.
Photo Courtesy of Missouri Valley Special Collections, Kansas City Public Library.

The labor of enslaved people, who were forced to migrate to Kansas City, would be used, quite literally, to carve out the downtown business district from the limestone bluffs that surrounded the southern end of the Missouri River (Shortridge 2012, 44). A majority of the early, and often still existing, town infrastructure was built by the enslaved African population in the 1800s—including most of the East Side of Kansas City, including the infrastructure for Westport, downtown streets, the first Jackson County courthouse, and nearby Independence, Missouri (Griffin 2015, 3). Enslaved Africans were integral in facilitating further westward expansion for settlers passing through Kansas City and were often employed as blacksmiths and wagon manufacturers; notably, Hiram Young, an enslaved man who bought his freedom in 1847, opened a wagon wheel and ox yoke repair shop in Kansas City and employed twenty freed Black men as his business grew (Gillis 2007). This labor was central to continued westward U.S. expansion.

Because of agricultural slave labor, Jackson County was leading the state of Missouri in aggregate wealth by 1850—the area became a leading producer of hemp, as well as a site of production for tobacco, corn, and cotton (Griffin 2015, 5). Most of the large-scale farming operations in the Kansas City metropolitan area were located in Jackson County, and by 1860, the area housed nearly four thousand captive Africans and seventy free Black residents (Griffin 2015, 4). The number of captive Africans in Kansas City, Missouri, was limited due to the proximity of free states—owning enslaved people was seen as riskier when they could escape to freedom without much of a geographic

An in-progress clearing of Delaware Street, 1868.
Photo Courtesy of Missouri Valley Special Collections, Kansas City Public Library.

Limestone bluffs on Delaware Street, after demolition and clearing for downtown Kansas City, 1868. Photo Courtesy of Missouri Valley Special Collections, Kansas City Public Library.

barrier—but slave owners still fought hard against Kansas abolitionists, in an era known as "Bleeding Kansas." This border war between Kansas free-staters (anti-slavery settlers) and Missouri pro-slavery forces was acutely felt in Kansas City, as it straddled the state line. By the start of the Civil War, some seventy people had been killed in the course of border violence, many in Jackson County (Griffin 2015, 15). While Kansas City was uniquely divided in its loyalties, Jackson County, it could be argued, leaned Southern—only 6 percent of Jackson County voted for Lincoln in 1860 (Griffin 2015, 17). Many enslaved people in Jackson County were forcibly transported South during this time, as slaveholders tried to preserve their existing system of control—Larry Lapsley, an enslaved resident of Jackson County, recalled being quickly taken, along with other captive Africans, down to Texas in 1861 (Griffin 2015, 28). Missouri outlawed slavery in January 1865, becoming the first state to begin the liberation process after the Civil War—largely because, as local political discussion at the time noted, the value of a captive African in Jackson County had plummeted and slavery made less financial sense than it had previously (Griffin 2015, 29).

After emancipation, waves of Black migration hit Kansas City as exodusters fled the racial violence of the South in hopes of stable labor and safety in the Midwest and North. In 1880 Kansas City's African American population had reached fifty-five thousand, and by 1890 that number had grown to over one hundred thirty-two thousand (Shortridge 2012, 53). These refugees initially found homes south of Truman Road, between Charlotte and Virginia streets, and along the levee in northwest Wyandotte County in "tent villages" (Griffin 2015, 36). A steadier migration of African Americans into Kansas City occurred throughout the rest of the 1800s; the city's African American population tripled between 1880 and 1910, despite a high rate of African American out-migration during the same time (Schirmer 2002, 28). In 1880 a majority of Kansas City's Black residents were still living intermingled in wealthy white areas of town—as it was easier for servants to live near the estates where they worked as domestic labor (Shortridge 2012, 27).

Residential location of Kansas City's Black population changed significantly, however, from 1860 to the beginning of the 1900s, as labor demands and the opportunities available to newly freed Black Kansas Citians changed. Industrial development began in Kansas City in the 1870s; investors saw potential in the large amount of available acreage and the city's close proximity to a river, which could be used both for transport and waste disposal (Shortridge 2012, 5). Another big draw for potential investors was Kansas City's immigrant (Latinx and Irish, predominantly) and African American population,

The homestead of the Bates family, unknown date. The Bates were exodusters who settled several hundred miles west of Kansas City in Nicodemus, Kansas. Photo courtesy of Library of Congress Archives.

which presented a large labor pool available to exploit for low-wage work. In 1865 this labor pool helped construct a system of radiating railroad lines that linked Kansas City with other major U.S. hubs and solidified the city as a site for investment. In 1871 Philip Armour and Charles F. Adams founded the city's first stockyard, which would grow to be the second largest in the nation behind Chicago and would attract other packing companies and investment in the West Bottoms area of Kansas City (Shortridge 2012, 36). Armour and Adams's investment also attracted other enterprises that used cattle by-products as their raw materials, such as soap and fertilizer manufacturers. Later, attracted by Kansas City's expanding railroad connections, manufacturers of agricultural machinery, furniture, and grain elevators opened warehouses in the West Bottoms as well (Shortridge 2012, 39). Adams would later write, "All the money I have made has been in dealing in real estate in Kanzas [sic] City" (Shortridge 2012, 37). The Armourdale stockyard would provide Armour and Adams with a 600 percent return on investment(Shortridge 2012, 37).

The new labor opportunities in the Kansas City stockyards, railroads, and meatpacking district would significantly impact the spatial realities of the city's

Stockyards investors in a cattle pen, unknown date. Photo Courtesy of Missouri Valley Special Collections, Kansas City Public Library.

Laborer in the stockyards. Caption on back reads: "Clearing the hog pen." Unknown date. Photo Courtesy of Missouri Valley Special Collections, Kansas City Public Library.

Two African Americans in Kansas City tilling their backyard farm at a residence located east of Troost and north of Truman Road, circa 1900. Photo Courtesy of Missouri Valley Special Collections, Kansas City Public Library.

African American population. Between 1880 and the first decade of the 1900s, this population (which accounted for about 10 percent of the city residents, at that point) was largely centered in small neighborhoods built up around sites of low-wage employment (Schirmer 2002, 32); specifically, African American laborers took up residence in three main areas in the West Bottoms (Shortridge 2012, 42). These West Bottoms residences started out as camping communities—sites where African American exodusters were able to find work and erect shelters nearby with what limited funds they had remaining after fleeing the violence of the South. The communities that grew out of these refugee shelters were described by white Kansas Citians in derogatory ways, as "shantytowns" and "shacks," and given place names such as "Hell's Half Acre," "Belvidere," and "Hick's Hollow" (Shortridge 2012, 42).

Hell's Half Acre, located squarely in-between the West Bottoms and River Market areas, was the subject of considerable white public scorn. The roughly 1.5 square mile area, located on the South side of the Missouri river, took shape as Black, German, and Irish immigrants working on the construction of the Hannibal bridge in the 1860s settled into permanent residence (Schirmer 2002, 34). Laborers who built the Hannibal Bridge facilitated Kansas City's expansion—the bridge allowed for the first railway span across the Missouri

Photo taken of the construction of Hannibal Bridge, 1868.
Photo Courtesy of Missouri Valley Special Collections, Kansas City Public Library.

A photo of an aerial view of City Market, in Kansas City's River Market region, circa 1900s.
Photo Courtesy of Missouri Valley Special Collections, Kansas City Public Library.

Shoppers at City Market, 1906. Photo Courtesy of Missouri Valley Special Collections, Kansas City Public Library.

River, connected Kansas City to the West and Southwest, and leveraged the influx of thirteen railroad companies that would traverse through the metropolitan area (Miriani 2015, 10). Without construction of the Hannibal Bridge, investors would have never seen Kansas City as a viable trade hub. Hell's Half Acre residents were also among those to construct the nearby City Market, an agricultural emporium and farmers market, which grew from one commercial stall in 1857 to more than sixty in 1888 (Miriani 2015). City Market was, at that time, central to Kansas City's economy. The labor of Black and immigrant low-wage laborers was a vital component that laid the groundwork for the growth of this market, one of the largest in the Midwest.

Hell's Half Acre became more geographically dense around 1880, as another wave of Black refugee families, from Texas and Mississippi, arrived in Kansas City (Shortridge 2012, 42). Housing conditions in the area were poor; while Armour and Adams were seeing 600 percent returns on their West Bottoms investments, the laborers who worked for them in the Kansas City stockyards and railroad industry were living in abject poverty, with an average of five individuals per household, in conditions that bred tuberculosis and pneumonia, with no clean water or sewage system (Griffin 2015, 47). The Toad-a-Loop neighborhood (likely a mispronunciation of the early French fur traders' name for the wolf-populated area) sat south of the West Bottoms, on the banks of the Kansas River, and was spoken of in public discourse as a site of rampant crime (Wilson 2016). Toad-a-Loop housed meatpackers and railroad workers and was also the site of saloons and gambling houses that welcomed Black and immigrant patrons (Wilson 2016). Expansion of the Santa Fe and Missouri Pacific railroads took up much of the remaining real estate in the area in 1890, and Toad-a-Loop residents were displaced (Wilson 2016). By the turn of the twentieth century all of the Black and immigrant low-wage laborers had been pushed out of their West Bottoms residences, the expansion of rail yards, stockyards, and packinghouses encroached on already cramped living space, and investors converted the area into an entirely industrial site (Schirmer 2002, 40).

City-Led Green Urbicide:
Furthering "Green" Development by Protecting White Rights

Concurrently, beginning in 1890, the City Beautiful movement took off in Kansas City: a national movement in urban planning that utilized parks, fountains, boulevards, and statues to cultivate economic growth and urban beauty (Schirmer 2002). With City Beautiful, park creation became a tool of Black displacement. Most of the extant green amenities in Kansas City were built between 1893 and 1915, as part of this movement (Shortridge 2012); a coordinated system of 2,050 park acres, linked together with twenty-six miles of landscaped boulevards, was used as a mechanism to displace low-income Black Kansas City residents from areas of the metropolitan area the city government wished to further develop. Nationally and locally, City Beautiful projects furthered segregation and the forcible removal of residents from low-income, "blighted," neighborhoods; the discourse and displacement of the era directly mirrors the urban greening movement in Kansas City today—as Danny's comment, referenced in the introduction, about curing blight by digging up weeds, indicated.

This development occurred under the guise of providing Kansas Citians urban beauty, clean air, and an increase in neighborhood land values. In Kansas City's West Bottoms, local City Beautiful planners George Kessler, William Rockhill Nelson, and Adriance Van Brunt demolished houses (primarily African American residences) in the bluffs above the West Bottoms to permit the creation of West Terrace Park (Schirmer 2002, 41). Black and Irish low-wage

A home in West Bluffs, with residents on the porch, before its demolition for West Terrace Park, 1890. This photo was taken for the purpose of proving 'blight' to claim eminent domain. Photo Courtesy of Missouri Valley Special Collections, Kansas City Public Library.

Looking southwest across the West Bottoms; a view from West Terrace Park after displacement of primarily African American bluff residents, 1915. Photo Courtesy of Missouri Valley Special Collections, Kansas City Public Library.

West Bluffs, a largely African American community in Kansas City, 1904. The Kansas City Parks and Recreation Department described this photo as illustrating "an unredeemable eyesore" (Mobley and Harris 1991:4). Photo Courtesy of Missouri State Archives.

The West Bluffs after demolition for the "City Beautiful" development. It is shown here as the newly rebuilt West Terrace Park. Photo courtesy of the Missouri State Archives.

House at 12th and Grove; may have been removed during construction of the Paseo. No date.
Photo Courtesy of Missouri Valley Special Collections, Kansas City Public Library.

View of the Paseo, after construction of the Greenway, at 13th Street, 1900.
Photo Courtesy of Missouri Valley Special Collections, Kansas City Public Library.

laborers living along O.K. Creek were uprooted for the new Union Railway Station (Schirmer 2002, 17). "Shanty"-dwellers, low-income Black residents living south of Westport, were evicted for the construction of Penn Valley Park. Even middle-class African American homes were labeled "blighted" and razed for the Paseo, an ornamented boulevard that ran north to south and was dotted with manicured trees and shrubbery (Schirmer 2002). The Hyde Park neighborhood, a then-white community directly west of Troost, was beautified and landscaped in 1897, as white homeowners complained to city officials about "squatters" living in a ravine along Gillham Road; in reality, Black low-income residents were pushed east of Troost to turn this space into Hyde Park and Gillham Park (Mobley and Whitnell Harris 1991).

Kansas City's greenspace, created on sites of Black displacement, was subsequently often racially restricted: available to whites only. In 1918 informal "park watchmen," a coalition analogous to today's "neighborhood watch groups," ejected Mrs. Julia Morrison from the Paseo Parkway, adjacent to the Black residential area, the Jazz District, telling her that "you niggers are not going to light in this Parkway between Ninth and Twelfth streets" (Schirmer 2002, 83). When Mrs. Morrison brought the issue to court, members of the Kansas City Board of Parks and Recreation denied that they had ordered segregation of the park and refused to take corrective action (Schirmer 2002).

Public participation in enforcing racial segregation in greenspace was celebrated in Kansas City. For example, an article in the *Sun* in 1914 congratulated two white men for getting Black patrons to leave Electric Park, a small amusement park formerly located at Forty-Sixth and Paseo, stating, "These two men are always handy when wanted. It will be remembered that they broke up the attendance of Colored people at Electric Park . . . and brought about 'jimcrowism' in many other public places" (Schirmer 2002, 84). Wealthy white developers blatantly used parks and greenspace to provide a buffer against Black encroachment on white communities.

Neighborhood associations copied this practice as well—Kansas City's Linwood Improvement Association (LIA) exemplifies this tendency. LIA, bordered on the north by Troost and Spring Valley Parks—which were at that time, in 1926, occupied by low-income Black families, requested that the Kansas City Board of Commissioners for Parks and Boulevards kick out the Black residents and combine the parks into one solid expanse of greenspace. The association argued that the park should be created "on account of the encroachment of negroes" and also requested that area surrounding the park be converted into greenspace as well, to expand this boundary, "for fear Negroes, or some schemers helping Negroes may by hook or crook cross over the park"

(Schirmer 2002, 112). The proposal was not successful, but only because several white families who would have been displaced by the greenspace, petitioned against it (Schirmer 2002, 112).

"Let the East Side Go Black":
Black Geographic Dispersal and City-Led Spatial Violence

By 1900 the forces outlined above had pushed an overwhelming majority of African American Kansas Citians into two East Side enclaves—the North End Hollows and the Vine Street corridor. Black Kansas Citians at the turn of the twentieth century found the housing opportunities available to them strictly regulated by the capital interests of local industry and urban development projects. Houses on the East Side, between Troost and Woodland and Twelfth and Twenty-Third, were bought up by speculation in the 1880s for the white middle-class market, but the financial collapse of 1890 left contractors scrambling to find buyers for the more than seven thousand properties. Prices dropped significantly in the area, and homeownership was thus also extended to Black buyers (Shortridge 2012, 86). Many in the Black middle-class jumped at the opportunity to buy quality housing in what was then seen as an up-and-coming area of town. Black-operated schools in the area attracted families—Jackson County's Hiram Young School, named after the ox yoke business owner, opened in 1874 and operated until 1934. The school operated what might have been the first schoolyard garden program in Kansas City.

Vine Street, in particular, became a hub of Black social and economic life. The area was originally settled by the Sweeneys—an African American reverend and his wife—who owned and operated a truck farm at the intersection of Eighteenth and Vine (Driggs and Haddix 2005, 26). At that time Eighteenth Street was a muddy, country lane that the Sweeneys lined with several acres of tilled fields, growing corn, tomatoes, and bell peppers. One block westward, where Paseo Boulevard would later intersect Eighteenth street, the Sweeneys cultivated a wild walnut grove, selling the hulled nuts locally (Driggs and Haddix 2005, 26). The Vine Street area developed as a major, largely Black-owned, commercial district serving Black clientele and housed more than a dozen Black churches—most of which moved from their original sanctuaries in the North End or West Side to join the growing community (Schirmer 2002, 41). More Black schools opened in the area, providing further incentive for Black families to relocate: the Attaucks School at Eighteenth and Brooklyn and the Lincoln High School at Nineteenth and Tracey (Schirmer 2002, 41). Vine Street housed the city's first movie theater for Black patrons

Hiram Young School Garden, circa 1935. Sign reads: "Public School Garden."
The school was named in honor of Hiram Young, who bought his freedom and
established his own wagon wheel repair business in Kansas City. Photo courtesy of
Independence School District.

(the Star) and an acclaimed Black newspaper (the *Call*). Vine Street was lined
with dry good stores, laundries, a fish shop, bakeries, cobblers, tailors, restaurants, a majority owned by, and operated for, the African American community (Driggs and Haddix 2005, 26). A coalition of African American baseball
team owners founded the Negro Baseball Leagues in the Vine Street corridor, during a meeting at the Paseo YMCA, and the Kansas City Monarchs—an
African American baseball team—drew crowds to the city to watch games
(Driggs and Haddix 2005, 26). Eighteenth and Vine would come to be known
as the Jazz District, as nightlife venues grew and musicians traveled to Kansas
City to develop the area's specific style of bebop; the district would come to be
known as a cultural Mecca for African Americans across the Midwest, which
attracted in-migration to Kansas City (Driggs and Haddix 2005, 26). In 1932
a Black-owned credit union and cooperatively owned grocery store opened
at Twenty-Sixth and Prospect, in the Vine Street corridor (Young and Young
1950). In 1900 the East Side of Kansas City was 29 percent African American,
but by 1920 that percentage had jumped to 75 (Shortridge 2012, 87).

The increasing geographic concentration, and thus visibility, of Kansas
City's Black residents over the first few decades of the 1900s led to concerted
efforts at displacement and containment by city officials, real estate agents,
and white urban residents. This increased attention was fueled by several
widely read housing reports and analyses conducted by local welfare agencies
in the 1910s—the *Report on Housing* (1912), *Social Prospectus of Kansas City*

A house located on the 1700 block of Troost Avenue. Housing conditions became increasingly cramped during the first several decades of the 20th century, as racialized renting and lending concentrated African American residents East of Troost. Photo courtesy of Missouri Valley Special Collections, Kansas City Public Library.

(1913), and *Our Negro Population* (1913) all located the cause of "blight," poor health, and poverty in Black neighborhoods (Fox Gotham 2002, 36). Asa Martin wrote in *Our Negro Population*, "There is the unsanitary condition of the streets and alleys in the Negro districts, which is due to a large extent to the negligence . . . ignorance and carelessness of the Negro in supplying the needs of his physical being" (cited in Fox Gotham 2002, 37). Reports such as these institutionalized and gave weight to popular racist linkages between poverty, place, and race and directly preceded containment policies and violence enacted by city officials, real estate agents, and white urban residents.

This concern with controlling the spread and inhabitancy of Black Kansas Citians was not a new phenomenon—since its inception as a city, Kansas City officials have worked to maneuver its Black population to best suit the interests of whites. In 1855 white settler inhabitants of Westport lobbied the Kansas territorial legislature to redraw state lines—hoping that the intensely proslavery sentiments held in Kansas City could help turn Kansas into a slave state as well (Shortridge 2012, 8). Politics had changed by the time the initiative was submitted, as Kansas had definitively positioned itself as a free state, where slavery was outlawed—but it is significant that from the start, control of Black bodies and Black labor was central to the formation and boundary definition of Kansas City. Later, as newly freed Southern captive Africans—refugees—traveled north, they were met with hostility in Kansas City. The mayor of Wyandotte City (present-day Kansas City, Kansas) banned exodusters in April 1879, stating that the city had received too many Black people already. The mayor and local businessmen paid to have Black migrants forcibly transported deeper into Kansas—many abducted and taken to Manhattan, Kansas, just to get them out of the newly developing metropolis (Griffin 2015, 38). It is not surprising that local government officials felt empowered to forcibly remove people of color from their state for development purposes; merely forty years prior the U.S. government had authorized the violent removal of Indigenous groups from Kansas City.

Two additional waves of migration north to Kansas City between 1900 and 1920—as wartime industry, coupled with decreased need for farm hands, changed labor requirements and sent African Americans north in search of work—were met with increased attempts to control the space that Black Kansas Citians occupied. Kansas City's Black population increased 72 percent over the first few decades of the twentieth century, reaching over thirty thousand residents by 1920 (Gibson and Jung 2005). The Vine Street corridor grew more densely populated, as racialized renting and loaning practices forced Kansas City's African American population into a containable area. To cope with this forced concentration, residents built "jerry-rigged" apartments, tacked on to tenement homes and jutting out into back alleys (Griffin 2015, 51). Black-owned businesses on Kansas City's East Side struggled, as banks refused to grant loans and producers and distributors overcharged Black business owners for their goods (Griffin 2015, 64). Kansas City capitalized on Black cultural contributions, yet excluded Black patrons—white-owned Jazz clubs and music venues utilized Black Jazz musicians but denied entry to Black patrons (Griffin 2015; Schirmer 2012). By 1910 Kansas City was facing hypersegregation; in 1915 one twenty-two-block area on the East Side housed 4,295 Black residents (Griffin 2015, 51). It is important to link these purposeful displacements to Black death—lack of clean water and forced geographic concentration led to high rates of pneumonia and tuberculosis in the Vine Street Corridor; in the mid-1920s the Black mortality rate in Kansas City was worse than in New York and Chicago (Griffin 2015, 52). The city government directly contributed to the contamination of Black communities; in 1926, the city installed its first major garbage dump at Twenty-First and Vine (Schirmer 2002).

As housing conditions became overcrowded in the Vine Street corridor, Black Kansas Citians attempted to spread the boundaries of their community and white Kansas Citians responded with force—both physically and through urban policy. By 1940, 71 percent of Black Kansas City residents lived between Troost and Jackson Avenues on the East Side; nearly 90 percent of people of color in the city lived in segregated neighborhoods (Griffin 2015, 79). When this growing community tried to push further south, past Twenty-Seventh Street and east past Troost into whiter neighborhoods, they were met with violence. City officials, as Colby writes, "drew a boundary right down the middle of the city along its longest north-south thoroughfare, Troost Avenue . . . Let the east side go black," (Colby 2012, 77). Every zip code, census tract, voting ward, and, until recently, every school district was split along Troost (Griffin 2015, 80). The north/south boundary line of Troost was purposefully developed by city officials and reinforced by the real estate industry, as a dam against Black migration west. The Kansas City School District reorganized its districts *each year* to keep Black schools Black, and white schools white; every public school east of Troost Avenue was 90 percent Black by the 1970s (Griffin 2015, 86). Racial violence during the time of school desegregation is an oft-discussed topic among Kansas City East Side residents who were in school during the '70s. One African American East Side resident shared, "Oh it was bad. Kids would line up outside the school and say 'go home niggers,' every morning." She and others felt fear of physical violence: "My cousin, she was as light [skinned] as you, but even she was bullied so bad she carried a knife with her to school. She was scared."

The real estate industry, banks, lending institutions, and developers redlined Kansas City with Troost; Black Kansas Citians found it impossible to buy or rent outside of the East Side's Jackson County. Banks denied home loans to Black Kansas City residents for decades—in 1977 alone, $642 million dollars was written in home mortgages in Kansas City, but less than 1 percent of this number was issued to home owners east of Troost (Griffin 2015, 81). Beginning in 1923 and ending around 1927, Black homeowners—primarily those moving westward near Troost Avenue, near historically white middle-class neighborhoods—were subjected to mob violence, bombings, and death threats from white homeowners. One neighborhood experienced seven dynamite attacks in one year alone (Shirmer 2002, 101). No deaths or major injuries occurred as a result of this violence, but arson and bombings led to many Black families losing newly purchased homes or being forced to move out of fear (Griffin 2015, 80). The local NAACP chapter attempted to bring a case against the city for complicity with these acts of violence, citing evidence that police failed to make arrests and left threatened houses unguarded to allow attacks (Schirmer 2002, 101). While housing-related violence in cities like Chicago and Detroit corresponded with times of housing shortage, in Kansas City this rash of attacks coincided with a period of housing construction; violence occurred not as a result of competition for finite housing, but rather as a result of Black residents trying to penetrate historically white neighborhoods (Schirmer 2002, 106).

The practice of utilizing racially restrictive covenants to segregate urban space was perfected in Kansas City by white developer J. C. Nichols, further restricting Black mobility in Kansas City. Between 1910 and 1940 Nichols acquired land and created several exclusive developments throughout the city—the Country Club Plaza, Mission Hills, and Prairie Village. Membership in Nichols's neighborhood associations was mandatory upon buying a home, and all members were legally required to enforce racial restrictions (Griffin 2015, 61). Nichols ensured that in Kansas City, racially restrictive covenants were self-renewing, meaning that the process of reforming these restrictions would be difficult (Griffin 2015, 61). As the Black population grew, whites fled—many to Nichols's restricted suburbs, aided by block busting enacted by local real estate agents (Griffin 2015, 61). Nichols's model was copied nationwide; he worked with President Roosevelt to design the Federal Housing Administration (FHA), which ensured that government-backed home loans would be denied to Black neighborhoods (Griffin 2015, 62). The work of enforcing racially restrictive covenants was also taken up by white homeowners; the Linwood Neighborhood Home Association started a metropolitan-wide effort to apply racial restrictions across the city, to "keep Negroes where they are"—an effort that included circulating threatening letters to Black families looking at homes in Linwood Neighborhood (Fox Gotham 2002, 45). The success of Nichols's exclusive suburbs, and their subsequent reinforcement by white Kansas Citians, is indicative of how strongly felt white segregationist attitudes were at this formative time in Kansas City's spatial development.

Nichols's Country Club Plaza, an open-air shopping district—46 percent of which is dedicated to greenspace—became central to Kansas City's economy and downtown development. The area where the Country Club Plaza would be developed sits in central Kansas City, Missouri, just north of east/west flowing Brush Creek. Nichols bought the forty acres he would later develop into a luxury-shopping district from an African American hog farmer, who had owned the land for several decades, and claimed a Black-only park—Razor Park—through eminent domain (Scanlon 2015). Black laborers were among those enlisted to build Nichols's open-air, Spanish architecture-inspired shopping district; simultaneously, they were written into racially restrictive deed covenants that kept them from establishing businesses or buying a home in

A laborer in downtown Kansas City helping to construct the Fidelity building at 909 Walnut Street, 1930. Photo Courtesy of Missouri Valley Special Collections, Kansas City Public Library.

View of the racially restricted Country Club Plaza, at the intersection of Mill Creek Parkway and 47th Street, 1945. Greenspace and walkability for white shoppers was an integral part of J. C. Nichols' design. Photo Courtesy of Missouri Valley Special Collections, Kansas City Public Library.

the up-and-coming area. The ability to establish oneself in the plaza led to the success of many small businesses; the white-owned Woolf Brothers clothing shop, for example, relocated to the plaza from Leavenworth, Kansas, and became one of the most profitable luxury clothing outlets in the Midwest (Scanlon 2015).

Urban renewal and highway development in the 1950s and 1960s sparked the next wave of displacement for Black residents in Kansas City. Urban renewal, across the United States, was guided by the interests of real estate boards, which favored "slum" clearance and private development in downtown areas over the creation of affordable housing. Eighty million dollars of mostly federal urban renewal funds were spent on eighteen projects in Kansas City from 1953 to 1970, locally called "negro removal" projects (Griffin 2015, 83). Nationally, Black residences accounted for more than 70 percent of those destroyed in urban renewal projects (Griffin 2015, 83). Locally, the 54.2-acre Attucks Project worked to clear out predominantly Black neighborhoods adjacent to downtown Kansas City, prepping the area for tourism development. In Jackson County, a Black neighborhood that whites called "Nigger Neck" was destroyed to create McCoy Park, part of local tourism development for the Harry S. Truman Presidential Library (Griffin 2015). The Harry S. Truman childhood home and historic site, where captive Africans had been enslaved for agricultural labor within living memory, was again a site of violence during 1950s urban renewal. African American residents of current day McCoy Park had their homes and farms dismantled to create public greenspace and "historic" monuments. Highway 71 was routed through mostly Black East Side neighborhoods—Ivanhoe, Beacon Hill, and Key Coalition—displacing more than ten thousand urban residents and plummeting the housing values for those residents that remained, whose homes were now located very close to roadways (Griffin 2015, 84). Highway 71 would cut through the site of numerous historic Black-owned businesses, such as Black Hawk Barbecue and Beer Garden at 1410 East Fourteenth. The small quantity of public housing that was built during this period was strictly segregated, in direct violation of federal civil rights legislation (Griffin 2015, 84).

The Current Landscape

Today, concerted renewal and redevelopment policy agendas are encouraging white and upper-middle class migration to historically Black, segregated, areas of the city such as the East Side. Many would agree that the East Side is gentrifying. Over the past two decades, nearly all of the African American

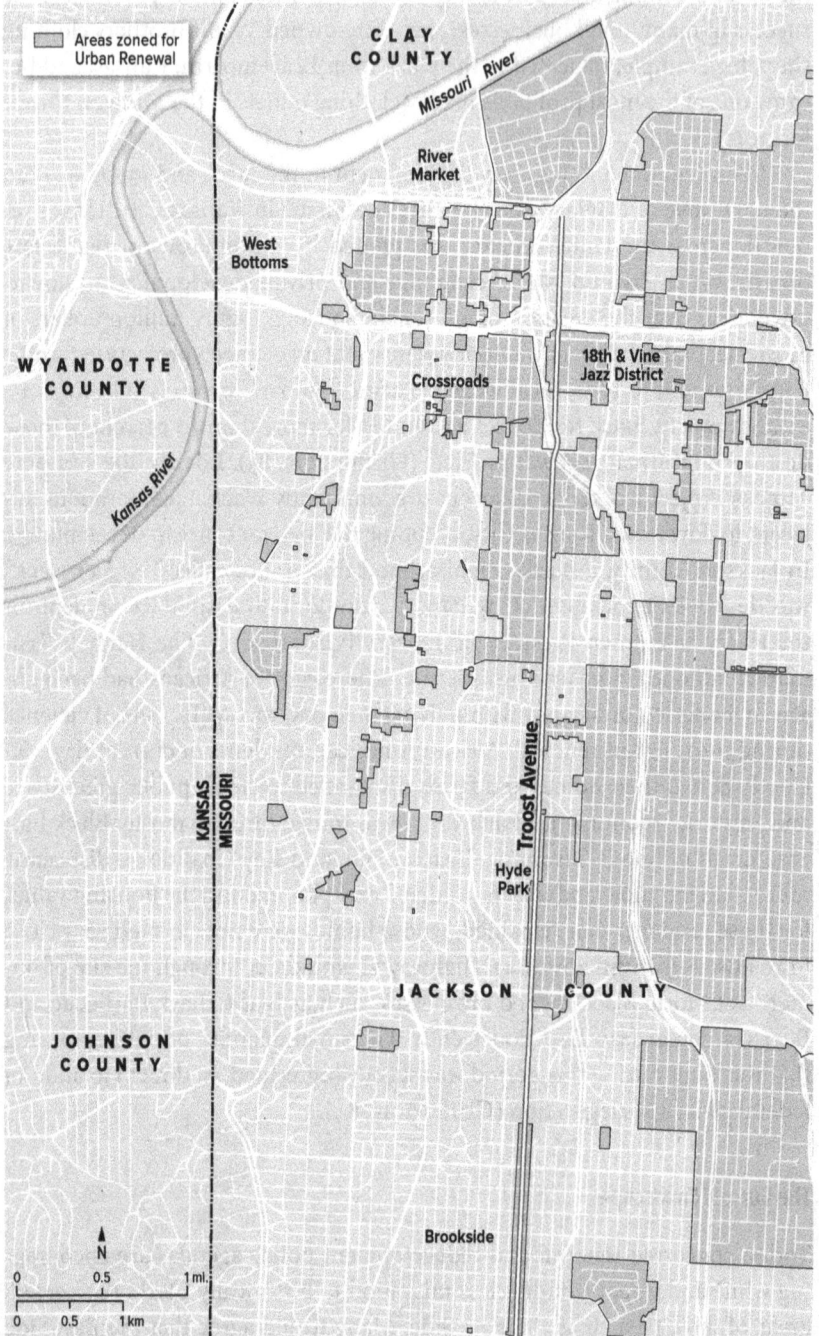

Areas Zoned for Urban Renewal in Kansas City

majority East Side and historic Black communities such as the West Bottoms have been designated as "Urban Renewal" zones or "Community Improvement Districts"—these renewal agendas have been spearheaded by both the city government and local policy mediators, such as the Economic Development Corporation (EDC) of Kansas City. These initiatives heavily promote private investment as a means of economic development; they offer incentives that "help to reclaim embattled neighborhoods by encouraging investment and removing blighted conditions that make neighborhoods unsafe or uninviting" (EDCKC 2014). For example, an EDC and KCMO city government collaboration, the Chapter 353 Program, enables private developers to acquire property in historically Black areas via eminent domain and offers 100 percent tax abatement for the first ten years of property ownership and 15 percent for the next five (EDCKC 2014; Shortridge 2012, 165).

Combined, these renewal designations and policy agendas have encouraged a massive surge in speculative development on the East Side. One development group, for example, is as of this writing seeking a twenty-year tax abatement for a $17 million dollar renovation project at Thirty-First and Troost—a project that involves transforming the area into a commercial district with offices, retail space, and museums. These projects are contributing to the unaffordability of the area for extant residents—in 2019, Kansas City, Missouri, raised property taxes in Jackson County an astronomical amount, in some cases more than 2,000 percent. Because of the speculative development and green infrastructure overhaul of Troost Avenue, homeowners on the East Side are seeing massive property tax increases. In one case, a homeowner's tax bill jumped from $1,200 to $4,500 dollars (Plake 2019).

Green urbanism accounts for some, certainly not all, of this (re)development; in Kansas City, urban food projects and other green development projects are often complementary or supportive of broader (re)development processes, being conceived in concert with the above development agendas (See also Alkon, Kato, and Sbicca 2020). Many of these renewal and redevelopment programs offer additional tax incentives for projects that incorporate "green" infrastructures—often interpreted as rooftop gardens, bike lane improvements, or attached community garden space. Around 2005 influential foodies began pushing for several policy mechanisms that would encourage urban food production—this included the adoption of KC's Urban Agriculture Ordinances (2010) and Urban Agriculture Zones (2014). Policy makers who supported private development–led revitalization of the East Side championed these initiatives, as they are complementary to broader efforts to attract the "creative class" to Kansas City's urban core. For example, a proposed comprehensive redevelopment agenda for the East Side (developed by KCMO city officials, Greater Kansas City LISC, Urban Neighborhood Initiative, and the Mid-America Regional Council) devotes $25–$40 million to urban walk-ability/bike-ability improvements, the attraction of small businesses and restaurants, and the development of urban greenspace. Foodie-led policies dovetail neatly with these agendas and serve to support new, green, urban priorities. The unaffordable living conditions that this sort of development often creates means that today's green urbanism is just as likely to displace Black and brown low-income Kansas Citians as City Beautiful redevelopment was in the 1890s.

It is primarily luxury developers and creative companies that take advantage, and benefit from, the above incentives—capital-rich investors see incredible potential in the East Side and West Bottoms disinvested warehouses. Spacious brick-walled warehouses can be reimagined as high-end lofts and co-working spaces; the deep history of the area is an added attraction for creative class consumers. The growth of the Stockyards District—a neighborhood association developed by a collaborative of high-end real estate developers—exemplifies this process. Their website encourages "urban-minded families" to relocate into the West Bottoms by prominently displaying an interactive timeline of the area's history, titled "History that's still in the making . . . our journey from cattle epicenter to cultural destination," and proclaims that this "historic neighborhood" is now home to artists and Kansas City's "most creative" companies (KCStockyardsdistrict 2018). Lloyd (2010) documents a similar process in Chicago's Wicker Park, where sites of "postindustrial decay" first become valued by artists and are then capitalized on by cities—where these disinvested spaces are newly realized as "edgy and glamorous" and valuable tools for attracting "the creative class" (18).

The projects created with these urban renewal incentives serve to further displace low-income Black urban residents, as they rarely include affordable housing options. Affordable rentals are increasingly scarce in Kansas City—one recent high-rise development project, for example, offered "affordable" $1,000 dollar/month rental units. Kansas City does not have any rent control or affordable housing policies in place.[2]

A majority of the historically Black neighborhoods described in this chapter have, through urban renewal funds, been reimagined as wealthy, predominantly white, communities. The River Market neighborhood was placed on the National Register of Historic Places in 1978, and consequent city tax incentives via urban renewal zoning and federal and state grants—totaling $100 million public, and estimates of $1 billion in private—went in to redeveloping this area as white public space (Miriani 2015, 22). City Market, located in the River Market district, now has over 180 outdoor stalls and attracts six hundred thousand shoppers and visitors per year. On summer weekends, yoga classes are offered on the City Market lawn. City Market is utilized as an asset for many real estate agents, who draw upon its proximity to market luxury lofts located nearby. One recent $59 million dollar River Market development project, a 276-unit multifamily complex boasting "energy-efficient" eco-units, drew on urban redevelopment funding and the area's blight designation to earn a ten-year tax abatement (EDC 2015); average rent in the River Market area is $1,400 dollars for a one-bedroom loft. The nineteenth-century architecture built with Black and brown labor has attracted the development of these high-end lofts, which in turn furthers Kansas City's growth as a destination city for upper-middle class white millennials (see also Alkon and Cadji 2015).

A huge influx of white twenty-four to thirty-four-year-olds has moved into KC's urban core over the past five years; Kansas City is often cited as one of the best cities for recent college graduates (Gose 2014). Conversely, racialized dress codes at KC-area nightlife spots and many bars' refusals to play rap or hip hop—because, as Black Kansas Citians note, they do not want Black patrons—have combined to encourage an exodus of young Black professionals from the city. A *Kansas City Star* article in September 2017—"Is KC Social Scene for Whites Only? Young Blacks Say They're 'Tolerated,' Not Welcomed"—notes that many Black millennials are choosing instead to move to Dallas and Atlanta, and other diverse cities.

The Jazz District, within the Vine Street corridor, has also received significant redevelopment support from public and private sources in Kansas City. This funding, however, has primarily been in service of preserving the area's historical narrative, rather than developing supportive services for current residents. KCMO city government appropriated $20 million to the area in 1989, funding the American Jazz Museum and the Negro Baseball Leagues Museum; and $100 million more has been appropriated since—funding roadway infrastructure, jazz festivals, continued museum funding, renovations of the old Paseo YMCA, and expansion of exhibits at the MidAmerica Black Archives (Janovy 2016). What East Side Kansas City residents often speak of as the "touristification" of the Jazz District, of Kansas City's "Black Wall Street," has not managed to address the history of disinvestment in and depopulation of the area. Between 1954 and 2007, the area lost 84 percent of its population (Martin 2016). Highway 71's cut through the district makes it geographically isolated, and disinvestment in the Black-owned businesses in the area has left the Vine Street corridor bereft of industry. The first Black high school in Kan-

Mural commemorating the Jazz District at 18th and Vine. Photo courtesy of Linda Fasteson.

sas City, the Attucks school, is underway to becoming an "arts and culture hub"—the city accepted a bid from Chicago-based artists to turn the abandoned school into a co-working space and gallery, turning down a bid to return the site to its original use as a high school (Collison 2017). In 2018 Kansas City Missouri officials further divested Vine Street corridor residents' political power by overturning the ability of neighborhood residents to have a say in liquor licenses and business development in the area—an act that singles out and suppresses voices in a historically Black neighborhood and does not affect development decisions in other entertainment districts in the city.

In 1951 a second devastating flood in the West Bottoms shut down Kansas City's meatpacking industry and changed the course of development for this river-adjacent site. Stockyard animals drowned, houses were swept off of their foundations, and oil company fuel canisters started widespread smoky fires in this mid-century flood; around nine thousand residents were evacuated from flooded areas, with only around three thousand ever returning (Shortridge 2012, 122). Today, the abandoned industrial warehouses in West Bottoms are home to high-end antique stores and flea markets, distilleries and microbreweries, New American farm to table restaurants, and speakeasies. Many of the historic buildings still feature triple-segregated entrances, now unmarked—one each for White, Black, and Latinx laborers (Campbell 2014). A City of Kansas City, Missouri, Community Improvement District (CID) sales tax is funding a green infrastructure overhaul of the West Bottoms. A key component of this "green" plan is bikeable pathways, in order to encourage the development of more high-end rental housing in the area, chiefly marketed toward the creative class. In 2015 the first luxury apartment complex in the West Bottoms, Stockyards Place, was completed—a studio apartment in the complex costs $1,600 dollars a month. The project received a 50 percent tax abatement for entering a blighted zone of the city.

Urbicide in Kansas City

In laying out a history of urban development in Kansas City, I have illustrated how displacement of (and violence toward) African Americans has been a key strategy city officials and urban policy mediators have used for capital accumulation and economic growth. Displacement of Black bodies, and exploitation of Black landed knowledge, was a central, unacknowledged, component of Kansas City's growth as a metropolitan area—and it was often enacted in service of creating greenspace.

It is useful, and important, to reframe these processes as urbicide, as this violence is often masked within neoliberal capitalist discourse that naturalizes linkages between blackness, poverty, and underdevelopment (cf. McKittrick 2011). These acts of urbicide—blight renewal, the "cleaning up" of slums, and the forceful displacement of marginalized populations—make clear statements about whose lives matter in the city (cf. Davis 2006). More broadly, these processes should be considered within the historical lineage of settler colonialism—globally, and locally, the removal of indigenous populations for profit is a key way that urban elites amass power and wealth. McKittrick (2011, 948) emphasizes how whites profit from this process—the economy of race is predicated upon the erasure of Black sense of place and the resulting undervaluing of Blackness.

Kansas City has profited from the exploited labor, and displacement, of African Americans and other groups of color. Black agricultural labor built sites that are central to Kansas City's economy, and Black bodies have been repeatedly, forcibly removed from neighborhoods that begin to be generative of economic growth. Infrastructural contributions made by Black laborers—such as Hannibal Bridge and the construction of railways and City Market—facilitated the very expansion of Kansas City. Many of these contributions have resulted in infrastructure that is aesthetically valuable for white urban developers; the industrial sites built by Black laborers in the 1800s, for example, are considered aesthetically valuable to green urbanists. Acknowledging these labor histories, and the way they are mobilized for current-day development interests, is important.

Further, green urban infrastructure initiatives that seek to address blight and disinvestment elide the fact that "blighted" spaces were often areas where Black urban residents were cultivating soil, food, community, and industry. Black Kansas City residents have been growing food in the city (for themselves, and as part of forced slave labor) for centuries, only to be displaced from these sites when city officials see value in the lands' redevelopment. Discussions of Kansas City's food deserts, today, do not include discussion of, for example, the Black hog farmer displaced for Country Club Plaza, the large-scale truck farmer at Eighteenth and Vine, or the schoolyard gardens at Black grade schools. Paradoxically, in many of these spaces of historical Black food production, racially marked bodies have become a target for discourse surrounding "healthy" eating and the promotion of personal food production. These histories—of the agricultural contributions Black urban residents have made—will provide useful context to inform discussion of food deserts and food aid in chapter 6. Highlighting how Black and brown urban residents have contributed significantly to Kansas City's growth, and how they have historically been displaced from their urban farms and gardens, is a necessary step in the process of reimagining a more equitable city—particularly within a context in which white-led green urbanism projects are most often praised for strengthening the urban economy.

The photos and histories of space presented in this chapter were difficult for me to track down. I learned about much of this history through moments of public eruption—like the young woman's outburst at the panel conversation on economic development. This is not surprising; space and its meanings are produced for certain goals and with benefits of a certain population in mind—the narratives shared here do not legitimate or lend support to those in power in Kansas City (cf. Razack 2002). Scholars of settler-colonial cities have noted that "sociocultural erasure" of indigenous residents, in addition to land acquisition, is key to the way settlers gain control of new territory (cf. McClintock 2018b). Dominant narratives about the history of Kansas City—those produced for the purpose of tourism promotion—are largely apolitical and color-blind. More broadly, narratives of U.S. history frequently make Black subjects invisible and render Black social lives ungeographic (cf. McKittrick 2006, x). This invisibility—the denial of displacement and violence—helps support and enforce white public space in Kansas City. As in, those whose presence is visible are those who can claim ownership (cf. McKittrick 2006).

It is important to foreground, in our narratives of urban growth and westward expansion, how the exploitation of Black and brown land and labor has been central to the development of U.S. cities and urban wealth. In the following chapter, I explore the dominant narratives in circulation about urban blight, hunger, and disinvestment in Kansas City.

CHAPTER 2

Creating White Public Space in the Urban Food System

Institutionalized Understandings of
Race and Space in Kansas City

On a Saturday night in September 2017, the largest, and arguably most influential, local foodie nonprofit—Grow KC—held its annual fundraiser dinner at the historic City Market farmers market. This year the event, titled "Dig In!" drew several hundred local foodies, who paid $125 per plate to support Grow KC's programs, which include grants and infrastructural support for small-scale urban farmers, administering the distribution of federal matching funds for SNAP recipients, and policy advocacy in relation to the local, urban, food system. Local chefs—in recent years, all white men—are selected to craft the farm to table menu; diners were lured in to the 2017 event with promotional advertising that read: "When you 'Dig In,' you help somebody else dig out of unhealthy food choices and food deserts!" As diners feasted under the open-air market pavilion on family-style servings of risotto, braised rabbit, pickled beet, and carrot salad, a promotional video played on a large projector screen. Produced by Grow KC, it outlined the history of the organization and highlighted what it sees as the positive changes it has enacted in Kansas City. I served as a volunteer waitress for the event and watched the video as I served guests Amigoni wine—a product of a local winery that grows and ages its grapes in the West Bottoms, where Black low-wage stockyard laborers lived half a century before. As the video began, an uplifting piano score accompanied sweeping shots of Kansas City's skyline, first showing urban vacancy before panning over to aerial shots of urban gardens and greenspace. Nancy, the white, fifty-something executive director of Grow KC, spoke over the piano:

> When I first came to Kansas City from being on the East Coast, one of the things I did was drive all over Kansas City, both sides of the state line, looking for land that I could farm as an urban farmer. And what struck me was just how much vacant land there was—and vacant land that really, most of us

don't see as we drive by. Today, what I see when I drive around, is I still see vacant land, I see a lot of it. But I also see farmers that have taken up vacant lots and are producing absolutely beautiful fruits and vegetables to feed people.

After Nancy's voice fades out, Mark Holland, the mayor of Kansas City, Kansas, comes on to the screen. What does he think about the work that Grow KC does, and why should we support small-scale urban farmers? "It's really fantastic," Mayor Holland says, as the video image pans to show gardeners in the local refugee agricultural training program, "It's using urban land that is available, that we need to put to good use, into productive use. And it's giving people a skill, and healthy food—in some of the areas that are the deepest food deserts that we have." The video cuts back to Nancy, who states, "We have the ear of our policy makers, we can influence the policies that make productive greenspace in the city something that becomes part of our everyday lives."

Nancy is correct about the influence her nonprofit has on local policy. In Kansas City, city officials across both sides of the state line, influential philanthropic donors, and other parties involved in urban development listen intently to the green urban infrastructure agendas outlined by Grow KC. Grow KC and several other local food-focused nonprofits have become leading voices in the metropolitan area, shaping discourse and action around how policy makers address urban "vacancy" and food insecurity. Because of this, Nancy's understandings of urban space and hunger are important—the fact that urban vacancy, to her, signals the potential for urban food production matters—because her reading of urban space will inform policies that affect the green (re)development of Kansas City.

Nancy was "struck" by just how much vacancy exists in Kansas City, and notes, "most of us don't see [it] as we drive by." Conversely, many African American Jackson County residents are acutely aware of the vacancy and disinvestment in East Side neighborhoods. Conversations—with strangers met at the bus stop, acquaintances, friends—about vacant lots, the industry that formerly existed there, and the details about how that industry went out of business—are an inescapable part of living on the East Side. In her interviews with African Americans about their engagement with nature, Finney (2014, xv) writes that for many, "their map of the world . . . demanded a particularly fine-tuned compass that allowed them to navigate a landscape that was not always hospitable." Likewise, Kansas City residents of color are particularly attuned to "vacancy"—a visual reminder of the discrimination and disinvestment Black communities are subjected to (cf. Lipsitz 2007).

Scholarship on the whitened ideologies that uphold local food movement activism has expanded quickly over the past decade. Many of the narratives shared in this chapter will not be new to those familiar with this literature—others working in this field have written extensively about how the paternalism and myopic celebration of agrarianism enacted by many foodies creates white, exclusionary space within the local food movement (cf. Alkon and McCullen 2011; Slocum 2007; Alkon and Agyeman 2011). Additionally, scholars have examined dangerous linkages between the vacancy rhetoric utilized by urban planners and green urbanism (cf. Safransky 2014). However, the important link between these two literatures—the way everyday ideology of local foodies informs urban policy mediators and impacts green urban agendas—has been less explored. Both this chapter and the following contribute to this body of work by clearly linking white ideology about local food systems to the development of spatialized whiteness within city space, enacted by urban policy mediators.

Specifically, in this chapter, I explore the ideologies about urban disinvestment, hunger, and poverty that guide the urban greening agendas of foodies like Nancy—ideologies that, centrally, revolve around concepts of vacancy, ignorance, and lack. What does it mean that in Kansas City, the most influential ways of knowing urban space and urban hunger are those shared by white voices, white readings of city space, white understandings of "vacancy"? This chapter examines examples of this dominant discourse on urban food projects, while paying keen attention to insurgent narratives of another history of urban agriculture in Kansas City and another interpretation of "vacant" land.

White Discourse, White Space

Studies of whiteness and white discourse are not a new phenomenon, nor are they unique to academia. As hooks (2009, 89) notes, African Americans have "from slavery on, shared in conversations with one another 'special' knowledge of whiteness gleaned from close scrutiny of white people." Historically, paying close attention to whiteness and white discourse was a way that people of color coped with and navigated white supremacist society. This reversed gaze has been, and is, forcibly protested by those with white privilege. Enslaved Africans, for example, could be punished for appearing to observe the whites they were serving, and today, discussions of whiteness are often countered with color-blind assertions of universal subjectivity (hooks 2009, 92–93). This refusal of whiteness to be seen serves a powerful function—to acknowledge that Black and brown subjugated "others" think critically about whiteness is to disrupt the fantasy that those who are imagined to be "subhuman" "lack the ability to comprehend, to understand, to see the workings of the powerful" (hooks 2009, 92). Refuting the existence of whiteness and white privilege allows whiteness to seem commonsense (hooks 2009, 94).

Oft repeated tropes and narratives about vacancy and blight are not harmless stories—when these sorts of stories are repeatedly told, they become naturalized as commonplace ideology. When it becomes commonplace, invisible, ideology gains power (Hall 1988). It is crucial to analyze foodie narratives because power is exercised within this discourse—it has a direct relationship to language, action, social institutions, and law (Foucault 1977). Analysis of these narratives can help us better understand both the individualized and collective process of constructing a dominant story about Kansas City's history (cf. Suzuki 2017), a story that directly works to support certain policy agendas and certain urban morphologies, while benefiting some urban residents over others.

As I outlined in the introduction to this book, I have opted to deeply anonymize foodie narratives—both out of respect for my interviewees and also to make a point about how discourse and power work. Here, I share excerpts from my interviews with over forty white, upper-middle class foodies—I have altered their life histories, and other identifiable characteristics, so that individuals would not be able to identify themselves in this text. I've adopted this methodology because discourse becomes powerful on a mass scale; while it is not helpful to vilify specific individuals,[1] looking at commonly shared metaphors, images, and narratives can help us understand how whiteness and systemic racism is embedded in Kansas City's urban food movement, and more broadly, how it informs the city's green urban development strategies.

"You Are What You Eat": Addressing Health Inequities and Community Dissolution with Fresh Food

For many foodies, the lens through which they think about urban space links pretty clearly to their own histories and transformative experiences with food and agriculture. An overwhelming number of my white interviewees had solved a health problem, relatively late in life, by adopting a "local" food diet. David, for example, a thirty-six-year-old farmers market manager, didn't take an interest in the local food movement until his son was diagnosed with ADHD. It wasn't until he had children of his own that David really started to cultivate an interest in the local food movement, and much of that interest had to do with his children's health. David told me that the chronic disorder is common in his family; many of his relatives are on medication to treat it. "For me, it made no sense for me to put my child on Adderall, what is basically cocaine, and then having to increase the dose as he got bigger." He went to the library and checked out a book called *Ritalin Free in 18 Days*, which told him and his wife that an all-organic diet free of processed food would help treat their son's ADHD. It worked; his next steps were to till up a spot in their backyard to garden and to start building a coop so they could raise their own chickens as well. A few years later, David founded both a community garden and a farmers market in his neighborhood in Northeast Kansas City, in order to help other families eat an all-organic, local, diet.

Similarly, Laura, a Grow KC staff member, left a career in pharmaceutical sales because she wanted to help people adopt "healthier" lifestyles through food instead:

> So I spent five years hawking drugs for type 2 diabetes and cardiovascular disease. Going in and out of doctors' offices every day for five years, seeing what happens when people have zero connection to the food they eat . . . and seeing what that looks like when its extrapolated out over a lifetime. We're talking about a three year old that weighed 120 pounds and was type 2 diabetic . . . so you know, these disease states that in a lot of ways can be preventable if the solution were less focused on the pill at the end or on the response to health issues, and sort of looking at it more proactively . . . and I did a whole lot of soul searching and figured out the very root of it . . . it came down to knowing where your food comes from. So I ended up volunteering out at [Grow KC's demonstration farm], and that turned in to two years there farming and spending another two years farming elsewhere, and learning all about sustainable vegetable production inside of the city, and learning about how food systems work and how they're broken, and the work that's being done to try to fix them in a very grassroots way, especially in Kansas City, and it all makes a whole lot of sense to me.

Laura, like David and other foodies, has come to believe that the best way to address structural health inequities is by encouraging low-income urban residents to produce and consume local, organic, food. This is also a well-documented ideology among local foodies nationwide (Guthman 2008; 2011a).

Nancy shares similar beliefs and approaches to addressing urban hunger and inequality. She grew up in central Kansas, not far from where parts of my own family were born and raised, and left for the West Coast immediately after high school—she hated the conservatism of the Midwest. She spent a decade apprenticing on small, organic farms, becoming heavily influenced by California local food activists like Alice Waters, and was inspired by the success of farm-to-table initiatives in the region. In 1995 she moved back to Kansas, to Kansas City, because land was more affordable than it was on the West Coast. Here, she grew food, sold food, and worked in restaurants for another decade, until 2005—when she co-founded Grow KC with a fellow farmer-friend. Since then, Grow KC has grown considerably; its goal, she said, was "getting more good food grown in city neighborhoods and more good food eaten in city neighborhoods . . . [our] programs all sort of layer in food access, community development, quality of life changes, and public health."

For Nancy, addressing hunger is a means of addressing other systemic inequities:

> One of my firmest beliefs is that we all have a right to eat local food that's culturally appropriate for us, regardless of our socioeconomic status. And I feel that not having access to that is one of the major killers of hopes and dreams, quite literally. You can take it back to Maslow's hierarchy of needs—food is one of the foundational needs that you have to have met, it literally fuels everything else, down to your biology. I mean, you are what you eat, and I very firmly believe that. If you're not getting the right fuel, then you're so sick that you're missing work and all this income . . . so addressing food, I feel like that's one of the ways we can start to address these other facets.

Because of their own personally transformative experiences with local food systems, white foodies in KC work to promote urban greenspace so that others can be personally transformed.

Guided by the impact dietary change has had on his family, David constantly works to make sure his neighbors know about, and care about, eating local, organic produce. He worked at a food bank for a few years in his early twenties, and some of his formative ideas about the diets of the urban poor were developed during that time: "I noticed that a lot of [food bank patrons] were people that were having to get low sodium [canned goods]. They have all these health issues and for some reason they don't see that the reason they have issues is because [they're] eating all this junk, and even if [you] just went out and gardened in a small spot, that would be helping your health. There was such a disconnect."

David assumes that food bank patrons are ignorant about healthy cooking and also assumes that none of them are growing food at home. Both his and Nancy's comments disregard well-established facts about health inequalities: poverty, not dietary choice, is the key predictor of health outcomes (Singer

1994; Guthman 2011b), and, regardless of poverty, people of color are more likely to be afflicted with diseases such as hypertension and diabetes—a fact which has more to do with racism than genetic predisposition (Dressler 1993). Leah, a local food nonprofit employee in her forties, shared similar assumptions about health, diet, and poverty when I asked for her thoughts on the high price of local produce: "I feel like if you're feeding your family nutrient dense food, if you're feeding them high quality food, you go to the doctor less. My family hardly ever has to go to the doctor. I can't remember the last time any of my children were sick. You can save money that way . . . I mean, I look at people whose children have just mega allergies and all these problems, and I'm kind of just like, there's gotta be some truth to it that you are what you eat."

Leah's comments frame poor health outcomes as a result of poor personal choices. For her, the solution seems simple: if consumers would make the choice to buy organic now, they would save money on doctors' bills later. Many studies indicate that diet is more intimately linked to economic capacity than nutritional knowledge or preference (i.e., when families earn a living wage, they often increase their consumption of fresh fruits and vegetables [cf. Alkon et al. 2013]). Regardless, Leah sees community gardens as important educational, transformational, sites in urban KC: "We get a chance to teach children where their food comes from. The garden is a place for learning where our food comes from, which we've become completely disconnected from. And if you grew up in the city and never got a chance to go to the farm, then you don't know . . . My goal is to see the needle move in terms of health outcomes in our neighborhood . . . I wanna see health outcomes change for struggling folks—a drop in obesity and diabetes, stuff like that."

Even though there is a rich history of urban food production in KC neighborhoods of color, Leah assumes that urban youth are unfamiliar with farms, nutrition, and health. Patrice (a community-garden manager in her fifties, who lives in an East Side neighborhood) echoes this sentiment but emphasizes that urban food production wouldn't even matter if local food advocates weren't putting equal effort into "educating" urban consumers of color about nutrition: "It's almost like, if this was a food desert, or if it wasn't, the result would be the same because of the lack of education. So it doesn't matter—if we're in the hood and we're next to the grocery store, or if we're in the hood and the nearest grocery store is five miles away—either way, everybody's eating potato chips. But if you can hit the kids early enough with education in the garden, show 'em how cool it is, you can have some influence on their life before you can't have any influence at all."

Patrice tells me she thinks her neighborhood is a better place because of her community garden—"less kids are joining gangs, more kids are having a brighter future." She thinks she sees less hunger in her community, and less "dependence on others." Much like David, Patrice is guided by the positive improvement in health and happiness she experienced when she began eating local food and feels confident that the local urban food movement can positively impact others. Similarly, Nancy, Martha, Laura, Anthony—and other white foodies—see absence, vacancy, and ignorance in urban space and within urban residents and neglect histories and current-day practices of urban food production within KC's communities of color. David, for example, doesn't consider that sites of Black food production like the Sweeney's truck farm, and myriad Eighteenth and Vine grocery stores and restaurants, have been displaced or demolished through racially discriminatory urban development. Instead, he tells me, "there's that old adage—give a man a fish, he can eat for a day, and teach him how to fish, and he can eat for a lifetime. So the idea is: can we teach that underserved population how to grow their own really healthy food?"

Vacancy, Emptiness, Crime: Urban Gardens as Urban Order Maintenance

Many foodies in KC speak about urban farms and community gardens as solutions to the issues highlighted above—disinvestment, poverty, and poor health. In these narratives, foodies frequently highlight vacancy and argue that urban agriculture can beautify, brighten, and populate the desolate urban core. Slocum (2007, 527) has analyzed this ideology as a "white geographical imagination"—where the concept of community is conflated with all things "good, proximate, wholesome, and local." These conceptions of "good" food and "beautiful" greenspace are arbitrary and based on white cultural norms.

Anthony, for example, speaking about disinvestment in the neighborhood he and his fiancé just moved into, shared, "It's hard to care about something that no one else cares about. When people start caring it's easier to care again." He told me that since the inception of his community garden, crime has gone down in the neighborhood about 80 percent—"when you're present in your community, the chances of violence are lower"—and people have started to paint their houses and pick up trash.

In some ways, Anthony's understanding of the role his community garden plays in the neighborhood is similar to ideologies that support broken windows policing, an "order maintenance" policing philosophy that prioritizes surveillance of low-level "quality of life" violations over violent crimes and has been critiqued for the harm it has inflicted on Black communities (Orisanmi 2015, 38). In this paradigm, urban crime and poverty is best addressed through increased surveillance and citations—the underlying causes of crime, such as unemployment and hunger, are unaddressed. Telling me about two blocks near his home that were currently being cleared for production as an urban farm, David stated, "A real benefit to those lots going into production is that it opens that space up—you can really see the garden, see the neighborhood. It all becomes much more open and it's easier to have eyes on the ground. You know, it's harder to have people steal from you when you don't have brush covering everything!"

Sarah, a community gardener in her late twenties, moved into the East Side of KC with a group of church friends. Describing a vacant lot near her new home, she said, "It used to serve largely as a dumping ground for trash, for people . . . .it was awful." Shortly after moving in, she and her friends planted several apple and peach trees on the lot. "As soon as we planted fruit trees there, nobody dumped anything. I tell people it was like a light switch, just on and off. We planted, and all of a sudden no dumping, no trash, now it's like a park." One of Sarah's friends created a community garden not far from the orchard lot and told me that his favorite part about gardening there was that it was good for "keeping a watch on people" in a crime-ridden area.

A white East Side police officer and local food advocate told me that he's seen crime reduction in his neighborhood since a nearby community garden was founded: "The community garden gets everybody out of their house— everyone's working to a common goal . . . it's helpful to help take ownership of each other and each other's property, simple communication. And then a big piece of it is: people are outside. They're watching, in the process of gardening, even though they don't really realize they're being witnesses, they're being witnesses [to deter crime]—because they're there."

The police officer, like other white KC foodies, discusses vacancy as a driver of crime and disinvestment, rather than a manifestation of disinvestment and poverty. Mathew, who manages distribution for a local food hub, shared remarkably similar sentiments about vacancy: "Vacancy breeds crime. But as each person steps up and takes care of their own property and is willing to go across the street and help their neighbor—it is incentive . . . if someone's house next to you looks nice, then it makes you think 'Oh, maybe I should sweep my sidewalk too, because theirs is swept.' If they're both not swept, then who cares?"

His partner, Kate, chimed in too—she's in the process of starting a small high production urban farm in a lot adjacent to their East Side home. "One of the big problems is the amount of vacant properties that we have here in the city. [Urban farmers] that are coming into the community—they care, they're taking ownership. In the process of taking care and ownership, they're outside working on the house. They're outside cutting the grass. They're outside weeding, they're picking up the trash. That tells a criminal that people care, they're paying attention, they're doing what they need to do—and if they do see something going wrong, they're more at risk of having the police called to deal with what they're doing."

The police officer, Mathew, and Kate all frame poverty and vacancy on the East Side as the result of crime and apathy. For them, and other white KC foodies, vacancy is a physical manifestation of individual poor choices, rather than a manifestation of decades of state-led disinvestment and racial discrimination. Nancy tells me that Kansas City's urban food movement has done a lot to address urban disinvestment and poverty: "It's absolutely wonderful. Over the last ten years urban agriculture has exploded, not just in Kansas City, but in areas all across the country . . . it makes a lot of sense—in the last ten years we've seen a lot of economic downturn, a lot of economic hardship. We've seen the number of vacant lots grow and grow. Urban gardens are a way to eliminate blight. They turn blight into neighborhood oases, and they make neighborhoods more attractive. To see lots that were a blight by anyone's standards be used as gardens is amazing. People are taking vacant space and making it absolutely beautiful and abundant."

Instead of questioning the purposive decisions that city governments and the real estate industry made to create "blight," Nancy's narrative shifts conversation onto how to beautify blight. Comments about urban vacancy, and beautification also ignore the rich history of industry, life, and culture that Black urban residents have cultivated in the East Side—by calling a neighborhood unequivocally blighted, Nancy denies that families build lives and communities in these spaces.

"It's *such* a great way to beautify the urban core," Constance, a retired nonprofit executive director who lives in J. C. Nichols's racially restricted Mission Hills suburb, told me one spring afternoon as we volunteered together to clear brush from a community garden on the East Side. "I just think when there's some vacant land, there should be some food growing!" Constance's comment seems innocuous, but for many, it painfully minimizes the racialized processes that resulted in urban vacancy. Similarly, in a discussion about economic decline and unemployment in Kansas City, a local food nonprofit executive director (ED) told me that she sees "urban agriculture as a web that helps make our city stronger." Both comments turn structural, deeply racialized, economic governance problems into depoliticized, race-neutral issues, easily fixed with raised beds and urban orchards.

Confronting Racial Inequality

Foodie desires to address "vacancy" with urban food projects are informed by misunderstandings of poverty and urban disinvestment. And, regardless of political affiliation, foodies often draw on neoliberal rhetoric of personal responsibility to promote these projects—for example, many assert that urban food production is important because it teaches the urban poor "self-reliance." Anthony, for example—a young white man who moved into the northeast of the city with his fiancé—hopes to start an urban farm business. The pair bought a home in an area of KC where roughly 54 percent of the population identifies as African American, and 41 percent experiences poverty (U.S. Census Bureau 2017). Here, there're an ample amount of cheap, vacant lots for Anthony to one day farm. They chose this neighborhood, Anthony told me, because he thought his farm (and an adjacent community garden) would help decrease crime and encourage "neighborly love" within the community:

> As the government gets too big . . . it takes the heart and the accountability out of things. It used to be that people had to—if they wanted help—they had to stick with the person who was going to help them, and people took care of their own. If their uncle, or brother, or cousin was acting up, they told them about it and they were on their way out. Now everybody's uncle, brother, or cousin is on the street and nobody cares because the government's taking care of them. So there's no accountability . . . no one holds 'em to the line so they never grow up, and then now you've got a bunch of ten-year-old adults running around. So I think you can't mandate love—as much as we want to love the poor, it's got to be done by individuals and not the government, because the government enables the poor.

Anthony, like many other white foodies I interviewed, thinks that urban poverty and disinvestment are the result of welfare dependency, dissolution of community, and apathy. For him, community gardens and urban food projects can be sites that encourage community and enforce accountability. His statement mirrors neoliberal global development discourse; particularly programs that encourage empowerment and vilify dependency, often in discursive service of explaining state retreat from providing necessary social services (cf. Miraftab 2010).

Similarly, Martha—a distribution manager for a food hub—told me what she thought led to the high rates of crime in the northern end of Jackson County, where she gardens at a community garden:

> There was a strong community here—maybe forty years ago?—maybe more like a hundred years ago. But some time ago that community of people—I think it's called white flight—that strong community of Italians left. They ran for the hills. They wanted to find better places for their kids. What made 'em leave all at once? I don't know. But once they left, the community fell apart. The folks who have means move out, and the folks that don't end up getting caught here in the only place they can afford to live. But the people with leadership skills move on, so there's nobody to lead the community to a better way. So what we have now is a population of people—40 percent of 'em are on disability—and they have time on their hands.

Martha's narrative about disinvestment in Jackson County doesn't include any of the discriminatory, racialized processes we discussed in the previous chapter: purposeful real estate and city government-led segregation tactics, such as blockbusting, racialized lending, and red lining (cf. Lipsitz 2007). As we have already addressed, racialized hiring practices, policing, and incarceration systems have also worked throughout the second half of the twentieth century to deplete Black neighborhoods (cf. Harrison 2013). Martha, and other foodies, instead frame narratives about urban disinvestment through a lens of neoliberal personal responsibility—in which individuals themselves are the ones responsible for either uplift or disinvestment in their communities.

Further, all of the foodies I interviewed for this book were extremely reluctant to discuss race, or to address it explicitly through their work—even though many of their urban farms, gardens, or nonprofits were situated in majority Black or brown communities. Again as previously alluded to, scholars within whiteness studies have argued that race-avoidance, or "color-blindness," is a key way whiteness functions—whites maintain power when they refuse to acknowledge that race impacts privilege (cf. Bonilla-Silva 2006). For example, when I asked Alice—a church friend of David's, who runs a program that places fruit tree orchards in low-income communities of color—about how she thinks about racial inequities in her work, she told me, "I'm gonna be really honest with you. I do think race layers in to this whole thing, but I'd be lying if I told you I'm really thinking 'where are the Latinos and how do I go help them?'"

Similarly, when I asked Leah about how she thinks food insecurity overlaps with racial inequality, she responded, "There's about a quarter of a million people in our Kansas City metro area that fall under the food insecure designation, and they come in all colors. Emergency assistance is important to all of them."

While Leah is right that many KC residents experience hunger, she misses the opportunity to explore the specific ways people of color are doubly impacted by food insecurity. Leah, discussing how her nonprofit approaches racial inequity, told me, "It's the Midwest, it's Kansas City . . . sometimes you get further by not naming something directly. And you know, I would say that while we're not direct about race, we are more direct about economic injustice. We work with a diverse array of groups across the metro. And we've got some mini grant funds that we prioritize giving to high need communities, which are generally lower income communities, inner-city communities . . . communities of color." KC foodies address race indirectly—through conversations about economic injustice, unspoken granting decisions that favor people of color, networking with "diverse" communities, and discussion of "urban" and "inner-city" hunger (cf. Bonilla-Silva 2006).

Even in explicit discussion of racialized barriers, many foodies pivoted to race-neutral explanations for inequities. For example, when I asked Nancy how Grow KC addressed Kansas City's racial boundary line, Troost, in its work— she told me I misunderstood the street's history. Troost, Nancy explained, was built wider than other streets to allow large produce trucks to pass through— there were a lot of farms east of Troost, and the street inadvertently became a racial boundary. I pushed—sharing some of the history I knew about how Troost was created as a purposive racial boundary, and Nancy shook her head: "[Racial division] came later. It was more the move away from agriculture in general that created that divide." Nancy's understanding of racial divisions in Kansas City is messy, confusing, and color-blind—she doesn't mention, for example, that the farms east of Troost were actually large-scale plantations.

Laura, another Grow KC staff member, told me how she works to address "diversity" through the programming she designs for local farmers. She used Grow KC's annual mini-conference, Farmers and Friends, as an entry point to the discussion:

> The first time we held our annual Farmers and Friends meeting . . . that was a really, really, diverse group. As the event has grown and more people have shown up, the diversity has gotten a lot less—it's gotten a lot more middle class. Most of it is that those early farmers, they got connected, they set up their relationships, so to some degree they don't need to come network. Some of the groups, like the Hmong, they're a somewhat closed off community. Also—our biggest challenges in the years to come is that we need to help

smaller scale farms get going. We need to turn them into mid-sized and larger. History and experience argues that that's going to be a more educated, whiter group of people who have more comfort with taking out loans, dealing with institutions for financing and the rest. How do we help them figure out financing and equipment appropriate for larger scale? So we want to really deliberately work on those barriers with this specific group of people.

Laura's comment indicates some ways that Grow KC's programming might prove ineffective in addressing racial inequality in the urban food system. First, she speculates that their events are whiter, and more privileged, because people of color have established their own support networks or are "closed off"—an assertion that might lead Grow KC staff to spend minimal time addressing inclusivity. Second, and importantly, Laura notes that they're working to help small-scale farmers scale up through loan assistance and financial education. Her comment that white, "more educated" people will have "more comfort" with this process paints an incomplete picture of the problem— people of color face historical, and current, racial discrimination from banks, the real estate industry, and the USDA that pose real barriers in their ability to scale up (cf. Havard 2001). By addressing farmer financing through a color-blind lens, with an imperfect understanding of historical racial discrimination, Grow KC misses the opportunity to meaningfully assist farmers of color.

As a result of these race-avoidant strategies and misunderstandings about poverty and urban disinvestment, many foodies feel uncomfortable when asked to directly confront racial inequality. For example, Nancy told me about her friend Hank—a Black farmer in his eighties:

It's funny, over the years his racial views have gotten even more polarized. Anytime I see him he makes a point of reminding me that if he and I had been talking like we were, standing as close as he were, he could've been lynched— you know, he grew up in rural Texas, in an agricultural community. [In contrast] One of the things I like about our refugee community in Kansas City is that these people, for most of them, farming is something that has respect and value. They've got emotional baggage about their refugee experience, but it's not so much about farming. So I feel like they are present in farming in a way that is pretty miraculous, and it's great to work with them.

Later, Hank tells me that he didn't just grow up in an "agricultural community." He grew up amid violence—his family sharecropped, and the landowner threatened them with economic and physical repercussions if they tried to leave. And, while Nancy implies that the refugee farming community has less "emotional baggage" than African Americans, this is not necessarily true—and white privilege is equally implicated in the displacement and violence afflicted against both populations. Nancy's comment highlights a number of key themes in foodie understandings of race and urban history—an avoidance of direct conversation about race and privilege, a messy and incongruous understanding of race, history, and politics, and a desire to reframe discussion of inequities into discussion about strengthening the urban local food system.

"Foodie"-Created White Public Space

The ideologies about urban hunger and disinvestment shared in this chapter are not innocuous—these oft repeated stories about Kansas City's East Side and its residents normalize harmful falsehoods about the urban poor that inform and support local green urbanism policies. Many white upper-middle class KC foodies share remarkably similar ideologies about urban hunger, poverty, and racialized histories of urban space—likely because of the local food movement's institutionalization through conferences, popular texts, and hegemonic discourse (cf. chapter 1). These ideologies hold true across political and religious divides; both foodies who confided in me that they helped vote President Trump into office, and those who proudly vote for Democrats down the ballot align in discourse surrounding urban vacancy and the benefits of urban food production. Their narratives depict Kansas City's East Side as vacant and desolate; its residents as unhealthy, ignorant, and lazy. Foodies assume that urban food projects will improve urban space, as they see it as a place of lack. Mobilizing around urban orchards in low-income communities seems commonsense, when one doesn't acknowledge, or isn't aware, of (1) deep racialized discrimination that has shaped and created "vacancy" in these spaces and (2) historical displacement of urban farms and gardens operated by East Side residents of color. Of course, discourse and practice are separate, sometimes overlapping, domains. Racial ideologies, especially the ones presented in this chapter, are uneven and messy and don't always concretely relate to action. For Kansas City foodies, however, the ideologies discussed here translate fairly neatly into policy outcomes and green governance strategies, as will be explored more in the following chapter.

For a vast majority of the influential local foodies in KC, this intense focus on promoting urban food projects, this idea that food can be personally transformative, came from their *own* personally transformative food experiences—such as David improving his son's health with organic produce, Nancy's experiences "coming of age" on West Coast farms, and Laura's years witnessing health-related inequities in the U.S. healthcare industry. These experiences and others place food at the forefront of many foodies' political ideologies; many of them shared with me their hopes that if others could have personal experiences with food, if they "put their hands in the dirt, "they would be transformed in the same way. This focus on food occludes the realities of deep structural urban inequality, but it has become the lens through which foodies imagine (re)developing urban space. It denies that, globally, the settler colonial process has involved displacing people of color from their land, the erasure of Indigenous foodways, and myriad other measures of violence.

Common foodie ideologies perpetuate untrue assumptions about the urban poor, racialized minority groups, and urban disinvestment. Chief among these is the idea that increased physical proximity to sites of urban food production will incite a number of positive changes among urban residents. Assertions that learning where "real" food comes from, being immersed in urban greenspace, and engaging in the act of cultivating food will improve the diets and health of the urban poor rest on dangerous falsehoods, such as the idea that poor health is the result of poor food choice and that poverty and crime are a result of lack of leadership and accountability. When Mayor Mark Holland, for example, emphasizes that urban food projects can help develop skills in food desert residents, he reinforces the idea that deserts, "vacancy," and blight are a symptom of urban residents' apathy and lack of skilled labor. This focus turns attention away from the structural, racialized causes of vacancy and blight and helps support neoliberal self-help policy agendas that are ill-equipped to address the real root causes of urban hunger and inequality. This narrative also rests upon a distortion of urban racialized history that elides the historical participation of people of color in urban food production and ignores the repeated displacement and violence Black urban residents have experienced in Kansas City.

Foodies in Kansas City draw heavily on race-avoidant discursive strategies in both their work and personal lives, falling back on language of blight and outright dismissal of race as an issue, asserting that the problems facing African Americans are not any different than the problems faced by all urban poor and people of color. Blight is not recognized as a byproduct of profit ventures and the urban growth machine (Molotch 1976); it is discussed as the result of individual disinvestment in the "beautification" of space. Foodies create white public space with these dismissals—in the assertion that Troost is merely an agricultural barrier and not a racialized one, in the discursive enforcement of the idea that health inequities are the result of food dollars poorly spent, in the discomfort and avoidance of associating with Black Kansas Citians who carry too much "emotional baggage" about agriculture, and in the policing of communities of color via "eyes on the ground" in urban farms and gardens. Policy makers enforce white public space on a citywide scale when they listen to those who "think there should be some food growing" when they see a vacant lot and dismiss those who ask about why that lot was disinvested in in the first place.

By sharing these narratives at the front end of this book I might, paradoxically, foreground white voices in representations of Kansas City. In the following chapter, I outline how these narratives manifest spatially in urban greening policies that further marginalize and displace people of color in the city. In each chapter that follows, however, I work to deconstruct this dominant, white-led, story about the East Side.

CHAPTER 3

Getting a Seat at the Table

White Local "Foodies" and
Green Urban Development Policy

Around sixty foodies gathered in a greenhouse. Rows of folding chairs had been set up to face a whiteboard; behind the seating, a buffet of vegan Indian food, prepared by a local, white, farm-to-table chef, was spread on a cream tablecloth. The greenhouse belonged to Danny—the wealthy owner of a micro-green business and high-tunnel company, who earlier reframed Neferet's concerns at the Grow & Tell. We had converged, on a fall evening in 2017, for what was being called a "Food Leader" meeting, hosted by a group of KC foodies, including Nancy and David. The attendees were overwhelmingly white and included local celebrity chefs, local-food advocates from nonprofit and philanthropy backgrounds, upper-middle class urban and peri-urban farmers, and foodie nonprofit directors. As we sat and ate channa masala, two nonprofit EDs annotated the discussion on the whiteboard, while they prompted participants to identify and share "challenges and opportunities in the urban food movement."

Invitations for this meeting, and others that would follow, were spread by word of mouth, within mostly white social circles. At each meeting, one attendee would raise the unanswered question: "How do we get more diversity in this room?" No substantive action, however, other than white foodies encouraging attendees of color to invite their friends, was taken to address the issue. At the January Food Leaders meeting, one of only two Black attendees posted an open invitation on Facebook, during the event itself. Andre, a Black farmer who has been selling food in the KC metropolitan area for more than a decade, wrote, "I am at a KC farmers meeting with pretty much everyone in KC that grows food and a few chefs. Event is catered by Farmhouse, Belfry, and Webster House chefs, who are also in attendance. I wish there were more brown faces here. Networking. $$$. What can I do to get you involved?" In response, other Black growers commented that they had no idea this event was happening. Some posted, "No one told us," and one Black woman, who owns a local-food centered small business, stated, "You know how I feel about those people."

The lack of diversity at the Food Leader meetings is a point of serious concern. Over the course of 2017, these gatherings—heralded as informal potlucks and held in foodies' homes and farm-to-table cafes—were formative spaces for the development of local policy and important networking opportunities for green entrepreneurs. Concerns and ideas initially scrawled on whiteboards were ultimately used to inform a policy document—"Strategic Framework for Adaptive Change in Kansas City's Regional Food System"—drafted by influential foodies who convened the Food Leader meetings. Foodies planned to take this document to local policy makers and philanthropists for funding. Because only upper-middle class white local food advocates' opinions were solicited during its drafting, the policy recommendations it outlines are color-blind; racial and class-based inequities in the food system aren't identified as a challenge, even though, arguably, they are the biggest challenge KC faces in its local food economy. Instead, the document lists three areas of foci for urban policy makers to address: helping create "a niche market for healthy food"; "overcoming divisions between conventional and organic urban farmers"; and "assisting urban farmers with business expansion." A result of the majority white, informal policy-making spaces—that people of color are either uninformed of or too uncomfortable to attend—is color-blind policy that supports privileged and white farmers and consumers.

Scholars working at the intersection of green urbanism and gentrification have called for more explicit examination of how "[urban agriculture], capitalist development, and racial difference work through one another" (McClintock 2018b, 2). This chapter meets that call, linking foodie ideology and discourse to the development of spatialized whiteness within city space. The narratives shared here demonstrate how the pioneer imaginary core to much urban agriculture discourse is animated by, and central to, the development of urban greening agendas (cf. Safransky 2014; McClintock 2018b). Through paternalistic discourse around health and "appropriate" land use, foodies displace Blackness and spatialize whiteness (cf. Rutland 2018).

In this chapter I explore the influential ways these largely white-only groups, such as the Food Leaders, create impact far beyond the potluck. Kansas City's green urban development agenda has been shaped by the ideologies and interests of white local foodies; policy agendas and foci are developed and refined in foodie-centric spaces—meetings at high-end farm to table restaurants, conversations at community garden workdays, potlucks at foodie ED houses. As a result, green urbanism in Kansas City centers around promoting urban agriculture as a solution to myriad problems. This chapter unpacks, in detail, these informal conversations and traces how they've informed urban greening policy. Ultimately, I argue this is a key way that whiteness takes up space in Kansas City.

Who's Present at the Table?
Influential "Foodies" in Kansas City

Nancy, the executive director of Grow KC, shared that when she first sat down with elected officials in 2005, on both sides of the state line, to discuss her vision for the city, she was laughed at. "'Urban agriculture? Ha, ha, goats in the city,' and so on. It was just totally not part of their framework," she said. Real estate agents even implored city officials to ignore her proposals, concerned that urban agriculture would bring down property values.

Now, however, there is extensive city government support for urban agriculture as a key mechanism of green urban development in Kansas City. "There's been an extraordinary developmental process for them," Nancy told me, referring to the metropolitan area city officials. More broadly, there is hegemonic support for—evidenced through citywide discourse celebrating urban agriculture—and capitalization upon urban agriculture initiatives. Part of that change came through persistence—Nancy kept scheduling meetings to explain her goals, even when faced with pushback—but it also came through strategic networking and social capital. Nancy told me that she, David, and several other foodies became close with several city council people, particularly one involved in urban land zoning and brownfields fund distribution. Convincing *friends* that urban zoning that allowed backyard chickens—one of the first policy changes that came about via foodie involvement in Kansas City—would also benefit food-insecure individuals was much easier than convincing an elected official whom they barely knew.

However, also key to local foodie influence were the national discourse valorizing the local food movement and "healthy" eating that arose in the United States at the beginning of the twenty-first century and the subsequent institutionalization of foodie discourse and ideologies through texts, conferences, and hegemonic discourse. This movement, for the most part, receives bipartisan support. Programs such as the Food Insecurity Nutrition Incentive (FINI), pushed through Congress by a bipartisan group in 2014, supports local food movement goals by funneling money toward farmers markets and small-scale farmers. It speaks to conservatives—whose voter base has a historical concern with "welfare queens" (Goode and Maskovsky 2001, 7)—because it ensures that SNAP recipients are spending their food dollars on "healthy" choices. On the Democratic side, First Lady Michelle Obama's revival of the White House garden in 2009 was a significant national move in support of the food movement and discursively enforced the idea that growing your own produce can be a curative for poverty-related diseases like obesity and diabetes (a KCMO city planner told me, for example, that the White House Garden "really, really did help incentivize the city"). Within the context of a national-level normalization of food movement ideologies, Nancy's proposal that urban agriculture play an extensive role in green urban development took hold in Kansas City.

In 2005, when Nancy cofounded Grow KC, the only other local food-focused nonprofit in the area was an organization that published a yearly organic farmer directory. This organization focuses on connecting organic producers to consumers and does not involve itself in any policy advocacy. Grow KC, in contrast, is explicitly focused on changing hegemonic understandings of urban space and what it should be used for (namely, agriculture). Nancy told me that at Grow KC, "We've done, over the years, tons of stuff that is about public education, cooperative planning, envisioning neighborhoods, envisioning the city, challenging people to think about different models than the rest—and we've done that through conferences, workshops, our annual Farmers and Friends gathering. So we've done a lot to stir the pot, make people think—and think not only about their specific situation, but think more in a systems way."

Grow KC uses a diverse array of programs to accomplish these goals. They offer yearly mini-grants to small-scale urban growers, run a demonstration farm (a high production, small, organic farm in Jackson County), and operate a biannual "Urban Grown" tour, which highlights urban farms and gardens in the metropolitan area. The tour—which featured thirty-one sites in 2016—is a key mechanism Grow KC uses to engage policy makers in their work; one day of the weekend-long tour is set aside for Grow KC staff to personally guide elected officials around the urban gardens. Grow KC administers a large FINI grant for the Kansas City metropolitan area, providing oversight and managing the distribution of SNAP-doubling benefits. Their most prominent work is a refugee agricultural training program, which they operate jointly with Jewish Vocational Services. The three-year farm training program provides language and marketing skills to newly arrived refugees. This farm is located beside the region's oldest housing project, whose residents—almost all African

American—refer to the site as a plantation. Many East Side residents of color refer to Grow KC as run by, and for—despite its claims that their programs help the urban poor—the white, upper-middle class.

In 2007 a food-policy focused nonprofit in the Kansas City metropolitan area—the Hunger Coalition—was founded through a large philanthropic donation; today, they are an influential force in urban policy in KC. A family foundation "had a ton of money and needed to spend it," explained Nancy, and funding efforts to address food insecurity seemed like a good idea. Because of this huge capital influx, free of the oversight or strings like grant funding would bring, the Hunger Coalition has been able to use its funds freely to sway policy makers and upper-middle-class foodies in KC. According to Nancy,

> So they had meetings and did things that no other nonprofit possibly could do. Like, they would have meetings at one of the best restaurants in town, they would pay for everybody's meal—they would like, basically, hand out a free forty-dollar meal and get everyone in the room, because it was [a high-end local Italian restaurant] and they wanted to eat. And then they'd talk to them about food and growing food, and of course most of us couldn't possibly afford that. So that's how they got people that were somewhat more mainstream, more in the sort of traditional and corporate worlds to pay attention and start showing up. That was an important dynamic.

For many foodies I spoke with, using philanthropic donations to fund conversations about food insecurity and policy change was thought of as an unequivocally good, charitable, act. Many told me they saw it as a productive use of wealth. However, it is also a highly privileged means of conveying policy agendas, which occurs outside the bounds of the democratic process. In contrast, the food insecure urban poor—who were not included in these lunchtime policy agenda setting meetings—must rely on voting in city officials who they hope will enact legislation that positively affect them. They have no means of influencing the policy agendas of those who attend these lunches.

The Hunger Coalition's goals are "to advocate for the Greater Kansas City food system and promote food policies that positively impact the nutritional, economic, social, and environmental health of Greater Kansas City." The organization accomplishes this primarily through lobbying—current issues include lowering the food tax and changing mobile vending laws in Kansas—and campaigning for Senior Farmers Market Nutrition funding in Missouri. The Hunger Coalition also mobilizes upper-middle-class foodies around food-access related issues, primarily via monthly meetings of the Food Desert working group and the Grocery Access Taskforce working group. At these meetings, individuals working on, or curious about, these topics are invited to come share progress and requests for assistance. In my two years of attending them, I've only ever been joined by five or six individuals of color; the attendees are also, consistently, upper-middle class.

The Hunger Coalition is run by Healthy Communities KC—a nonprofit that emphasizes cultivating healthy bodies through the creation of healthy urban environments (researchers have critiqued this framework, arguing that this focus on obesogenic environments should be shifted to a focus on economic conditions, cf. Shannon 2014; Guthman 2011). Founded in 2005 through a philanthropic donation from a retired physician who was worried about childhood obesity, Healthy Communities KC's mission statement asserts that "when our neighborhoods support healthy habits, we are less likely to suffer from obesity . . . heart disease, and poor mental health," and of their work, states: "to make a lasting impact, we shape policies that improve our food system and physical surroundings, and ultimately, the places where we live, work, learn, and play." To accomplish the above, the Hunger Coalition provides incentives to restaurants for purchasing local food, organizes farm-to-school training for teachers and advocates, and performs and publishes the results of urban walk-ability assessments.

While Grow KC, the Hunger Coalition, and Healthy Communities KC are the foundational and most influential foodie-run, policy-focused nonprofits in Kansas City, there a few other nonprofit organizations, whose programming focuses on the promotion of local food projects, that exert policy influence. Our Daily Bread, a faith-based nonprofit, was founded in 2011 by a group of suburban Kansas Citians who had become "deeply concerned for the growing number of hungry people and [were] seeking a way to provide them more sustainable, nutrient-rich food." Our Daily Bread plants orchards across the city, in vacant lots and places labeled food deserts, in order to "feed the hungry." Having planted around 150 orchards in the metropolitan area, Our Daily Bread is often cited—by city officials and in dominant discourse—as a key player in providing for the poor and for reshaping urban space. Within the past five years, the organization secured partnerships with the Parks and Recreation departments in Kansas and Missouri that will allow them to plant orchards on city-owned properties. Kansas City Grower's Club is another nonprofit with significant influence in KC's urban landscape; they offer very low-cost membership, seeds, compost, and backyard gardening classes for low-income gardeners and small-scale farmers. Additionally, they provide infrastructural support and guidance for schools or businesses who wish to incorporate a vegetable garden into their landscaping; administer $100,000 dollars of KCMO city funding, yearly, for water audits for small-scale growers; and offer a small grant system for gardeners and farmers who need help with water catchment systems or municipal water line installation. Finally, the Pantry is also key in shaping KC's urban food policy—this is a nonprofit that mobilizes foodies to harvest second-best produce from area farms, which it then distributes to the food insecure via various food pantries and programs across the metropolitan area. Because of this, the Pantry is highly influential in green urban governance and shaping local discourse that heralds urban farmers as important players in the fight against urban blight and food insecurity.

In the United States, national and state governments increasingly redirect public revenue to third-sector organizations, empowering them to take active roles in formerly public responsibilities, such as welfare disbursal and governance (cf. Russell and Edgar 1998). In Kansas City, where local-food movement advocacy dominates the third sector, the organizations mentioned above have been elevated as powerful urban policy mediators, whose thoughts on food insecurity and urban vacancy are incorporated into green urban governance, that is, into policy that prioritizes the use of urban space for food production. The third sector is, arguably, especially influential in Kansas City: KCMO ranks fifth nationwide in a study of cities ranking nonprofits in terms of size, influence, and financial capacity (Charity Navigator 2010). Thus, it's important to shed light on the organizational ideologies, agendas, and policy-making processes of those within this sector.

Advocating for Farmers Markets: Arguing the Value of Farmers Markets as Vital for Food Security, Urban Economic Growth

In July 2018, at the height of farmers market season in Kansas City, two small local businesses operating at two urban farmers markets were shut down by the health department—an incident that sheds light on how third-sector foodie ideology becomes policy, and, more broadly, how the spaces in which policy is developed have expanded beyond City Hall. One of the businesses, a small yet high-end locally sourced bakery, has a physical storefront in the wealthy Brookside neighborhood and also sells coffee and baked goods—like their $4-dollar homemade toaster pastries—at the Brookside farmers market. The market imposes strict nearly-organic requirements on its vendors and is praised and heavily trafficked as a weekend outing by Brookside residents. It is also known throughout the city as the most wildly expensive place to buy eggs. The second business that was shut down was a flavored snow cone business, run by a ten-year-old East Side youth. He sold cones of fresh-made shaved ice with bottled syrup for $1 apiece, weekly at an East Side farmers market. The young entrepreneur raised money for a cash register, ice-shaving machine, and other infrastructural costs by doing odd jobs around his neighborhood. Both the bakery and the snow-cone business were shut down during surprise health department visits to their respective farmers markets, and both were charged with violation of processed foods codes. The bakery was told it had prepared its baked goods without proper certification, and the snow cone business was told, similarly, that it had not prepared ice in compliance with health codes. For both businesses, the codes violations involved food preparation code gray areas—Missouri allows prepared products to be sold at farmers markets without being cooked in a certified kitchen, under what is called Cottage Law, but Kansas City, Missouri's, city health department requires all goods to be prepared in a certified kitchen. Missouri law should technically supersede the city requirement, but health department officials, in practice, enforce this law inconsistently and unpredictably. Refuting codes violations depends a great deal on a producer's ability to contest the citation and argue that their practices are in line with health department codes.

While the bakery owner is prominent within foodie circles and locally respected by white foodies (because the business sources consistently from urban farmers), the snow-cone business owner—popular on the East Side—could not draw on any influential social networks. The ten-year-old's snow-cone stand was shut down permanently, as neither he nor his mother had the means to address the code violations, and within the broader "food scene" in KC no one mentioned or discussed the demolition of his business. In contrast, a group of foodies went to bat for the bakery, including several influential local farmers, market managers, and Brookside Market vendors. They formed a coalition to change the city's farmers markets codes to allow the bakery to continue selling their products at market.

This coalition drafted a set of complaints, looped in a representative from Healthy Communities KC to help facilitate the conversation, and set up a meeting with officials from the Kansas City, Missouri, Health Department to petition for change—a meeting that I was invited to attend as well, as some foodie friends thought I might learn valuable information about regulatory barriers affecting urban farmers. The Health Department was amenable to hearing foodie concerns and scheduling such a meeting, given the long history of collaboration and involvement foodies have with the KC city governments. During this meeting, the foodies argued that the KCMO health department codes had not been enforced consistently over time, causing confusion, and that the codes made no sense. Because the bakery can no longer sell at the Brookside Market, the coalition argued, the Brookside Market's traffic and economic viability has been reduced. Farmers markets, they pressed, depend upon product variety to draw in and retain customers; the markets are vital to downtown Kansas City's image and economy, as people moving back into the urban core shop at these markets; finally, Brookside, as a community, gathers around this market. The coalition drew on and leveraged its members economic contributions to Kansas City's urban economy, making the case that this "green" image is central to Brookside and to economic development in the metropolitan area.

Foodies used the meeting as an opportunity to bring up other policy changes they wanted enacted. Laura, a market manager at an East Side farmers market (who had previously been a market manager for a market in the Northeast) interjected halfway through the meeting to mention how vital cooking demonstrations are to a market's success. Cooking demonstrations, and offering free samples for customers to taste, are game-changers, she said. Farmers sell more produce, and food insecure customers, she argued, learn how to cook with fresh food. "Low-income families don't really know how to cook the food we're selling. It's really important to show them," she said. However, current codes require either individual vendors to pay for sampling permits, or for samples to be prepared at a stationary sink that has undergone a strict inspection—this just is not financially feasible, she said, at her market. Although numerous studies (see also chapter 4; Minkoff Zern 2012) indicate that food-insecure individuals are often quite adept at cooking well with limited means, Laura's argument was well-received by those in the meeting— who, though they would likely describe themselves as racially and ethnically diverse, were on the whole an upper-middle-class privileged group.

A number of policy outcomes emerged from this and several follow up meetings. First, the Health Department agreed to increase education and outreach involving farmers market codes, so that all vendors are better aware of what is required of them. A specific codes inspector was assigned to the Brookside Market, and a get-to-know-you meeting between the inspector and the vendors was scheduled, partially in order to help the bakery at the center of this imbroglio better understand how to bring their business back into health department compliance. Because of her comments at the meeting, Laura was offered a variance for her East Side market—she's now allowed to offer samples to customers without the costly expenses and time involved in setting up a certified market kitchen. Laura tells me, regarding her victory, "If you're gracious to city officials, just like you'd be gracious to cops, you get what you need."

Though Laura probably did not mean to, her reference to interactions with police officers highlights important facets of the coalition's meeting with the Health Department. Just as interactions, and their outcomes, with police officers are highly racialized (Johnson 2003; Balko 2013; Burton 2015), so too are these interactions with city officials. In their ability to petition the Health Department for a meeting, foodies draw on a wealth of unacknowledged racialized social capital and privilege (Bourdieu 1984; Glover 2004). This privilege, combined with citywide valorization and promotion of foodie ideology, allowed the coalition to approach the Kansas City Missouri Health Department and identify, define, and suggest solutions for urban problems—ultimately allowing them to shape green economic policy in ways that benefit white farmers and foodies.

Cultivating Urban Investment:
Urban Agriculture Zoning, "Blight,"
and "Revitalizing" the Urban Core

"Blight" designations are common in city plans and ordinances nationwide; in Kansas City, they are central to the way urban agriculture ordinances operate and the way racialized urban space is created and (re)enforced in green urban development. The groundwork for these urban agriculture policies was laid during the end of the first decade of the twenty-first century, when foodies began petitioning KCMO and KCK city governments for ordinance changes to expand opportunities for urban farm businesses. A KCMO city official explained the genesis of developments to me—around 2005, her now-friend Charlotte began scheduling meetings at City Hall to loosen local restrictions on urban chicken coops. Charlotte—an upper-middle class white self-identified "urban homesteader," wanted to keep chickens within the urban core and eventually wanted the option to sell the eggs at market. In her petitions, Charlotte argued that changing these ordinances would accomplish a number of things: it would beautify urban space by repopulating it with nature; it would allow urban residents in food deserts to access fresh food and animal products; and it would create job opportunities for urban entrepreneurs. The city official told me that she, and other KCMO staff, were so impressed by Charlotte's arguments that they invited her and other foodies to start collaborating with them on plans for green urban development in the city. Going forward, Charlotte and others in her foodie social circle—directors and staff at Grow KC, Healthy Communities KC, and the Hunger Coalition—would have a major impact on urban land use policy in Kansas City, as their insight and policy suggestions for green urban development were actively sought out by city officials.

The first major policy outcome of foodie and city official collaboration was KCMO's urban agriculture ordinances, which were enacted in 2010. KCMO city officials invited Charlotte and other foodies to evaluate all of the city ordinances regarding urban food production and to propose any changes they could identify. True, crop agriculture has always been legal in residential neighborhoods in Kansas City—urban residents have always been allowed to grow and eat their own food. The major changes the foodies suggested and enacted via the urban agriculture ordinances increased the ability of urban residents to start and expand urban food businesses—this was a key priority for numerous members of the foodie advisory team who worked on drafting the policy. A number of them already sold produce to their neighbors informally and wanted the ability to grow their businesses.

So, while heralded as a solution to urban hunger, disinvestment, unemployment, and the supposed dissolution of "community," the 2010 ordinances chiefly operate to ease restrictions on urban farm businesses and paved the way for a wave of white, upper-middle class in-migration into historically Black communities in the urban core. A flier explaining the ordinance changes, published by the city and Grow KC, states, "There was a need to bring the codes more up to date with what is actually happening on the ground in city neighborhoods . . . [These codes] help communities reap the benefits of urban food production: [offering] increased access to home-grown healthy produce, economic opportunities from the sales of agricultural and horticultural products, employment and learning opportunities, and the creation of productive, community-building green space in a rapidly changing city landscape."

As the ordinance flier text indicates, these policy changes were locally championed as a sort of public health intervention that would loop marginalized urban residents into emerging green urban development schemes—helping Kansas Citians sell produce to their hungry neighbors and offering apprenticeship opportunities to community youth. But, while the codes are marketed as a panacea to a number of urban ills, they were never mentioned to me by small-scale backyard growers or by any urban residents of color. None of the East Side residents of color I spoke to even knew about the ordinances. Additionally, many gardeners and small-scale farmers of color I spoke with told me they actively avoided even looking at city ordinances and health codes related to their activity; they have, and will continue to, grow food and distribute it—no matter what restrictions urban policy may place on these practices.

Those who did tell me about these ordinances, and how they paved the way for their small-farm businesses in the urban core, were white, upper-middle class, and were selling their produce not within food-insecure neighborhoods but to high-end restaurants. A number of white foodies bought low-cost, so-called blighted, land in the urban core of Kansas City to start farm businesses shortly after 2010, when these ordinance changes were passed. During the time I lived on the East Side, I knew of seven white urban farmers—in my neighborhood alone—who had taken advantage of the urban agriculture ordinances and other food project incentives to move into the urban core and start farm businesses. This isn't anomalous. Other scholars have identified that in the United States, there is a predominance of white farmers and gardeners in communities of color (cf. Reynolds 2014; Meenar and Hoover 2012).

Even more influential, however, than the 2010 urban agriculture ordinances is Article VI of Kansas City, Missouri's, Urban Development ordinances—the Urban Agriculture Zone Ordinance (UAZ). The roots of this ordinance lies in Missouri Senator Jason Holsman's interest in urban food production and consumption. In 2010, around the same time that *The Omnivore's Dilemma* was published and national discourse was promoting urban sustainability and local food initiatives, Senator Holsman formed a joint committee on urban farming to investigate the possibility of strengthening Missouri's urban local food economy. This committee consisted of five senators, five members of the House of Representatives, and a subcommittee including eight foodie representatives from urban farming or sustainable agriculture organizations within the Missouri area. The committee held four public hearings across the state of Missouri in 2010; at the one in Kansas City, area stakeholders in urban agriculture came to speak about their aspirations for urban agriculture and green urban development. As a result of these foodie-informed conversations, the joint committee published a report proposing statewide zoning ordinances supporting urban food production. Senator Holsman's initial proposition for a statewide urban agriculture zone ordinance was ultimately voted down; he then sought support in Kansas City to pass a citywide ordinance. In partnership with Senator Holsman, City Councilman Scott Wagner, the assistant city manager, and representatives from Grow KC, the Kansas City Grower's Club, Our Daily Bread, the Pantry, and the Hunger Coalition drafted a policy designed to support urban agriculture businesses across the metropolitan area; this local UAZ was passed into law in 2014 in KCMO. Thus, again, food-

ies were intensely influential in the shaping of green urban policy futures—
the seats they held on the committee, and the opinions they expressed in the
public hearings, would ensure that city officials would eventually adopt policy supporting urban farm businesses as a key component of green urban
development.

An Urban Agricultural Zone (UAZ), as defined by these foodies, is an area
designated by the local government to "promote food production as a healthy
strategy; create new land use opportunities for unused land; increase positive
economic activities in blighted communities; [and] facilitate and support surrounding housing and business development."

In short, the UAZ offers economic incentives to encourage urban food production and distribution, namely, lowering property tax and sales tax rates
for businesses that propose to grow, process, or distribute/vend locally produced products in urban space that has been designated as "blighted." Individuals or businesses must apply to have their land zoned as a UAZ. In order
to do so, they present their case to the Urban Agricultural Advisory Commission—a board that consists of Nancy, David, and several other local foodies
and does not include local homeowners or other community stakeholders;
if they receive the designation, they will gain a twenty-five-year property tax
abatement. They are also eligible to apply for discounted water rates. There are
no direct incentives listed for urban residents who live near the incoming UAZ
business, other than potential employment opportunities (though the business is not required to create more than one job in order to apply for a UAZ),
and increased "access" to locally grown and processed healthy food (despite
the fact that physical access does not equate with actual access, or affordability). In fact, local communities near UAZs may be actively disadvantaged—
all taxes from the sale of agricultural products within a UAZ are collected and
deposited into a UAZ-specific fund, to contribute to future urban agriculture
projects, meaning that already-divested urban tax bases are further depleted
(cf. Gordon 2008).

In the ordinance, "blight" is defined as "an area of the City which the City
Council determines that by reason of age, obsolescence, inadequate, or out-
moded design or physical deterioration has become an economic and social liability, and that such conditions are conducive to ill health, transmission of disease, crime, or inability to pay reasonable taxes." The ordinance
requires the applicant to document blight, which the advisory commission
will then verify. In effect, this gives an all-white, upper-middle class board the
ability to geographically define the urban core and blighted areas in need of

beautification and development. This vague definition of blight—determined on a case by-case-basis—facilitates development in any urban area the advisory commission deems to be blighted, based on their racialized and class-specific interpretation of city space. The signifiers of "blight" listed in the UAZ definition—physical deterioration, conditions conducive to ill health, inability to pay reasonable taxes—are discursively naturalized as urban conditions, rather than as the result of purposive racialized discrimination.

African Americans in Kansas City are subjected to a number of policies that "blight" their neighborhoods: labor markets that are less likely to hire them than white applicants (Sugrue 1996), continued racialized renting and loaning practices, and purposive state policy that has prevented Black accumulation of generational wealth, resulting in higher rates of poverty (Oliver and Shapiro 1997). This broad array of policies and practices—better thought of as racialized violence on a structural scale—actively disadvantages people of color. Combined, these policies push African Americans into lower housing stock in geographically contained swaths of the city, which are then identified as blighted and are cleared for more "productive" use—a process that is masked with the seemingly apolitical discourse of "ending food desertification" and "promoting healthier urban communities and lifestyles."

Furthermore, UAZs may only be created on "underutilized urban parcels," which in effect translates into the identification of "underutilized" space as primarily low-income African American occupied space. "Underutilized urban parcels" are defined in the ordinance as vacant or "economically obsolescent, outdated or failing," which is further explained as a parcel of land that is located in a census tract having a poverty rate of 20 percent or greater, or in a tract where at least 33 percent of the population lives more than one mile from a supermarket. This idea of urban productivity, which is predicated upon and reinforces white public space, finds the most value in creating urban areas for the "creative class," who create and circulate capital in state-preferred ways (Lloyd 2010). It denies the creativity, contributions to the urban economy, and resourcefulness of the urban poor, who are displaced from underutilized space. In reality, residents of "economically obsolescent" space prop up postindustrial urban economies by holding down two, three, or four low-wage service sector positions at a time; this is a huge contribution to the city. In Chicago, for example, the low-wage service sector is estimated to constitute more than 30 percent of local revenue generation (Wilson and Keil 2008, 843).

A member of the city government told me that one of their goals with the UAZ was "to really incentivize people to come back to the urban core, to

blighted areas, to use urban agriculture to do that." UAZ's became a key mechanism, in their thinking, for moving toward a green urbanism in Kansas City
that would be attractive to the creative class. Many of the Black East Side residents I spoke with considered this development strategy akin to settler colonialism (Safransky 2014), as it is, in effect, similar to historical global claims
of *terra nullius*—a zoning law that allows a white-only commission to identify
areas of urban space that they see as vacant and deteriorating and to incentivize the in-migration of wealthier, predominantly white, urban residents to
"develop" the space. One Black East Side resident told me, in reaction to another white upper-middle class urban farmer buying land in his neighborhood, "They see so much value in our land. They see wealth beneath it, above
it, and every place in-between it."

Another intended outcome of the Urban Agricultural Zones, as stated in a
workshop presented to urban farmers on the issue, is to "facilitate and support
surrounding housing and business development." UAZ's are quite likely to do
so, if development refers to an increase in rent for nearby residents; as Joassart-
Marcelli and Bosco (in Curran and Hamilton 2018, 101) found in their analysis
of the San Francisco housing market, landlords and real estate agents capitalize upon farmers markets, community gardens, and urban farms to both market their properties and raise their value. While some homeowners—those
who can afford increased property taxes—might appreciate this consequence
of urban agriculture, over 50 percent of Kansas City East Side residents, where
a majority of urban gardens are placed, are low-income renters (U.S. Census Bureau 2017). A similar process to the urban renewal agenda identified by
Joassart-Marcelli and Bosco in San Francisco is occurring in Kansas City: for
example, a three-bedroom home at Forty-Second and Forest is advertised by
its realtor on Craigslist as "located directly across the street from Mannheim
Park Community Garden!" Its rent rose $100 between 2017 and 2018, alone. It
is common for rental listings in Kansas City to advertise the property's proximity to nearby farmers markets and community gardens; real estate agents
with properties near Grow KC's newly built urban farm, at Thirty-Ninth and
Gillham, actively advertise this amenity in their listings.

The idea that urban agriculture can combat blight is common in policy circles in today's Kansas City. In 2016 Kansas City, Missouri, city staff attended
a green urban development design program in Washington, D.C. There, they
workshopped their idea to rehabilitate the now-abandoned municipal jail
land into a sustainable greenspace. This EPA-funded greenspace redevelopment plan includes two large-scale commercial, organic farms. A comprehen-

sive redevelopment plan for the urban core, east of Troost Avenue, began in 2016, spearheaded by KCMO city officials, and several nonprofits: Greater Kansas City LISC, Urban Neighborhood Initiative, and the Mid-America Regional Council. This $25-$40 million redevelopment program has dedicated $200,000 for one specific neighborhood to combat blight by expanding its community garden and urban garden activities; as the program report notes, the hope is that this will "cultivate a local, vibrant economy." At a local foodie panel, invited speaker Kansas City Missouri Councilman Scott Wagner said that in his "formerly blighted" Northeast Kansas City community, urban agriculture has sparked a lot of change: "[The city] looks at urban agriculture as a way to create economic development, create jobs. We have at least five thousand pieces of property, vacant property, that we have control of. We can use urban agriculture there to move toward job development, economic development—that is our future."

In contrast, African American East Side residents of Kansas City frequently voice understandings of blight as analogous to historical state-led projects of racialized violence such as redlining, discriminatory urban zoning, and Jim Crow. In interviews or during walks around urban space, Black urban residents would point to crumbling buildings and tell me "*they* totally blighted that." During public meetings where white speakers would use the term "blight," my Black and brown companions would mime quotation marks and roll their eyes. All of these Black urban residents indicate that for them blight and "blight designations" are just another tool for racialized control.

Kansas City foodies have championed the implementation of urban agriculture zoning as a means of simultaneously addressing a number of urban problems: chiefly blight and inner-city food insecurity. In practice, however, urban agriculture zoning serves to make historically African American neighborhoods vulnerable to speculative development. Rather than addressing urban hunger, UAZ ordinances in Kansas City have facilitated land acquisition for food-secure white urban migrants looking to start or expand extant farm businesses, the products of which are chiefly distributed to high end markets outside of the urban core. Blight designations can, and should, be seen as a continuation of historical projects of segregation and racial control, such as redlining and discriminatory urban zoning (cf. Sugrue 1996), and, from a global perspective, settler colonialism. Much like these historical processes, blight functions in twenty-first-century urban greening initiatives to displace Black bodies from urban space deemed to be of economic value (cf. Safransky 2014).

Cultivating "Healthy" Bodies in the Obesogenic Environment: Farmers Markets and Bus Stops as Tools against Urban Hunger

A second key outcome of foodie influence in green urban development policy is a focus on urban space as obesogenic, accompanied by a discourse that promotes urban food production, distribution, and consumption, as a remedy— even as the actual policies that emerge from this discourse serve to benefit urban farm business owners and do little to address food insecurity or other public health concerns. In informal discussion with policy makers, in meeting minutes, and within planning committees, discussion surrounding urban agriculture focuses on how to increase land and water access for farm business owners and how to decrease other zoning barriers standing in the way of business expansion. Conversely, in official reports and news releases, these policies are framed and emphasized as solutions to urban hunger, "food desertification," and the "obesity epidemic."

This disjuncture between how policies are conceptualized privately and publicly marketed is most evident in the University of Missouri Extension report *Urban Agriculture: Best Practices and Possibilities*. Minutes from the 2010 meeting, when the report was drafted, indicate that food insecurity, affordability, and access were not discussed at all (Hendrickson and Porth 2012); discussion instead centered on how to ease zoning restrictions for urban farm infrastructure. However, the report, once published, foregrounds the ability of these urban agriculture policies to reduce urban hunger. The 2010 extension report on urban agriculture was presented to sustainability directors in major Missouri cities—St. Louis, Columbia, and Kansas City—and has been used to guide green urban development policy and urban food insecurity amelioration strategies statewide.

Thus, a central way that policy makers advocate for green urban development, locally, is through its supposed ability to create healthier environments and healthier people. This idea is the core thesis behind the concepts of obesogenic environments and food deserts—conceptual frameworks within urban planning that emphasize how disparities in urban infrastructure access result in health disparities (for example, one common refrain of proponents of the obesogenic environment thesis is that urban minority populations face higher rates of obesity because of the greater number of fast-food restaurants, compared to grocery stores, in the urban core). These frameworks have been refuted by scholars on a number of counts—for one, they are propped up with the ideological fallacy that mere proximity to "healthy" produce creates healthy bodies (cf. Guthman 2011; Guthman 2012; Alkon et al. 2013). Moreover, this lens frames the problem of food access as a *condition*, which leads policy makers to address symptoms (i.e., hunger) instead of root causes (racialized inequality, wage disparities, and systemic racism) (Sbicca 2014).

Additionally, a growing number of activists and scholars argue that these terms support white privilege by implying a barrenness in Black and brown urban neighborhoods and by ignoring the robust food networks that already exist in these spaces. Reese (2019) explores this idea effectively, uplifting the "hucksters" and Black food networks in a historically Black D.C. neighborhood by arguing that they are overlooked because they are not "conspicuously consumed or marketable greenspace tied to a return to urbanism." Narratives of emptiness and abandonment parallel colonial narratives that justified white rule; for white settlers, historically, lands could be legally deemed uninhabited if the people who lived there were regarded as not "evolved" or educated enough (Razack 2002). Similarly, portrayal of a place as a food desert justifies the absence of "desert" residents' input on food policy (Razack 2002; Stovall and Hill 2016).

A section of the 2010 urban agriculture report initially provides a nuanced view of the concept of food deserts, noting that Missouri officials should understand that the term has been debated and that urban residents have protested it, arguing that it paints their communities as "wastelands devoid of people, hope, or wealth" (Hendrickson and Porth 2012, 24). However, the report then confusingly suggests that food desert residents "may also fear that cities will adopt strategies that work solely to attract grocery stores . . . without considering other options that may make the community more food secure, including incubating food businesses to promote community economic development or redeveloping empty green lots as green spaces for recreation as well as healthy food production." The report then emphasizes that urban agriculture is one of the best ways to address food access and that easing zoning restrictions on agricultural production and incentivizing SNAP-dollar spending at farmers markets are two ways that cities can utilize green urban development infrastructure to improve food security (Hendrickson and Porth 2012, 24). As a result, this locally influential report, which guides green urban development and urban welfare agendas in Kansas City, Missouri, foregrounded the creation of urban farming projects as a solution to a number of urban problems, chiefly food insecurity.

Kansas City East Side residents have voiced other preferred methods of ameliorating urban food insecurity, but they are not represented in green urban development agendas. East Side residents are vocal about the urgent need for more full-service grocery stores in Jackson County. Ivanhoe neighborhood residents campaigned for years to bring an Aldi's grocery store to Thirty-Ninth and Prospect; when several homeowners delayed the process by refusing to move for the parking lot development, other neighborhood residents provided public testimony and campaigned to encourage the store to begin development, regardless. A SunFresh grocery store opened east of Troost in 2018—in Jackson County, its construction was a central topic of discussion for years prior, and a cause for celebration months after its completion. Despite this, foodie promotion of urban food projects as a solution to urban hunger has been incorporated in policy agendas as a viable, cheaper, and often preferable solution to food insecurity in comparison to the development of urban grocery stores. To echo Reese's observations, an Aldi isn't a marker of green-space and urban sustainability that's likely to draw the high-earning creative class to the urban core.

In the years after the 2010 report was distributed to Missouri sustainability officials, several key foodie, KCMO, and KCK collaborations related to food-security emerged. Foodie-suggested solutions to food insecurity were incorporated into local policy agendas in earnest. In 2011 Jackson County allocated $40,000 dollars to the Pantry for its programs that partner with urban farmers to share second-best produce (bruised or "unattractive" produce) with food pantry users. In 2013 Wyandotte County established a water grant program to encourage food-insecure urban residents to grow their own food and reached out to Healthy Communities KC for help in administering it. And importantly, in 2012 Healthy Communities KC and the Hunger Coalition partnered with elected officials to develop a "Healthy Food Access Resolution." This latter codified the city council's support of the Hunger Coalition, a foodie-led non-profit, as a "key partner in building a healthy, sustainable, accessible and economically beneficial food system" and established a strong interdepartmental support of the Hunger Coalition's work. The resolution lays out their combined intentions to:

- Improve access to healthy food . . . in under-served communities by identifying and establishing incentives, zoning efforts, and other policies to establish and support farmers markets and to increase the number of full-service grocery stores
- Identify and adopt land use policies and zoning regulations that encourage citizens to produce as much food as possible at home, in community gardens and urban farms
- Educate and empower citizens to responsibly grow and distribute food to Kansas City, Missouri, residents, institutions, and businesses

- Support diversified production and distribution within all communities by creating new economic opportunities and initiatives that encourage investment in food and farm production, processing, and distribution
- Support educational programs that inspire and empower the community to make healthy food purchasing decisions
- Evaluate transportation projects that offer safe and convenient pedestrian, bicycle, and transit connections between residential neighborhoods and community gardens, food pantries and community kitchens, and farmers markets.

This 2012 city-sanctioned resolution—a policy agenda for addressing urban hunger in Kansas City—focuses overwhelmingly on urban food projects; five out of six of the resolutions assert policy commitment to encouraging the poor to grow their own food and increasing food production in food deserts. This intense focus on urban food production means that even the creation of farming season-extension infrastructure—such as high tunnels—is championed as a solution to food insecurity. A staff person at a Healthy Communities KC workshop on local food businesses told me that "for food deserts in particular, these season extension projects are so important. We can extend the amount of time fresh food is brought into these areas, the amount of time people get to be *near* fresh, healthy food!"—as if being *near* food could be equated with being able to *afford* food. This resolution develops and institutionalizes a programmatic focus on empowerment (encouraging the poor to provide for themselves) and emphasizes the creation of green urban infrastructure that increases, and better links the poor to, urban food projects.

The "Healthy Food Access Resolution" isn't informed by any empirical data about KC residents' food access strategies. Many food- insecure East Side residents I spoke with, for example, placed food access at the end of a long list of other budget priorities. The Kansas City Grower's Club gave a presentation on their small water grants program during a monthly meeting at an East Side neighborhood coalition: a Black woman I was sitting closest to laughed, leaned in, and whispered to me, "I don't care if I have to starve, I pay my house payment. The roof over my head comes first. Where's the grant to help me with that?" When one considers that instead, a resolution could be drafted that outlines goals to provide an affordable minimum wage and develop a transportation infrastructure that better links public transport–dependent urban poor to their jobs, the energy that is directed toward empowerment and paternalism toward "food dollar" spending looks like a painful constraint on the already constrained lives of the urban poor.

One of the most powerful mechanisms through which foodies play a role in the lives of the urban poor is via distribution of a nutrition incentive grant. In 2017 a coalition of nonprofits, including Grow KC, applied for and received a $5.6-million matched Food Insecurity Nutrition Incentive (FINI) grant from the federal government. This grant, implemented in Kansas City via Grow KC management, doubles SNAP-recipient dollars when spent at specified grocery outlets. The grant funds are distributed only to specific farmers markets and grocery stores, sites that are identified by an all-white, upper-middle class foodie committee. In 2017 the FINI grant program was available for use at thirty farmers markets and fifty grocery stores in the Kansas City metropolitan area.

Through distribution of this grant, foodies play an integral role in shaping green urban development and the geographies of food acquisition for the urban poor. The SNAP-doubling program requires shoppers to spend at least one dollar on "locally produced" products before the savings will be applied to their grocery purchases. Because of this, the program is constrained to stores where local products are already regularly stocked. The SNAP-doubling program is available, for example, at all Whole Foods stores within the metropolitan area—something that, in my experience, low-income shoppers often laugh at when looking over the list of FINI-grant approved shopping locations. A majority of the low-income East Side SNAP recipients I met shopped regularly at Family Dollar, Dollar General, Save-a-Lot, and Aldi's—low-cost, small, full-service stores that offer mostly canned goods. The FINI grant is not being rolled out at any of these grocery providers. As a result, the grant assistance does not meet food insecure shoppers within their already-existing food networks. Instead, increased emphasis is placed on creating more urban farms and more farmers markets where the grant funding can be disbursed—regardless of whether or not these are the grocery outlets that low-income SNAP recipients prefer. While the FINI-grant constraints do play a role here, alternatives are possible—for example, foodies could stock small full-service stores with locally produced products, which would increase the grant's reach into low-income shoppers' extant food networks.

The geography of the FINI grant rollout is further constrained by neoliberal paternalism toward the poor—a pervasive ideology that blames the poor for their own poverty and couples aid with close monitoring of recipients' diets and morality (cf. Guthman and DuPuis 2006). Foodies in KC often express worry that the grant will be "misused" and subject the grocery stores where the FINI funds are rolled out to intense scrutiny. During a Food Deserts working group meeting in early 2017, a representative from Grow KC came to explain the grant process to other foodies. Martha, a representative from the Pantry, raised her hand to ask, "But, is there a way, at grocery stores, to make sure that the money isn't spent on nonfood items? Will a [fruit] rollup be counted as fruit?" The Grow KC representative assured her that the markets and grocery stores will be required to follow National Institute of Food and Agriculture guidelines on fruit and vegetable classification. Martha's sentiments, a concern that food-insecure aid recipients wouldn't know how to spend their aid dollars wisely, are not uncommon. Paternalism is a common theme when foodies discuss expanding food access for low-income urban shoppers. This helps explain why foodies are more amenable to distributing the grant funding to Whole Foods Grocery stores, rather than Family Dollars—where they wouldn't be able to restrict shoppers from purchasing "unhealthy" groceries.

Paternalistic policy regarding Black diets persists despite empirical evidence directly contradicting foodie assumptions. For example, in 2019 the Hunger Coalition released two white papers—one on urban local food production and one on "food insecurity and education"—developed based on working group meeting discussions. These white papers list challenges, opportunities, and policy recommendations in several urban food domains. The white paper on "food insecurity and education" lists findings from the Hunger Coalition's 2011 food habits survey of over three thousand metro residents—the document states that when asked why they don't purchase fresh fruits and vegetables, 45 percent of respondents cited cost, 41 percent cited fear of spoilage, and less than 10 percent cited lack of knowledge about how to cook the items. However, on the following page, a section labeled "threats" lists the following barriers the Hunger Coalition identifies to addressing food insecurity:

- Limited skill/knowledge/interest in nutrition and cooking fresh/seasonal food
- Barbeque [sic] culture
- Lack of knowledge about where food comes from + what local food is
- Declines in home economics education

The list of barriers doesn't touch on real issues in addressing food insecurity —many scholars would note the primary barrier is income—and actually looks like a list of barriers to getting urban residents to shop at farmers markets. Most upsettingly, the Hunger Coalition has identified "barbeque culture" as a barrier to food security—a thinly veiled critique of Black diets (barbecue, as a tradition, is historically linked to Black and Indigenous struggles against colonizers, cf. Twitty 2015). Further, while their own survey results indicated that shoppers are well aware of how to cook fresh produce, the white paper suggestions all promote education. So while the white paper's mission statement is to identify and ameliorate barriers to urban food security, the Hunger

Coalition has, in effect, compiled a list of ways to promote shopping strategies that benefit urban farmers and ultimately support the development of urban amenities that are "green" in a highly marketable way.

One of the most baffling food-security projects to emerge out of foodie collaboration with city officials is the Grocery Shop with Ride KC project, a paradigmatic example of paternalism and ignorance about food networks and food-procurement strategies of the urban poor. The project was born out of Hunger Coalition Grocery Access Task-Force working group meetings—working group participants conducted a year of research into how to improve grocery store access for food-insecure Kansas City residents. Without the input of food-insecure Kansas Citians, the working group settled on a path forward—creating a list of recommendations for both the Kansas City Area Transport Authority (KCATA and those who use public transit to reach the grocery store on how to streamline the grocery shopping experience. Funding and support for this project came from the Wyandotte County Kansas unified government, several Wyandotte County health-focused nonprofits, KCATA, and the Hunger Coalition. During a presentation to the Hunger Coalition about the inception of the project, their research, findings, and recommendations, Katie, the white, twentysomething project leader of the all-white team, told us they "realized" that a lot of people were using public transit to get to grocery stores. After this realization, they began visiting bus stops to assess how improvements could be made to infrastructure there. One outcome of the project was that the working group submitted a list of recommended repairs to metropolitan area bus stops to KCATA—suggesting improvements for sidewalks, ADA curbs, and signage. Their main project, however, rolled out at KC bus stops in 2018—a signage collaboration and marketing project created in partnership with KCATA. "We're really excited about this collaboration, and what it can do," said Katie, "We've developed signage that promotes healthy food and consumption, and lets people know they are welcome to use the bus system to shop for groceries." Katie then passed around a copy of the signage that would soon be posted at KCATA sites in the city—the signage includes directions to the closest full-service grocery store and sports a bulleted checklist: "Double check your shopping list; Use insulated bags; Use a pull cart." It also includes a link to the Hunger Coalition website, where, Katie tells us, visitors can find "pedestrian friendly healthy recipes that are lightweight, affordable, and low-calorie." The Grocery Access Task Force is currently fundraising for another signage campaign; this signage will also be posted at bus stops and will list, Katie said, farmers market hours, some healthy eating tips, and WIC information.

The "pedestrian friendly healthy recipe" website, linked to on KCATA bus stops, uses language that implies food-insecure shoppers are incompetent. The website offers a free printable meal planning template that intones "Make a list (and stick to it)" and tells shoppers "Healthy ingredients don't have to be expensive or heavy." It links to a list of recipes, including "healthy chocolate delight," posted just before Thanksgiving 2017. A narrative included with this recipe cheerfully tells low-income shoppers that the ingredients for this recipe will fit heavily in one bag, or comfortably in two; and that "yes, the holidays are a time for us to indulge and enjoy celebratory foods, but these recipes prove that we can do that without 'breaking the bank' on money spent or calories consumed."

This collaboration between KCATA and the Hunger Coalition highlights several painful themes. First, it draws on and furthers neoliberal paternal rhetoric that asks the poor to better manage their own bodies and health, while ignoring and denying economic constraints (Guthman and Dupuis 2006). For many urban poor, "junk food" or low-cost sweets are one way they can treat their children or themselves, in a context where they live under socioeconomic constraints that constantly necessitate saying "no" (cf. Fielding-Singh 2017). To suggest that these families combat higher rates of poverty-related health diseases by replacing pecan pie with a sugar-free chocolate dessert at Thanksgiving dinner denies the root cause of inequities and places the onus back on individual self-regulation. It also denies the importance of familial traditions and cultural heritage, which may include holiday sweets. Finally, the project ignores the ingenuity and resourcefulness of those experiencing food insecurity, likely because no empirical research was conducted and no one experiencing food insecurity was consulted for the project. Katie thinks that her project will "let people know" that they are welcome to use the bus system to shop for groceries—the urban poor already know this and have developed sophisticated means of transporting themselves, via bus, social networks, and otherwise, to places where they can buy food (Alkon et al. 2013, Page-Reeves 2014; see also chapter 4 of this book).

Counternarratives and Conclusions

Much of this land-use policy has developed as a result of welfare rollback and the resulting inclusion of third-sector actors in urban policy and welfare disbursal. As foodies are locally influential in Kansas City's third sector, they have a tremendous impact on land-use policy within the metro area, particularly within the context of citywide adoption of green urban infrastructure. Foodie

ideology centered on entrepreneurship, self-determination, and a myopic focus on food and diet interventions as a solution to myriad urban poverty issues has resulted in the green urban planning policy enacted in Kansas City
today—policy that encourages urban food production through tax incentives
that further deplete urban tax bases, contributes to inner-city gentrification,
and spatializes whiteness. It is not my intent to make a case for whether these
policies are developed in explicitly race-based ways or are just racist in function. What I do illustrate is that they are developed without empirical evidence
by all-white, privileged advisory boards; ignore histories of racialized urban
inequality and displacement; serve to (re)develop urban KC in ways that support spatialized white privilege; and are viewed by many East Side residents
as settler colonial projects.

Foodie narratives about blight and hunger, and the uplift and empowerment that policies incentivizing urban agriculture can bring, are widespread
in Kansas City policy circles, upper-middle class social groups, and in dominant media representations of the city. However, this does not equate with
unequivocal acceptance of these ideologies; in private conversations, several
policy makers and foodies voiced reticence about using green urbanism to address myriad problems and as a lens through which to shape urban space. As
one Kansas City, Missouri, councilperson shared with me, during a discussion
of urban agriculture's current political popularity with in the city, "To get on
the ballot in Kansas City, you gotta get petitions signed. So when I was trying
to get on the ballot in 2015 [to be voted into City Council] I stood outside of a
grocery store in Brookside—which is not in [my] district, but it is voter rich.
A high number of African American women who did not live in the neighborhood close to [the grocery store] were signing my petition. They had zip codes
from my area. To an extent, the food desert conversation just doesn't really
speak to the end-run consumer—you know, they'll travel to the good grocery
store that's over there, or you shop by work, what have you."

When talking with me, the councilperson was unsure that local policy
could address food insecurity in a meaningful way—"we're kind of playing
whack-a-mole [by promoting urban farms in food deserts] . . . chasing a problem that exceeds local government's ability to solve." However, these privately
shared concerns do not often translate into publicly advocated-for policies.

Local foodies, however, are certain—and vocal about their certainty—that
urban food production, distribution, and consumption can address urban disinvestment and hunger. This foodie certainty and persistence, in Kansas City,
has offered policy makers a ready-made, bipartisan approved green urban
development plan, one that also speaks to secular and religious urban resi-

dents and is, because of nationwide discourse, seen as an unequivocal—often profitable—boon to urban space. While some city officials have told me they think of urban food production as "a palliative, at best" for food insecurity, hegemonic support and welfare rollback that elevated foodies as urban policy mediators has resulted in this becoming a key facet of green urbanism and the metropolitan area's chief means of addressing hunger. The following chapter considers these dominant paradigms for addressing food insecurity from the perspectives of the urban poor.

CHAPTER 4

"Don't You Know You Live in a Food Desert?"

Food Charity Programming and the Lived
Realities of Seeking Food Aid in Kansas City

Matt, a young, white, blonde reporter stepped in between raised garden beds in an East Side urban garden and addressed the camera: "Urban gardens have been sprouting up in Kansas City. A lot of people are finding it's a great way to grow some food and save some money on their food bills!" The news segment aired in June, the week before Grow KC's 2015 Farm and Garden Tour—a popular metropolitan-wide event, in which local farm businesses, community gardens, and backyard gardeners open up their homes to show off the diverse methods of food production taking place in the city. In preparation for the tour, Matt interviewed community gardeners at Oak Park Community garden. The camera panned to show an urban garden-space full of gardeners, all weeding and tidying in preparation for the tour: "They're hoping for a lot of visitors, hoping to maybe inspire others to start their own garden, maybe feed their hungry neighbors," said Matt. He walked over to Tom Winston, an African American man who we're told is a ninety-two-year-old community gardener at Oak Park. Matt asked "Tom, how long you been gardening over here?"

> TOM: "Oh, I've just been here for three years now."
> MATT: "Yeah? And what are you growing?"
> TOM: "Oh, just broccoli, beets, onions, carrots, and tomatoes."
> MATT: "Why? Why are you doing this?"
> TOM: "Well for one thing, I need to get out and do something. And if I do this, at least I'm doing something I know how to do. See, I've been farming since I was eight, ten years old."
> MATT: "So you know how to grow these seeds!"
> TOM: "Yeah, I know how. In the slave camp we used to do this too."
> MATT: "You were in a slave camp?"

TOM: "Yeah."

MATT: "Oh my goodness, that's terrible."

TOM: "Yeah it was. Down in Mississippi."

MATT: "Well now you're here, and it's gotta be rewarding to be able to eat fresh healthy vegetables every single night!"

While Tom is not old enough to have actually been enslaved, he may have been referring to a labor camp or myriad other sites where Black labor was exploited—the historical accuracy of his comment is less important than the trauma he was hoping to express. Matt moved on from this uncomfortable interaction with Tom to interview a white Grow KC staff member, whom he asked, "Why are you hosting this tour?" She responded, "You know, I participate in this because I absolutely love it. Watching communities come together, watching people come together, around something that is so central to the human race—food and eating. That's what inspired me."

There are several points that this moment of public discourse on urban agriculture and food insecurity illustrates. First, while the Grow KC staff member asserts that people can come together around food, that food is central to the human race, Matt and Tom's interaction is exemplary of why this is not true. Food is not a common language: while many white Kansas City residents might draw on family narratives about gardening as patriotic duty—as with Victory Gardens—or might think of neatly ordered English kitchen gardens when they imagine the act of growing food, for many Kansas City residents of color, the act of growing food is intimately linked to forcible migration, violence, unpaid or underpaid labor, and alienation from land and product. There is also, of course, intense heterogeneity of opinion within this simple binary that I have just implied. Lower-income white families with histories of tenant farming might today react painfully to hegemonic discourse about the joy of gardening and getting one's hands dirty; several Black East Side residents I spoke with had mixed, sometimes positive, family memories and narratives about sharecropping. For Tom, food production can index all of the above emotions, perhaps simultaneously. These examples illustrate the myriad differing emotional associations people can have with food and the act of growing it.

A second point I wish to make by sharing this narrative, the point central to this chapter, is that food charity programming in Kansas City—as a result of myopic focus in green urban development agendas on urban food production—is painfully out of step with the lived realities of those seeking food aid. Regardless of personal food and agriculture histories, and regardless of a local context in which city officials and the real estate industry have displaced or demolished sites of African American agriculture—such as the Hog Farm at Brush Creek, or the Sweeney's Truck farm at Eighteenth and Vine—food-insecure Kansas Citians who seek aid are "assisted" by being taught to grow their own food, and by being taught to identify and select "healthy" food for their diets. The fact that Tom says he was forced to learn how to grow food in a slave camp in Mississippi is disregarded—at least Tom can grow and enjoy healthy produce every night now.

Recent scholarship on the lived experiences of food insecurity has focused, primarily, on highlighting how paternalistic discourse affects aid seekers (cf. Kato 2013; Counihan 2012; Mares 2014). An additional line of scholarship has focused on refutations of the "food desert" analytic: scholars have highlighted how this term implies emptiness and robs "food desert" residents of agency (Reese 2019, 6). Others have argued that the "food desert" analytic leads activists to address symptoms of inequity (hunger) rather than root structural causes and have advocated for the use of "food apartheid" instead (cf. Sbicca 2012; Bradley and Galt 2014). Less deeply explored, however, are the multiple scales at which this discourse about food deserts and food insecure populations functions to support green urbanism (although Pettygrove and Ghose 2018 analyze this well). The narratives shared in this chapter build on these analyses. I explore how programmatic work at the food charity level also reflects and (re)creates understandings of food deserts that prop up green urban development. This sort of programming and discourse provides justification for the greening of urban cores, as it perpetuates a hegemonic misconception that the urban poor are ill equipped to cultivate healthy bodies and environments. Racialized discourse that constructs inner-city communities of color as infrastructurally insufficient provides justification for redevelopment and capital extraction in these spaces.

Specifically, in this chapter I document how green urban development has shaped food aid in Kansas City. Since 2010, as policy makers began to embrace green urbanism, food charity programming in KC shifted to partner food aid with nutrition education and classes in urban food production. Here, I illustrate the programmatic inefficiencies this partnership has created and highlight the narratives of Black food-insecure KC residents who creatively navigate programs that attempt to control their bodies and diets.

Historical Regulation of Black Bodies
and Black Diets in Kansas City

This focus on regulating the diets and bodies of Black Kansas Citians is not new; white Kansas Citians have been forcing African Americans to grow food in "food deserts" for more than one hundred years within the city lines. While today these state biopolitics—mechanisms through which governments control citizens' health and bodies—are recast as empowerment programs within green urban development agendas, historically, this process took the form of agricultural slave labor and sharecropping. In the 1800s, James Hyde McGee used captive African labor to reap profit from the land on his nearly two-hundred-acre working farm in today's West Bottoms, bordered by Holmes Street on the east, Broadway on the west, Independence Avenue on the south, and topped to the north by the Missouri River (Austin 2017). Hyde McGee used his wealth to buy over one thousand more acres in the Kansas City area—land that houses, in 2018, downtown economic hubs such as the Kansas City Convention Center, the Kauffman Center for the Arts, and the Crossroads Art District. Much of Hyde McGee's vast acreage was cultivated with the labor of enslaved people (Austin 2017). The current-day Troost corridor, which would later be developed through purposive policy into Kansas City's racialized dividing line, was bought up by millionaires in large tracts of land during the 1800s. In Jackson County, the area between Twenty-Third and Thirty-First streets and Locust and Paseo became known as "Millionaire's Row." Here, large mansions abutted open-acreage and the labor of enslaved people was used to grow hemp for trade and to cultivate kitchen gardens for whites (Shortridge 2012, 53).

While Black bodies were controlled *physically* during the era of slavery, via forced agricultural labor, states explored other methods of control after emancipation. One way in which whites with power attempted to exert racial power was through data collection and biased research, for example, through sociological survey and welfare agency research into Black diets. Early sociological focus on urban pathology drew on theories of social disorganization and suggested behavioral fixes as a solution to urban poverty (cf. Burgess 1925; Drake and Cayton 1945; Lewis 1966). Locally, in Kansas City, numerous sociological surveys were funded by local welfare agencies as the city's Black population grew; most notable was Asa Martin's *Our Negro Population*. Martin's survey was enacted with the goal of explaining high rates of Black death in Kansas City—actually attributable to racism, experienced through lower housing stock, crowding, and racialized access to health care—and argued that the source of this problem could be found in deficiencies in Black diet. Surveys such as Martin's worked to categorize and label "problem" populations, a strategy that helps the state give credence to its preferred solutions, setting the ground for policy by making the problem seem "common sense" (Hacking 1991). Martin chronicled the percentage of income Black families in Kansas City spent on food in 1912: for many of the poor, this ranged from 38 to 50 percent (Martin 1913, 66). Martin didn't even believe those he surveyed were being truthful; he wrote that the Black women he surveyed likely did not accurately account for the food dollars they spent, and he interviewed butchers and grocery store owners in Black neighborhoods to get a more "accurate" understanding of the food Black families were buying (Martin 1913, 67).

Martin suggested that at least 25 percent of Black Kansas Citians in the 1910s were "underfed" and located the cause of this, partly, in "the lack of economy in management and of wisdom in the buying of food." He added, "In 95 per cent of these cases there is also evidence of exceptional expenditure on drink" (Martin 1913, 67). He added that many poor Black families cannot—will not, he implied—afford an oven, and thus "everything must be fried" or purchased from a bakery: "The food so prepared is unhealthful, and in the second, very expensive" (68). Martin's study is just one local example of nationwide efforts to place blame for poverty and poor health on racialized individuals (cf. Fox Piven et al. 2002). Such state-sponsored efforts to locate causes of poverty in racialized pathology—meaning, patterns of behavior that cause self or community harm—help those in power displace responsibility for the structural injustices and violence that have actually led to inequality.

Along with sociological racism vilifying Black diets, popular culture in Kansas City often drew on depictions and mockery of Black diet and stereotypes of Black food to maintain white public space. Advertisements for food-unrelated businesses—such as a shoe store and a sporting goods store—commonly drew on depictions of African Americans clinging to watermelons. This trope emerged in the U.S. post-emancipation, as many newly freed Africans secured economic independence through the cultivation and sale of watermelons (Black 2018). White Americans racialized the watermelon in public discourse and associated it with ideologies of laziness, childishness, and uncleanliness to undermine its associations with emancipation and Black self-sufficiency (Black 2018). Watermelons were used to denigrate Black freedom on a citywide scale in 1922, when the mayor of Kansas City, Missouri, scheduled a watermelon-eating contest for Black children, as part of his free summer picnic (Schirmer 2002, 150; see Greenlee 2019 for discussion of enduring impact). Instances like these—historical, state-sponsored efforts to manage and contain racially marked bodies—help contextualize today's current-day food charity focus on Black diet and nutrition.

It is also important to note that nationally, scientific understandings about healthy food and bodies have been shaped by white discourse. The Body Mass Index (BMI) calculator, which is still widely utilized by doctors, social service workers, and within food charity programs in Kansas City, was developed with white bodies in mind and has been shown to be inaccurate at best when used on racialized bodies (Jackson et al. 2009; Guthman 2011). Likewise, dominant understandings of healthy food, such as milk—which is incorporated into USDA recommendations for a healthy diet—privilege one culturally specific form of eating at the expense of other food practices; around 70 percent of African Americans have some level of lactose intolerance and are unable to access this recommended diet (DuPuis 2002; Slocum 2010). These racialized understandings of health are conducted by whites, draw on studies of white bodies, and prop up the food charity programs that address food insecure, Black Kansas City residents.

The act of growing food and eating it is highly constitutive of racialized identities and their politics—what we eat, and how we eat it, says a lot about race, class, and inequality. It is vital to consider, given how personal food production is a widely sanctioned proscriptive for food insecurity, that historical attempts at Black autonomy and agrarianism have been met with state violence or discursive erasure. African American food traditions have either been co-opted (such as how "Soul Food" has been whitewashed and rebranded under a banner of Southern gentility, cf. Witt 2004), or elided, such as the erasure, from popular health food discourse, of the fact that kale was brought to the United States by enslaved Africans. Black liberation movements that emphasized back-to-the-land philosophies were branded as violent by the state, even though these ideologies were widely celebrated among white U.S. residents in the 70s. Members of MOVE for example, a Black liberation movement grounded in agrarianism, had their homes bombed by the city of Philadelphia (Boyette and Boyette 2013). There is also a Kansas City–specific history of state-sponsored violence against Black self-determinism, especially in regard to food and food security. In 1969 the Kansas City Police Department collaborated with the FBI to destroy Black Panther food stores, produce that would have been distributed via school breakfast programs and to food insecure Black Kansas Citians (Griffin 2015, 108). More broadly, KCPD launched a campaign to arrest Black Panther members and discourage support and membership (Griffin 2015, 108).[1] This context—a historical legacy of forced, unpaid agricultural labor, sociological and scientific racism concerned with containing

Black bodies, discursive co-optation and erasure of Black food traditions, and state-led violence against Black food-security efforts—necessarily shapes how food charity programs are seen by low-income U.S. citizens of color. It shapes how urban residents of color react to green urbanism proposals that valorize the use of city space for food production and the production and maintenance of "healthy" bodies.

"We Have Forgotten How to Grow Food in the Urban Core": Food Charity and "Food Deserts" in Kansas City

Food charity in Kansas City is managed by organizations and actors from within the local food scene, foodies, which leads to a focus on promoting the production, distribution, and consumption of local produce as a key mechanism for solving urban hunger. Foodie-led organizations that are particularly active in addressing urban food insecurity include the Hunger Coalition, the Pantry, and Our Daily Bread (which also receive significant institutional support via grant funding from the Health Care Foundation of Greater Kansas City). Various initiatives spearheaded by these organizations, such as a large-scale schoolyard garden program, Missouri house bills that incentivize the donation of fresh produce to local food pantries, and local efforts led by the Hunger Coalition to decrease the high food tax in Kansas—but *only* on fresh fruits and vegetables, preferably local—illustrate that attempts to control the diets and bodies of the urban poor are strong both historically and currently.

KC foodies use the "food desert" framework to prop up and support programs that align with their green urban development agendas. Narratively linking urban food projects to food insecurity initiatives allows foodies to secure funds from a wider variety of agencies—often from healthcare-focused ones, as the development of things like community gardens, mobile grocery stores, and urban orchards can be advertised as mechanisms of feeding the poor. A Hunger Coalition promotional video, discussing a grant the organization received for soil improvements in local urban gardens, states, "We have forgotten how to grow food in the urban core—healthy soil makes healthy plants makes healthy kids!" In this way, even the distribution of compost is celebrated as an effort against food insecurity. The Health Care Foundation funds hobby-gardening classes in East Side neighborhoods as a means of feeding the food-insecure, a market-based effort of addressing poverty that asks the poor to learn how to better provide for themselves (see also Lyon-Callo 2004).

This focus on food desertification and nutrition education persists even when met with head-on opposition. For example, one East Side neighborhood

hosts monthly housing meetings at which neighborhood members join together to vet new development; ensure that new developers prioritize creation
of more affordable housing; and strictly regulate the influx of urban farms
and gardens. Affordable housing is a major crisis in Kansas City; the East Side
in particular faces additional compounded problems, as much of its housing
stock is more cheaply bulldozed than renovated. After one of these housing
meetings—where a white urban farmer's potential land acquisition plan was
scrutinized—a local foodie who runs her own successful urban farm snapped
at me, "Why do they care so much about housing? Don't they know they live
in a food desert?" In discursive ways such as this, and through policy and
funding focus, foodies redirect more pressing neighborhood concerns (housing, livable wage concerns, etc.) back to the issue of healthy food production
and consumption.

Coincident with foodie promotion of urban food production is a focus on
nutrition and "educating" the urban poor on healthy eating practices. A Health
Care Foundation blog post advertising one of its new grantees—a Spanish-
language nutrition education course—states that Latino immigrants in Kansas
City "face chronic health risks often made worse by their limited knowledge
of nutrition." Numerous scholars have documented the ingenuity, resourcefulness, and nutrition knowledge of the urban poor and have indicated that
ameliorating the economic conditions that create poverty would be a much
more effective measure to improve nutrition in the United States (Page-
Reeves 2014). Yet in Kansas City's food charity paradigm, as in other nonprofit
spheres, it has become taken for granted that "decisions about production, ap-
propriation, and distribution of the local surplus will remain in the hands of
a few," and efforts to address food insecurity take the form of neoliberal self-
empowerment and the redistribution of capitalism's waste (Lyon-Callo 2004,
47). As a result, a large amount of time and money is spent on ineffective pro-
graming that is found by participants to be demeaning (cf. Kingfisher 1996)
and does nothing to address the root causes of food insecurity. The remainder
of this chapter explores one such program, a nationally replicated model I'm
calling Feast!

Feast! Curriculum

Feast! is a nutrition-education curriculum developed by Feeding America, offered for free to nonprofits across the United States. Locally, Feast! is offered by
the Pantry and funded in partnership with BlueCross and BlueShield Insurance. Feast! in Kansas City is taught primarily by young, white, female Amer-

icorp volunteers, who administer the two-hour-long weekly classes over the course of seven weeks. I attended four cycles of this class; each time the curriculum and lesson plan remained the same. Each Feast! class begins with goal setting and accountability—participants are asked to make one dietary and one physical goal for the week—and then the class reads through (out loud) that week's curriculum packet, completing activities such as quiz questions, fill-in-the-blanks, and crosswords. The curriculum packet also includes weekly stretches and exercises, led by the instructor. Afterward, the class instructor passes out copies of that day's lunch recipe; each week, the Feast! class cooks and eats a "healthy," low-cost meal or snack. After cooking, eating, and cleaning, the Feast! instructor will ask the class quiz questions based on that day's curriculum, and prizes of leftover cooking materials—half onions, partially used cans of tomato paste—are claimed by those with the correct answers. Each class ends with distribution of bagged groceries—a large paper shopping bag full of canned vegetables and fruits, typically a box of cereal and a bag of pasta, mac and cheese and other boxed mixes, and a loaf of bread. Participants are also given a sack of fresh produce from the Pantry's partner-farms. When the class falls during garden season, and when available, participants are also given seed packets to grow their own food. If participants arrive more than ten minutes late to class, they are not allowed to receive that day's groceries—a rule that I saw enforced often, as many Feast! participants worked at fast food restaurants and their shifts never ended at a consistent time.

Feast! is consistently perceived by Feast! participants as paternalistic; they often laughed, scoffed, and shared jokes after receiving their weekly curriculum packets. During week 1, participants are asked to calculate their BMI and set goals for the class, such as eating more leafy greens each week, or taking a walk every morning. In week 2, participants are taught about food-borne diseases and are walked through—and forced to practice, for a grade—how to wash their hands properly. Week 3's curriculum covers how to read a food label and offers shopping tips that can help participants save money on groceries, such as "eat before you go so you do not shop hungry." In week 4, participants are taught about the warning signs and management of heart disease and diabetes; a fill-in-the-blank exercise teaches participants to look out for trans fats: "Limit saturated and _ _ _ _ fats!" Week 5 covers media messaging about food and asks participants to learn to discern what terms like "'natural,' 'real,' and 'healthy' mean. In week 6 participants are given calorie charts for popular fast-food restaurants and asked to calculate the calories and sodium of their favorite meals. The final week covers physical activity and offers ways that busy individuals can still fit exercise into their days.

Some Feast! instructors seem to understand that this program is limiting and often insulting. One instructor, in particular, would slip in comments during class about how childish the curriculum was and would acknowledge larger forces at play in food insecurity by discussing wage stagnation. However, most of the instructors I encountered through Feast! seemed unaware of, or complicit with, the stereotypes of the poor conveyed via course curriculum; relatedly, actors in other state and private welfare disbursal circles have been shown to assume the majority of their clients are "bad," deceitful, and manipulative (cf. Kingfisher 1996, 99; Edgar and Russell 1998). As a result, food insecure individuals find the process of accessing food aid deeply stigmatizing (cf. de Souza 2019).

The very ideological basis of Feast!—that increasing nutritional knowledge will increase the health of the urban poor—has been undermined by qualitative research suggesting otherwise. Tepper et al. (1997) find that nutritional knowledge plays a modest role in food choices, and Mancino and Kinsey (2008) find that more immediate concerns, such as hunger and stress, are stronger predictors of food choices than nutritional knowledge, across class divides. Likewise, Rose (2014) finds that low-income women in Detroit are highly knowledgeable about nutrition but are forced to make food purchases that contradict their nutritional preferences because of time and transportation constraints. Policy makers have, in many ways, overestimated the effects of nutrition education on health behaviors.

I participated in Feast! four separate times between 2015 and 2018; each class was held at a different location, with different participants, and a different instructor, though the curriculum remained the same. Through Feast!, I met and spent weekly time with (both inside and out of class) thirty-one food-insecure Kansas City residents, around three quarters of whom would describe themselves as Black or African American. I was always the youngest class participant, aside from the course instructor—most Feast! participants in Kansas City are between the ages of thirty and eighty. In each Feast! class I took, there was always one grandmother taking the class to acquire groceries for their child and grandchild. Several women told me that their children worked full-time and didn't have time to participate in the course, just to get the free groceries; participants are not allowed to bring children to class. Around 60 percent of the Feast! participants I met were women, and the course was always led by white female instructors—this is not surprising, as the burden of both food acquisition and nonprofit welfare work falls disproportionately on women (Kingfisher 1996). I took Feast! classes held at an East Side public library, a low-income housing complex in North Kansas City, a low-income senior living center, and a community center on the East Side. Conversations relayed in this chapter primarily occurred during class, or while driving fellow-Feast! participants to the grocery store or doctor's appointments.

"We Used to Grow Food but the USDA Fucked Us Over"

Even though popular discourse in KC suggests that food deserts are a central concern of East Side residents, most of those I spoke with dismissed the applicability of this concept to their lives. For example, in 2015 the local public radio station, KCUR, broadcast a series of interviews with influential urban farmers in Kansas City. One interviewee, a Black farmer and long-time resident of Northeast KC, said, "I've just been told [the Northeast] is a food desert. I didn't understand 'food desert' when I first got into this, but there's not a supermarket within a fifty-block square radius in this area which I live in. So now I know what a food desert is." The reporter responded incredulously, "You lived there and that wasn't something that you thought about?" The farmer replied, "Nah. I guess, for me . . . we always, when my parents were living, and my mother and my grandmother—they all canned. My grandmother had a little small garden on the side of her house. My mother would grow tomatoes and okra, just particular things on the side of the house where the water comes out of the gutter, so they didn't have to water. We didn't think of it as a food desert because my father was a hunter, a fisherman. I never thought of it as a food desert."

The farmer rejects a characterization of his neighborhood as one of lack. His family has always grown food in the area, has always preserved food for later use, has always utilized existing resources—like gutter water—in ecologically thoughtful ways. Public discourse elevates ideas of food desert residents as devoid of agency and draws on visual depictions such as corner store shelves stocked with brightly colored junk food to paint a bleak picture of the urban foodscape.[2] This farmer, however, had no idea he lived in a food desert; this depiction of urban life did not accurately reflect his experiences and belied the incredible resourcefulness of his family.

I met numerous other Black East Side residents who grew their own food and had been doing so in the city long before it became fashionable as part of green urban development. During research for *Well-Intentioned Whiteness*, I tended raised beds at a number of community garden plots across the East Side of the city. This meant that I was often walking around city space with a tote bag full of produce I had just harvested, that I made several weekly trips to Home Depot during the summer to purchase items like tomato cages and seeds, and that the trunk of my Honda Civic was stuffed full of a large hay bale, which I used as mulch. Almost daily, low-income Black East Side residents would comment on these items or my presence at these places, as they themselves grew their own food, too. A member of janitorial staff at a local community center, who once walked past while I was checking my tomatoes for pests, stopped to identify blight on my plants' leaves. A court-ordered community service volunteer, helping build a gazebo at one of my community garden locations, once called out to me—"Your peppers are looking good, but not as good as mine this year!" A pair of elderly women waiting at a bus stop to catch a ride to Walmart explained to me that the nasturtium seeds I was carrying would one day make edible flowers, which would "look lovely on a cake." Once, at a monthly neighborhood meeting for an East Side community, an elderly Black woman who noticed my garden gloves announced to me, "I grow food in two and a half gardens. My momma bought several pieces of land when I was young, and we grow food on them for our community. We give it all away. That's just something we've always done." And on my way home from this meeting a cashier at a CVS on Troost pointed toward the chard sticking out of my tote bag, mimed smelling a good meal, and said, "I smell fresh, fresh vegetables! Maybe I should pick greens from my garden tonight, too!" These daily utterances and assertions of personal food production stand in direct opposition to discourse that asserts that Black Kansas City residents have forgotten how to grow food in the urban core. While many East Side residents I spoke with did desperately wish there were more affordable full-service grocery stores in the urban core, the vast majority felt that the food desert framework denied their agency and actual lived experiences.

Because the Feast! curriculum so often denied these historical legacies of food production in Black neighborhoods, Black food-insecure participants in this program frequently made a point to counter this narrative and assert that they did know how to grow food and had been doing it for years. Once, while slicing cherry tomatoes for that week's lunch—a cold pasta salad with avocado and olives—our Feast! instructor told the class, "These are cherry tomatoes, you can find them at pretty much any grocery store." A mid-fifties African American woman interrupted her sharply, "We know what they are. My mother sure could grow them, too." In a different Feast! class, the previous year, a middle-aged Black woman yelled at our instructor as she told us how to plant the kohlrabi seeds she was passing out, "I know how to do that. My family farmed a couple hundred acres in Arkansas. We used to grow food before the USDA fucked us over." Another week, while Feast! participants and I cooked a mole sauce to pour over ground pork and brown rice, I brought up my concern about pork, saying I had always been scared to cook it because my grandmother said it could harbor worms. Our instructor interrupted me and said, "That's not right, no, it's a very clean meat." The rest of the class participants all yelled out at once: "No, they eat anything, that's why so many religions don't want us to eat pig"; "You gotta be careful with pork"; and "They're a nasty animal." Our instructor pushed back—"these are old wives' tales." To that, an older Black participant snapped at her, "They eat *anything*. We used to have pigs and they are disgusting, just like chickens." Another participant chimed in, "I can tell you that chickens are every bit as dirty as pigs. We had chickens growing up and they will eat whatever you give them." These assertions disrupt the white public space of the food charity programming, as low-income urban residents push back against depictions of their communities as spaces of lack and speak against representations of their families as ignorant about healthy, fresh food.

Some Black East Side residents did use the framework of food desert when we spoke, but often to highlight structural policies that created the "desert" and food insecurity and to highlight areas where the state has failed to support urban residents. This usage is similar to how Neferet used "blight" to highlight policies that disinvested her community and stands in direct contrast to how food desert is utilized by foodies, who use the term as a descriptor of a place, not as an inquiry into structural inequality. This was particularly apparent in one specific interaction, between a Feast! participant and instructor, during the iteration of Feast! that I took when it was held at a public library. The cohort enrolled in this course was small—there were only about seven of us who consistently attended class, a group that included a young Black man who wanted to one day become a chef, a white mother and her thirtysomething daughter who had both just been diagnosed with diabetes and wanted to learn more about its management, a Latina grandmother and her granddaughter—both great chefs, but who told me they were having a hard time affording groceries after a string of job losses in the family—and a middle-aged Black woman named Sherene, who always wore skirt suits and had her hair neatly pulled back. While I, and many other, class participants, often displayed visible signs of offense at course material, Sherene always seemed doubly injured and angry at the fact that she had to sit through this curriculum to receive groceries. Each week, she would refuse to participate when our instructor would call on her to answer questions, and she would sigh, huff, and roll her eyes during particularly patronizing course lessons. One week, when we were all asked to go wash our hands and return back to partition up the cooking assignments for that week's recipe—pizza pasta salad—Sherene stayed in the bathroom and did not return to the kitchen area until we were halfway through cooking, at which point she refused to accept any cooking tasks. As we cooked, she sat, raised her eyebrows, and watched.

The class session in which Sherene finally spoke up, and addressed the topic of food deserts, was the week our instructor, Mona, led us through a lesson plan on obesity and causes of poor health. Our class met in a private library meeting room, where we all gathered around a square grouping of tables and read over our curriculum packets together. The first page of that day's packet contained an illustration of a line graph chronicling the trends in overweight and obese U.S. citizens over the past century.[3] The chart demonstrated that most recently, the number of overweight Americans has gone down but the number of obese Americans has risen (the chart ignored, and did not discuss, how poverty manifests as obesity in the United States and more often afflicts communities of color; cf. Alkon et al. 2013). Mona, a white woman, explained, "This trend has a lot to do with eating out, and the rise of processed food." We turned the page of our packet to find a BMI chart, and as Mona started to walk us through how to find our number, Candice (the white mother) interrupted her, "Have you ever noticed, it's the things that are healthy that cost more money, though?" Mona sighed and said, "I know. I know. But not oatmeal— old fashioned oats are very healthy and very cheap." Candice continued, "I don't want oatmeal though. I used to love shredded wheat. Hot, in the morning with milk—my mom used to give me that before school. But now, shredded wheat has frosting on it, you know? And if you want the one that's unfrosted and called 'healthy', its two times as much as the frosted stuff. How is that fair?" Sherene suddenly spoke up, sharply, for the first time in four weeks of class: "Food we don't want and food we can't afford. That gives a new definition to the term food desert, doesn't it?"

Sherene's interjection on food deserts says a lot. For one, it indicates some of the specific reasons why Feast! is so painful, and offensive, to her. The class emphasizes "making do"; its curriculum covers how to rinse off canned fruits to remove excess sugar and make it "healthier," discusses how to modify family-favorite recipes to utilize the cheapest items at the store, and emphasizes choosing the cheapest healthy option, such as oatmeal, instead of your favorite healthy option, such as Candice's shredded wheat. Sherene does not want to be taught how to make do; she's likely been "making do" for years. Sherene likely resents the fact that she has to sit through proffered strategies on cheaply shopping and cooking, to receive a bag of groceries that she desperately needs, when she would much rather have the economic freedom to make her own food choices (cf. Page-Reeves 2014). Sherene's comment also refutes common usages of food desert to point toward the need for increased access to grocery stores in the urban core. Sherene doesn't want increased access to stores, or free bags of food; in her statement she indicates that she currently has access to many different grocery outlets. Instead, Sherene's comment highlights dissatisfaction with how her city is being developed in ways that clearly exclude her, are not meant for her, and are not affordable to her. In this way, Sherene uses "food desert" to index this top-down control of development that excludes her. Many low-income Black East Side residents I spoke with refuted the conceptual framework of food desert because of this, and because it led to hegemonic understandings of their communities as barren, when in fact they have long been populated by resourceful, ecologically mindful residents.

"I Don't Want Anything That's in Those Bags"

Feast! participants are knowledgeable about how to acquire food that they understand to be nutritious and healthy and are often far more insightful than the Feast! instructors about how to utilize meager WIC, SNAP and food charity benefits—because they have been making do with these programs for years. During Feast! classes, I frequently witnessed participants using and sharing creative means for stretching food dollars. Participants in several courses shared with me their yearly plans—one woman had mapped it out in a back page of her pocket calendar—for utilizing food aid. Participants are only allowed to take Feast! twice in any given year; numerous people planned to take Feast! in the spring and then in the fall—the fourteen-weeks total of food aid provided nonperishable items, such as weekly jars of peanut butter and bags of pasta, that could be stretched throughout the year. To supplement these items, Feast! participants visited myriad food charity sites to acquire food that they liked to eat. Betty, for example, a Black food-insecure woman in her sixties, told me that she went weekly to a church on Prospect street that "gives out the best bread, the good artisan stuff" and that she came early on Mondays to the senior center she frequented because that's when they distributed frozen food items. "You can get good stuff, like Hungry Man, sometimes," which, she explained to me, "there's a lot of salt in that, but protein too." These strategies for feeding oneself and one's family throughout the year take incredible time-management and resourcefulness; a creativity and agency that, in Kansas City, is denied in popular discourse regarding the urban poor (Wilson and Keil 2008). As other scholars have shown, for many of the urban poor, these supplementary and emergency food programs are incorporated as permanent, life-long food provisioning strategies (Stanford 2014, 23).

Feast! participants, despite food insecurity and economic precarity, often vocally dismissed and refused food aid that was not suitable to their family diets. One week, during a series of Feast! classes I took at an East Side community center, our instructor Pam walked us through making vegetarian chili. As we cooked it, my classmates, an entirely African American group, all over fifty, critiqued the dish: "I don't want to eat that. Where's the cornbread?" "Maybe if it had some beef? My kids wouldn't eat that without beef." "I know it's supposed to be vegetarian, but I need meat. Maybe shrimp. Shrimp would be good." With these comments, Feast! participants reject their implied passivity in the transfer of knowledge between instructor and food-insecure student: they know how to cook these meals and they know how they'd prefer to eat them. At the end of class, when Feast! participants are presented with pre-packed grocery bags, trades are common. Feast! participants are not allowed to look in the sacks, or trade what's in the sacks, during class; these trades often occurred in the hallway outside of where class had occurred, after our instructor had left the building. One week, for example, after Pam left the room, one Feast! participant called out, "I don't want cabbage, who'll take this?" An African American woman in her seventies reached for it and told us that she'd use it to make a slaw. I held up a box of frosted flakes—no one wanted it. Later, on our way out, we all left our frosted flakes in the community center's donation box. Terry, an elderly African American man, held up a bag of millet and laughed, saying, "No!" No one else wanted the millet, so I took it from him, though I had never cooked with it and was not sure how. As we continued our trades, one of the oldest class participants, Bernice, stood up and tied on her head scarf, getting ready to leave, and said, "I don't want anything in that bag. I'm just going to walk to the store. You all can take it." Terry asked her if she was sure, as he dug in her bag for peanut butter, and she responded, "I don't want cabbage, I don't eat cereal, and I'm not going to start today." The food given to Feast! participants is collected from large Feeding America donation bins—found in the lobby of nearly every grocery store in the metropolitan area. Promotions such as discounted amusement park tickets often encourage suburban shoppers to donate canned goods. On several occasions, I have been told by Feast! participants that they will drop off unwanted food items, received in class, back into those bins; canned green beans are the universally most unwanted item in Feast! grocery bags and are often donated back to the Pantry by food-insecure Feast! participants.

Feast! participants are often, but not always, skilled or decent cooks—an ability that is denied in class curriculum language and in hegemonic discourse in Kansas City. Some farmers markets in Kansas City have applied for and received Health Care Foundation funding for programs that "teach" urban residents how to cook with fresh produce, as increasing awareness and knowledge is often spoken about as the way to increase farmers market attendance and capital flow. Narratives shared by food-insecure Feast! residents refute this understanding of the urban poor. While cooking lunch together as a class, I watched food-insecure urban residents demonstrate kitchen skills and comfort—such as a Latina grandmother who neatly rolled basil before chopping in a chiffonade, or Donna, a Black woman in her forties who was receiving disability payments and had limited mobility, quickly and efficiently dicing a bag of onions from her seat in her wheelchair. This skill was often ignored by Feast! instructors, who, while class participants cooked, walked around and corrected our "errors"—this took the form of chastising participants for measuring with slightly rounded, rather than strictly leveled, tablespoon-fulls, or correcting participants who were cooking with time-honed techniques—such as personal understandings of how long to sauté onions or beef—rather than following given recipes to the minute. This paternalism was most obviously refuted during one particular class at the community center. As class participants cooked, a middle-aged African American man came by to grab a bag of bread out of the food pantry located behind us. Pam, our class teacher, called out, "Why don't you join us and learn how to cook?" The man replied laughingly as he strode out of the kitchen, "Honey, my mom raised me in the deep south. I know how to cook. I could cook you if I had to!"

Feast! participants often have highly developed social networks that they utilize to acquire the cheapest, most desired, food items. This network meant that instead of utilizing the most spatially convenient grocery outlet, food-insecure Feast! participants often traveled outside of the urban core to visit full-service grocery stores that they knew to both have lower prices and carry the variety of product they wanted (see also Barnes 2005). During class, Feast! participants would quite often end up discussing prices of various food items at area grocery stores, highly aware of where the best deals could be found, engaging in rigorous price surveillance (cf. Carney 2014). An interaction between our white instructor, Pam, Michael (an African American man in his mid-fifties), and Donna—as we discussed where to find strawberries—exemplifies this. Our snack recipe for the day was jicama with pureed strawberry sauce, and no one in class knew what jicama was or where to get it. Donna said, of the recipe, "Getting fresh fruit is too hard, Pam, it's too hard to get something like jicama over here on the East side." To this, Pam responded sympathetically but paternalistically, "I know, I know—it's tough because you're in a food desert. Don't you know you live in a food desert? But you can absolutely substitute canned fruit here in this recipe." Donna snapped back, "But I want *fresh fruit* and it's hard to get those. Fresh fruit. Fresh fruit. There's too much sugar in that can stuff." Pam attempted to offer a solution: "Have you tried the Rollin' Grocer?" Michael chimed in about the Rollin' Grocer, a mobile grocery store that sometimes makes stops outside of the community center, adding, "Yeah they have bananas at 59 cents a pound. Fifty-nine cents! At Price Chopper in Brookside you can get 'em for 39 cents a pound—" "You gotta be able to get there, though," said Donna, "even better is Roeland Park— you can buy the brown bananas there for 10 cents a pound." Laura, a young Black woman, chimed in, "That truck just isn't the same, anyway. They have everything on the South side, you can get everything there, and the stuff in that truck isn't fresh." "There's a grocery store coming this year to Prospect," said Donna. "No," said Michael, "It's groundbreaking this year and opening in 2018." "Well until then, I've got my granddaughter to drive me to Price Chopper in the Southside every month," said Donna.

Contrary to popular discourse and foodie understandings of the urban poor, Feast! participants have keen understandings of where the best available produce is located and have highly developed mappings of the urban foodscape, which they draw on to discern the most affordable grocery outlets. Many of the Feast! participants I met enjoyed cooking for their families and utilized all available social networks and charity resources—a task which takes considerable work—to find the produce and items that they most liked eating. Carney (2014) has theorized this time and expertise as "food work," primarily enacted by women, and argues that this labor is extremely undervalued and near impossible to enact alongside the long hours required by low-wage jobs. One useful outcome of Feast!, in my experience, was that it provided an expanded social network for food-insecure urban residents, who utilized these new connections to find new transportation mechanisms. For instance, it was ascertained early on within each Feast! cohort which participants had cars or access to family members with cars, and inquiries—"where do you live? When are you heading to the store?"—and requests to ride along to grocery shop, would be made. While the food aid and nutrition education were not always helpful to Feast! participants, for many, the networking and solidarity opportunities were meaningful outcomes of the class.

"I Worked in a Packing House for Thirty Years, I Know How to Handle Meat"

Feast! course curriculum and the way it was conveyed offered painful dismissals of structurally violent forces that shape food insecurity; food-insecure participants frequently and forcefully called out and corrected these dismissals. In small ways, Feast! participants assert their agency and call attention toward the structural forces that have combined to make them need of food charity programming. For example, when Pam asked Terry, an elderly African American man, to set a goal for the seven-week course, he responded, "My goal is to get a quarter of a million dollars. Then I can eat what I want!" Assertion of knowledge, skill, and structural forces that have subjugated them were common in Black Feast! participants' comments to white Feast! instructors. Once, for example, during a lesson plan about food safety, Bernice, an elderly African American woman, reminded our white middle-aged instructor Pam of her white privilege. Pam walked us through our lesson for the day, which included instructions for how to safely defrost and cook meat, how to safely store food, and how to wash one's hands, and then asked us to mime washing and drying our hands together, as a class. Pam added, we should dry our hands with paper towels, then turn the faucet off and open the door with that same paper towel, in order to keep our hands clean. Bernice chuckled to herself, and Pam asked her what was funny—to which Bernice responded, "I cleaned houses for people like you for a long, long time. You don't have to tell me not to touch those bathroom doorknobs." Later, when we had moved on to proper protocol for defrosting meat, Pam thought she would surprise Terry, who looked like he was ignoring the lesson, with a quiz question: "Terry, do you know which way to defrost? Should you do it on the counter, or under cold water, or in the microwave?" Terry, an elderly African American man with broad shoulders, looked visibly insulted at having been asked this question and snapped at Pam, "Woman, I worked in a packing house for thirty plus years. I know how to handle meat." Pam, and other instructors, certainly do not mean to insult Feast! class participants; instructors are given only nutritional training, not structural or sociological training, and are often young—straight out of college. But uncritical transmission of culturally and historically tone-deaf nutrition education—which ignores that participants like Bernice and Terry labored in underpaid and precarious domestic and food-processing positions in Kansas City's segregated labor market for decades—is felt as incredibly marginalizing by food-insecure participants.

Another notable instance of class participants reminding Feast! instruc-

tors about structural inequality occurred when I took Feast! at a senior assisted living complex in North Kansas City. Our instructor at this location,
a white middle-aged woman named Patti, was leading us through a lesson
plan on obesity and obesity-related illnesses. Our information packet for the
day contained a worksheet, which we worked through together as a class. We
were asked to list the causes of obesity on a left-hand column, and the hazards of obesity on the right. Patti listed out some suggested causes of obesity—
overeating, inactivity, and then called out—to our almost entirely African
American class of ten—what are some hazards of obesity? Class participants
shouted out, "heart problems," "diabetes," "you can lose a leg," and finally one
class member—a Black woman who walked with a cane—said "Hey, but we
get all of that because we're Black, too, though." Patti responded, well, with
diet and exercise you can "give yourself a fighting chance," and the woman
again retorted, "But being Black makes us get some of those things, and the
only hospital I can afford is 'dead man's hospital.'" Here, she references Research Medical Hospital, commonly referred to as one of the worst hospitals
in the metropolitan area. Patti tried to move the class along, stating, "Okay,
turn to page four. Let's calculate our BMIs," to which an African American man
said, "I read that that isn't a good indicator of my health." Patti snapped, "Well,
no, we're gonna use it and it works fine for us." Here, Feast! participants rightly
bring attention to the fact that racialized inequalities make them more likely to
be subjected to certain diseases (Dressler 1993; Albritton 2013). They highlight
the fact that unequal access to healthcare makes it harder for them to manage
these diseases they are disproportionately disposed to (Page 2006). They protest that the indicators of health, promoted in Feast!, do not accurately account
for all of the socioeconomic forces in their lives.

Feast! participants also often referenced and brought attention to the fact
that they were under much stricter economic constraints than the Feast! instructor would acknowledge. During one class cooking segment (we were
making "lady bug pizzas"—English muffins, cut in half, and topped with pe-
sto, cheese, tomato, and black olives) our instructor, Laura, a white woman in
her midtwenties, told us "I always buy the block of cheese instead of preshred-
ded cheese. It's just so much cheaper, and it spreads and melts easier!" Carla
and Joan, two Black-middle aged women who had been attending the class together, as friends, scoffed. Joan said, "At least you have a choice. We're not even
allowed to buy the shredded cheese." Laura was confused and asked who was
keeping them from buying the cheese they wanted. "Shredded cheese has ad-
ditives that they say aren't good for babies. You have to buy the block cheese.
Block cheese is a WIC food." While Laura likely has the time to shred cheese

and enjoys saving money, for Carla and Joan, taking time away from parenting to shred cheese likely feels like an imposition. The extensive time, paperwork, and procedures involved in obtaining WIC in the first place are difficult for the urban poor to manage (Page-Reeves 2014). Likewise, during a Feast! class at a community center, participants and I had a long discussion of making do while experiencing poverty. Bernice told us, as we ate the vegetarian sloppy joes we had cooked in class that day, "There was one time, when I had three boys to feed, and all I had in the fridge were some biscuits, a pound of ground beef, and a can of sloppy joes. I cooked up that beef, I put in the sloppy joe sauce. I put the biscuits in the oven, and then we poured on the sloppy joes when they were done. That was so good. And it fed us all." Terry laughed, "that's nothing," and added, "When I was growing up there were twelve of us. Twelve of us plus my momma and dad, and we had one chicken to split. I would kill that chicken in the morning, pluck it, and we'd have it for dinner. One chicken for all of us!" Stories such as these served, in part, as a way for food-charity recipients to demonstrate to Feast! instructors that they were under great constraints—had been for quite some time—and had developed sophisticated means of dealing with these barriers without the help of foodies.

Paternalism and the
"Public Spectacle" of Nutrition Education

African American Kansas City residents have a storied history of self-sufficiency and resourcefulness in a racialized food landscape, built high with roadblocks restricting their agency and access. Racialized urbicide, enacted by powerful white Kansas City residents undergirds the very need for food charity in the urban core. These acts of violence are unacknowledged, and food charity paradigms designed to assist victims of this violence focus instead on techniques of "self-making," in which the racialized urban poor are asked to identify causes of poverty, and their solutions, within themselves (Lyon-Callo 2004, 154). These programs present a continuation of historical efforts to quantify and contain Black bodies and Black diets in Kansas City. Feast! has inspired similar models of food charity programming in Kansas City, and likely other U.S. cities. Locally, numerous foodie-led nonprofits offer classes, programming, and farmers market events that exchange groceries for the participation of food-insecure residents in nutrition education. In the case of Feast!, such programming denies the historical and current acts of self-sufficiency by the urban poor, disavows their ability to judge and monitor their bodily health, and elides purposeful acts of disinvestment experienced by the poor—enforcing, instead, unwanted and inaccurate frameworks, such as food desert, in order to locate the cause of their suffering. Studies have indicated that the vast majority of those who receive Food Stamps "feel their own need as a personal failure rather than, or often as much as, a reflection of structural dynamics over which they have no control" (Page-Reeves 2014, 13). While the Feast! participants I encountered often forcefully asserted that they had been subjected to violent structural policies, many of those seeking food aid experience doubled forces of blame and stigmatization, as both they and food-charity workers blame them for their poverty.

A significant amount of time, energy, programmatic development, and money—state and private—is appropriated toward food charity programming like Feast!, though studies have indicated they become long-term strategies for survival rather than the temporary assistance they are intended to be (cf. Fox Piven et al. 2002). Comparatively, unconditional cash transfer programs— common state-led strategies for poverty reduction in "developing" countries— are on average 20 percent cheaper, comparatively easier to administer, and have been shown to offer the same or better nutritional outcomes as food-based programs (Hidrobo et al. 2014; Cunha 2014). Foodies express great concern about the food choices of low-income urban residents—best illustrated by the comment made by Martha, an employee at the Pantry, about a SNAP-dollar doubling program: will they be able to spend that money on fruit roll ups? However, studies in rural Mexico and a recent experimental cash-transfer program in New York City demonstrate that assistance recipients do not spend this money on tobacco or alcohol (Cunha 2014; Miller et al. 2015); instead, they spend money on "more and better food," with the result of preliminary findings of health improvements (Paes-Sousa et al. 2010). Cash transfer programs are also mindful of the time constraints faced by the urban poor—who in this study often rushed out of work to make it to Feast! on time and struggled to find childcare during class hours—and acknowledge agency and the ability of the urban poor to judge what food is best for their families. Instead, in large part because nutrition education, teaching the poor to grow their own food, and farmers market vouchers fit in with foodie plans for city space (and are heavily incentivized and funded at a national level), models like Feast! inappropriately and inadequately address food insecurity in Kansas City. Unconditional cash transfer programs are unpopular in the United States, despite their proven successes, where the "public spectacle" of welfare recipients' subservience is required (Fox Piven et al. 2002, 27).

Feast! is exemplary of the fact that, in Kansas City, many programs that purport to address food insecurity actually seem to function as promotion for farmers markets, community gardens, and other local food outlets commonly uplifted in green urban development. While all of these spaces have a place in cities, research shows us they aren't an effective means of addressing hunger; a myopic focus on instilling green urbanism into all facets of municipal policy has led to their adoption in Kansas City, regardless. The following chapter explores how even Black urban food producers—those who also, like white foodies, support local food movement goals—are disadvantaged in the white public space created through Kansas City's green urbanism.

CHAPTER 5

"We Know We're Being Treated like Tokens"

Black Urban Farmers Navigating and Contesting Structural Racism in Kansas City's Local Food Economy

Adrienne, a short Black woman who wears her hair in braids, was born and raised in Kansas City; one morning as we shared donuts and black coffee at Lamar's on Troost, she told me that she had grown up in a "back to the earth-type" of family. She was raised vegan, and her parents grew every bit of food they ate—canning and preserving for the winter and barely needing to purchase anything at the grocery store. In her early fifties, Adrienne decided to try her hand at selling her extra produce. She knew how to grow food. Every spring for the past several decades, she and her sons had tilled up their backyard and put the space into use for intensive vegetable production. "Local food" was taking off in Kansas City. More and more restaurants were listing the small-scale urban farmers they partnered with prominently at the top of menus, on chalkboard signs propped up outside on the sidewalk, and cross-advertised on Instagram, where restaurants would tag photos of local Kansas City farmers holding up brightly colored produce. Adrienne had heard that you could make shockingly good money if you secured a restaurant contract, but she had felt nervous about approaching any of the local farm-to-table establishments. So far, she sold to her neighbors and family on an inconsistent basis. One fall season, she told me, an early frost forced her to finally try approaching chefs:

> One year, I think it was November, we had a cold snap, and I had this whole bunch of tomatoes that hadn't ripened yet. And it was like this mad rush to get all these tomatoes off the vine. Turns out I had four hundred pounds of green tomatoes, right? Well, Black folks like green tomatoes, we like to make chowchow and all that—but I still had too many. I started going around to the small, locally owned farm to table restaurants and I looked pretty rough, you know, I'd been harvesting all day. And I remember this one place, a pretty

popular one. I walked into their kitchen with a box of tomatoes, in my overalls, and they were like, "*No*, we don't need anything from *you*. We don't need
anything you have." So I said okay. I went to another place, and I'll tell you the
name because they were so cool—Succotash—and they were like, "Yeah! We'll
take 'em!" There were ten heirloom varieties. They liked that. But, they sold
them as an East Side fried green tomato plate—a soul food sort of deal . . . so
on some level we know we're being treated like tokens. And for now that's
okay, its working okay for now. There may come a time when it's not gonna be
okay, but I can deal with it for now.

Adrienne's encounter was not exceptional in Kansas City—numerous Black
urban farmers have experienced systemic racism in the urban food movement,
particularly in local food sales. Even though Adrienne's upbringing means that
she shares a lot of ideas about food and ecological stewardship with white,
upper-middle class foodies in KC, her racialized and class-based positionality
still separated her from market-based outlets until she marketed her products
as a racialized commodity, a token of East Side entrepreneurship for upper-
middle class white consumption at a restaurant in the gentrifying Hospital Hill
neighborhood. While there are farmers of color who earn a significant income
from urban farming, particularly the farmers in Grow KC's refugee agricultural training program (a model in which refugee status is an integral aspect
of product marketing), on the whole, white farmers in Kansas City are much
more likely to "scale up" and earn a stable income than Black farmers.

Scholarship on whiteness and the local food economy has chiefly focused
on a few themes: the "white farm imaginary" (cf. Alkon and McCullen 2011)
and its shaping of a color-blind, class-neutral history of farming and agriculture; valorization of community and locality that embodies white ideology
(cf. Slocum 2007; DuPuis and Goodman 2005); and alienating discourse that
prioritizes environmental sustainability over social and racial justice concerns
(cf. Alkon 2012; Alkon 2013; Guthman 2008; Guthman 2011). This literature
has developed rich theorization about how foodies shape exclusionary whiteness in local food spaces, but it has primarily focused on how this experience affects local food consumers. Missing, in this literature, is substantive
discussion of how inequities manifest in the realms of production and distribution of local food, and how the whiteness of local food impacts nonwhite
local food producers. Nonwhite urban growers face all of the discursive and
culturally exclusionary themes noted above, in addition to having to navigate
the way whiteness impacts consumer preference and market networks. Rachel
Slocum (2007, 529) touches on some of these issues, highlighting how the way

that cilantro is harvested and sold (sans roots) lends to its use in white kitchens, rather than Indian or Thai households (where roots are typically utilized as well). This chapter builds on these observations of how race "congeals" in commodities by analyzing the extensive barriers Black urban growers face in the production and distribution of locally grown produce.

Specifically, in this chapter I analyze the extensive barriers Black urban growers face in the local food economy, within the context of green urban development infrastructure that heavily promotes urban food production and entrepreneurship. In doing so, I seek to disrupt the dominant claim within Kansas City that green urban development (as opposed to more conventional models of urban planning and economic growth that center profit, rather than economic sustainability) can create more equitable and accessible opportunities for entrepreneurs.

The Rise and Fall of the Potato King:
Discrimination against Black U.S. Farmers

Adrienne's experience resonates historically, and on a national level—reflecting broader forces of discrimination that have affected Black farmers in the United States. United States Department of Agriculture (USDA) discrimination against African American farmers, a case Black farmers brought to court, and won, in a class action lawsuit, has irreparably shaped the socioeconomic opportunities available to Black farmers in the United States. The suit, Pigford v. Glickman, alleging racial discrimination against African American farmers in USDA allocation of farm loans and assistance in the 1980s and 1990s, was settled for more than $2 billion in 1999 (Benson 2012, 117). Still, discrimination continued following this court decision; the USDA failed to notify affected parties that they could apply for settlement payouts and crafted a near-impossible process that required claimants to produce numerous documents and records backing up their claims of discrimination (Benson 2012, 117). This process included requiring Black farmers to track down white farmers who had applied for and received assistance from the same benefit program, and who had "the same acreage, the same type of crop, the same credit history, and who had received a higher payment or better treatment" (Benson 2012, 119). The USDA has spent nearly $330 million in public funds challenging the claims that were advanced, with the outcome that less than half of the compensatory funds have been paid out and 31 percent of those eligible for compensation have been denied (Benson 2012, 119; Schneider 2013). In 2010 Congress appropriated $1.2 billion more to these discrimination claims, as seventy thousand Black farmers claimed that they had not had their cases heard; studies through 2008 have illustrated continued discrimination enacted by the USDA (Schneider 2013).[1]

Discrimination against Black farmers should not just be conceptualized as differential loan allocation; as Adrienne's story indicates, discrimination happens in insidious ways through interpersonal interaction. Scholars have indicated that any real accounting of national-level discrimination against Black farmers is hindered by our inability to quantify these racialized interactions (Thurow 1998). Such racial discrimination occurs even within racially "equitable" policies, as these are enacted by myriad individual actors with their own ideologies. For example, USDA and agricultural extension agent discrimination against Black farmers can occur in ways such as charging a higher interest rate to Black farmers; offering information about special programs, such as reduced loan rates or disaster assistance, only to favored farmers; assisting favored, white farmers with government paperwork; and granting loans to Black farmers but purposefully delaying payout until summer, long after the loan was needed to start spring production (Schneider 2013). These national processes are reflected and (re)enacted locally within racialized access to local food markets in Kansas City.

Additionally, the concepts of "local food," and "local food markets" are fraught with racialized and class-based complications. Discursively, with lived effects, the local food movement is painted as upheld by white farmers for white consumers (see also Van Sant 2016). Much like Benson (2012) illustrated within the tobacco industry, with the erasure of the crops' plantation history and migrant laborer involvement, local small-scale urban food production—-a sector that is, historically, racially and ethnically diverse—has been whitewashed and incorporated as part of the production of a specific white foodie identity. Weiss (2011, 456) points toward some of the implications this has for Black involvement in local food markets. In North Carolina, for example, African American hog farmers reject categories of "local" and "cooperative," even though their practices can be categorized as such, and resist outreach from extension agents. The uneven adoption of these market categories indicate that local is "not simply an existential condition of being in a place, it is a specific orientation to how space is produced" (Weiss 2011, 456), an orientation that has significant implications for the racialized operation of the local food economy.

Why does racialized inequality in agriculture and the local food economy matter, locally, in Kansas City? Green urban development discourse currently heralds urban agriculture as an equal opportunity occupation that provides a stable income and involvement for all in the burgeoning green economy. This discourse is (re)produced at a number of scales. A "Food Hub Feasibility" study conducted by Grow KC, Kansas City Chamber of Commerce, the Hunger Coalition, Healthy Communities KC, and several green, urban, development-focused architecture firms advertised that there is high demand among food-buyers in Kansas City and stated that there is $177 million in unmet demand, in Kansas City, for local produce (Kansas City Food Hub Working Group 2014). Capacity studies such as these further city-level efforts to promote green urban development and urban food production as a viable means of creating urban job growth. Kansas City residents are repeatedly told—in media celebrating the success of local urban farms, and in daily discourse—that urban farming can provide a livable wage. David, for example, the white, East Side farmer and farmers market manager discussed in chapter 2, once gave a presentation at a Jackson County Third District community meeting to recruit urban residents for a farmer training course he was helping sponsor, in which he said,

> We're holding a beginning farmer class—a SPIN farming class, which is intensive farming on small plots—and working with our Kansas City farmers this year to be more productive, so they can actually supplement their income or replace their income with urban farming. SPIN farmers in Canada and the United States—they're making anywhere from $20,000 to $100,000 dollars a year, urban farming. And so we want you in the inner city to learn how to do that too. We want the 3rd district to have the best GMO-free, locally grown, organically grown, sustainably grown produce to feed their families at a good price. And the money that purchases that produce will be put back into the local community. It's gonna be great.

In reality, most urban farmers in the United States make significantly less than $10,000 dollars per year; Dimitri et al. (2016) find that a majority also must rely upon supplemental income or inherited wealth. While studies have not analyzed urban farm income in relation to race, structural inequalities likely result in even lower incomes for urban farmers of color. David's discourse also denies that historically, Black farmers have been divested of land and wealth and have been met with violence—structural and physical—when their businesses have succeeded.

The violence that farmer Junius G. Groves, "The Potato King," experienced exemplifies this process of dispossession. Groves was born in Louisville, Kentucky, and moved to Kansas City as an exoduster after emancipation. There, Groves saved money while working as a laborer in the stockyards; eventually, he was able to purchase eighty acres of land west of Kansas City. Groves became a prolific farmer—reportedly growing more potatoes than any other farmer in the United States—and a major produce distributor in the Midwest (Kansaspedia 2012). As his wealth grew (at the height of his career, Groves was a millionaire), he built a twenty-room, electric equipped home and also began selling tracts of his land to other Black farmers. At this point, the local KKK launched a series of attacks, setting fire to his home and property three separate times, twice after Groves had rebuilt and recovered from the previous destruction (Kansaspedia 2012). Historical violence such as this is not considered in David's assertion that Black urban farmers can make $20,000 to $100,000 in the urban core.

Generational Wealth and Racialized Access to Farm Startup Capital

An accounting of start-up costs for an urban farmer must be understood within the context of racialized governmental policies that denied African Americans the right to accumulate wealth and own land. Public discourse, today, celebrating the incredible affordability and availability of vacant urban land to farm parallels homesteading discourse and policy in the 1800s, such as the 1862 Homesteading Act, which disbursed acreage to white settlers in the hopes that they would "cultivate" and "tame" so-called uncharted spaces. Captive Africans were, by law, not able to own property or accumulate assets until the Southern Homestead Act in 1866 provided legal basis and incentives for Black land ownership (Lanza 1990). By 1910 whites owned more than 99 percent of all property in Kansas City (Griffin 2015, 51), an early foundational monopoly that makes it difficult for Black land accumulation to occur today. Though federal policy post-1866 technically allowed African Americans to apply for land through the Homesteading Act, racialized discrimination—such as "black codes," state laws that denied Black asset accumulation—in land allocation kept Black farmers from fully realizing its benefits (Oliver and Shapiro 1997, 15; Lanza 1990). Public opinion also stood in opposition to Black land ownership; a white southerner quoted in Gunnar Myrdal's *An American Dilemma*, responded to a question on the merits of Black-owned farms: "Who'd work the land if the niggers had farms of their own?" (Myrdal 1944, cited in Oliver and Shapiro 1997, 15). Between 1940 and 1974, the number of Black-owned farms fell 93 percent, from 681,790 to 45,594 (Daniel 2013), a result of USDA discrimination described above, individualized discrimination enacted by white southerners, such as the one quoted by Gunnar Myrdal, and a number of specifically racialized economic policies, described below. Today, African Americans comprise less than 2 percent of U.S. farmers (Daniel 2013).

Segregation, redlining, and racialized lending combined to drastically reduce Black Americans' abilities to accumulate generational wealth, all while home ownership and home value appreciation provided white U.S. citizens a key mechanism for upward mobility (Massey and Denton 1993). Whites have benefited from the massive equity buildup made possible by Federal Housing Administration (FHA) policies that facilitated their entry into home ownership; today, a majority of young white homeowners receive financial assistance from their parents, who themselves were able to accumulate generational wealth because of these FHA policies that restricted Black home ownership (Oliver and Shapiro 1997). Racially restrictive covenants enacted via FHA policy continued, legally, into the 1950s, and the practice continued informally afterward. This policy has created spatial realities of white suburbanization, and Black urban cores (Gordon 2008). African Americans who own homes face unique racialized disadvantages: it is much harder for Black applicants to get approved for mortgages (a 2022 study by Bachaud finds that banks reject Black applicants twice as often as whites); mortgages offered to Black applicants feature significantly higher interest rates than those offered to whites; home-repair loans are more often denied to Black applicants; and Black-owned housing stock in urban communities do not rise in value nearly as much as homes in white communities (Oliver and Shapiro 1997). Today, the U.S. tax codes further privilege whites—by favoring property owners—and disadvantage asset-poor African American citizens (Oliver and Shapiro 1997).

These barriers to asset accumulation are compounded with specific racialized policies that have a significant impact on the ability of Black U.S. citizens to build and maintain successful enterprises. Until the middle of the twentieth century, Black entrepreneurs were limited to a restricted African American market, to which white-owned businesses also had access (Walker 1986). Black entrepreneurs were excluded from lucrative mainstream white markets, which has today resulted in a higher preponderance of small-scale, rather than large-scale, Black-owned businesses (Walker 1986). Black business owners have been systematically blocked from low-interest government-backed loans and barred from other means of wealth accumulation that white business owners have access to (Oliver and Shapiro 1997). For example, several states had laws blocking African Americans from investing in the stock market up until the early twentieth century (Oliver and Shapiro 1997). Racialized discrepancies in credit-card issuance also have important implications for understanding the challenges Black entrepreneurs face. For example, whites often receive cards with higher credit limits and lower interest rates than African Americans do (Williams 1996, 352). White entrepreneurs offered competitive cards with interest-free grace periods can use these incentives to invest in their businesses, unlike applicants of color, who receive lower credit card limits and less added perks.

These racially discriminatory policies have an enormous impact on the ability of African Americans to participate in the local food economy. Black urban farmers typically start their farming enterprises with less generational wealth and familial financial support, a decreased likelihood of being approved for a low-interest rate business loan or credit card, and significantly decreased likelihood of being hired for a low-wage job to support themselves while they establish their new farming business (Pager et al. 2009), a strategy used by many white urban farmers. African Americans are also forced to operate within a racialized real estate industry that is more likely to rent or sell urban land to urban farmers with "white" sounding names than stereotypically "Black" sounding names (Turner et al. 2013). These racialized employment and entrepreneurship dynamics contradict David's assertion that any urban farmer can make a living growing food in Kansas City and highlight the problematics of national-level celebration of the potential "green jobs" that can be created by green urban development in postindustrial U.S. cities. (cf. Alkon 2012). And, as Alkon (2018) reminds us, "green" jobs can still be imbricated in the process of gentrification.

Infrastructural support for urban agriculture businesses is vital, as start-up costs are varied and expensive. Knowledge acquisition is expensive in and of itself. In Kansas City, apprenticeship programs and workshops that are widely regarded as having trained the most successful urban growers are costly to participate in. One apprenticeship program—which includes farm planning workshops held by area experts and offers (requires) forty-hour unpaid work weeks with host farms in the Kansas City area—costs $500 dollars to enroll in and demands a time commitment that would be difficult to balance with a paying job or child care. Apprenticing, and other variations of unpaid manual labor, are valuable currency in the Kansas City food economy.[2] Apprenticing with a respected urban farmer will set a new farmer up for success in local grant applications and in sales network connections. While some apprenticeships pay a low-wage salary (most often around $3 dollars an hour), the hardship imposed by unlivable wages with no benefits is not recognized within the foodie community. For example, when I discussed the difficulty of acquiring affordable farm training, a white middle-aged foodie responded to me, "Why don't people just go apprentice with Stony Crest [urban farm]? It only pays ten dollars an hour but you get to work with rockstars." This discourse assumes that in-training farmers will be able to supplement their income in other ways, or will be able to rely on family assistance—as many young, white, new urban farmers in fact do. This is not to say that self-made urban farmers are not common, nor successful; rather, apprenticeships are a valuable currency, bringing respect and legitimacy to a new farm-business entrepreneur, but are costly to participants in ways not always visible even to those offering the apprenticeships.

Land acquisition is also a barrier for beginning urban farmers. While the Land Bank offers vacant plots of land for often around $100 dollars, and popular foodie discourse incentivizes the idea of buying a "fixer-upper" and its conjoined vacant lot to farm on, the infrastructural investment in making such homes livable, and such land ready to farm, is high. Racialized lending continues today and makes it significantly more difficult for African Americans to receive home improvement loans. Preparing urban land for farming requires soil testing (a service offered by the University of Missouri Extension, which costs around $15 for a basic test, or significantly more if a land-owner worries about arsenic or other urban pollutants). Soil amendments (compost and fertilizer) are necessary to start high production SPIN vegetable farming, and can cost around $3,000 to $5,000 dollars per quarter acre(approximately 3 urban lots), depending on compost quality. Tilling and land clearing will also likely be necessary on urban plots; both are labor intensive (if carried out by oneself) or expensive (if hired out). Water infrastructure is possibly the most expensive addition to a vacant lot an urban farmer needs to make. Installation of a water line is necessary (otherwise, one must carry or transport water from their house, or ask a neighbor near the farm for permission to tap into their line) and expensive, costing several thousand dollars. The city government offers water grants to urban farmers, administered through the Kansas City Grower's Club, but applicants must demonstrate that they have already grown on the plot for at least one season—meaning that farmers must struggle through one farming season, piecing together water sources, before receiving assistance. Farmers who attempt to farm communally shared land (such as in community gardens) or borrowed land (offered up, often, by elderly neighbors who have no plans for its use) run into costly problems. I spoke with several Black urban growers who grew food to sell at market on numerous community garden plots, across the city—sometimes as many as four—meaning they would drive to four different urban locations, almost daily, to water and check on their crops. One farmer told me how at one of her community gardens, a fellow gardener froze the water pipes by leaving them on over the winter—a problem which the city did not come to fix until June, at which point her spring crops had died and she lost out on nearly two months of profits at the farmers market. Another had his garden flooded when a fellow community gardener forgot to turn off the water hose. Farmers who do not own their own land lose autonomy over their market production, which has a drastic effect on farm profitability.

The infrastructure involved in produce preparation, storage, and transport is also highly expensive. Urban farmers have to consider where they will wash produce before market (many, who can afford it, build wash stations near their crop fields), the added water costs of vegetable processing, where and how to store produce before market, packaging for products, and aspects of transportation (such as a large cooler, or a cooled-trailer, so that produce does not wilt before reaching its market). Availability of a large walk-in cooler is one of the most valuable farm assets, because it allows farmers to harvest and process vegetables on a more manageable schedule (instead of harvesting right before market, so vegetables will be their freshest) and allows farmers to scale up (many Black urban growers I know could not grow more vegetables than would fit comfortably in their home fridges). A less expensive alternative to a professional walk-in cooler, advocated by many farmers I spoke with, is a shed with a high-powered air-conditioning unit installed. While this is a lower-cost option, the startup expense involved in buying a shed and air conditioner and paying for a constantly running sub-zero cooling bill can be extravagant, especially for those who have not received any income from their urban farm as of yet.

Other infrastructure costs include season-extension products, such as hoop houses, high tunnels, and green houses. While they are not necessary for an urban farmer, they offer a significant market advantage; farmers with high tunnels can plant crops earlier in the season and be the first to bring certain products to market. USDA high tunnel grants are advertised locally, and foodie-led workshops assist farmers in applying for this infrastructure. But the grants offered are matching grants and reimbursements, meaning that farmers will have to have several thousand dollars available for this expense before applying for a grant. Farmers unable to afford these costs have told me they feel embarrassed about asking for help, or for assistance with low-cost alternatives. For example, at one of the SPIN farmer training classes David co-hosted, the topic of discussion centered on low tunnels—essentially mini high-tunnels, only several feet off the ground, that provide minor weather and bug protection, vital in protecting against locally devastating squash bugs, for instance. One white farmer in the room, a woman who had recently left a high-income marketing career to buy peri-urban land to farm, told us how she had found a "cheap" low tunnel kit—$400 dollars for around a thousand square feet. A Black urban farmer sitting next to me, a middle-aged man who had been farming small-scale for several years, whispered, "would hula hoops cut in half work, covered with sheets?" and declined to ask this question to the group, when prompted by the course instructor. Foodie discourse denies that these costs are prohibitive (in this case, glossing over the fact that several decades in a high-paying career could allow some farmers to draw from stores of wealth that are out of reach for minority farmers) and create a privileged space in which farmers unable to afford basic infrastructure feel ashamed and unable to seek outside assistance.

Farmers markets are spoken of in Kansas City as a market accessible to all, even hobby farmers; this is untrue. Farmers who earn a consistent profit at farmers markets meet considerable infrastructural costs in order to do so. While a farmer can sell uncut produce at market without having any certification, other market products and services, which often lead to higher market earnings, can cost quite a bit. Vendor fees to sell at the city's most trafficked and profitable markets, such as City Market, can be several hundred dollars per market day, or around $15 dollars for smaller East Side markets. Some markets, such as City Market, require vendors to have proof of up-to-date car insurance, as their cars will be on market property. Vendors need to apply for a market sales permit through the health department, which costs $25 dollars per year. Additional permits and inspections are required if a farmer sells eggs or meat. It is often recommended that farmers apply for food liability insurance, as a customer illness can be a costly mistake. One of the cheapest food liability insurance plans costs around $300 dollars per year. Offering a free berry or radish could result in higher sales, but if farmers wish to offer samples of their produce to customers, they either need to sell at a market that has been certified to offer samples (meaning, they have an inspector-certified sink and kitchen on site), which often means vendor fees will be higher, or they need to apply for a sampling permit themselves, in which case they need to illustrate that they have a working sink, gloves, tongs, and other food service materials. Additionally, local farmers market managers have told me that farmers sell more at market when they offer produce priced by weight, rather than per piece. In order to sell produce priced by weight, farmers need to purchase and pay for inspection of an N-chip certified scale, a piece of equipment that starts at around $250 dollars. Farmers need to bring sufficient cooling mechanisms for their products at farmers markets—which are often located on tarmac in parking lots, where heat is reflected back onto produce. Without adequate ice and cooling (ice at such a scale that it needs to be bought by the bag, rather than created at home in trays), produce appears limp and is less likely to be purchased. In addition to all of these regulatory and safety costs, infrastructural investment in market aesthetics is a costly endeavor that consistently leads to greater farmer profit. Higher-earning farmers have invested in farm logo and branding development, large banners for their farm stand, table cloths, decorative jars and baskets to display their produce, and consistently carry a large variety and volume of produce—this kind of bounty attracts customers. Offering a high volume of a wide variety of products involves, of course, infrastructural investment and labor in developing a diversified farm, or the social networks to partner with farmers who offer products you do not, such as honey, which you offer to sell for a cut of the profit.

During another SPIN farming class, a Black urban farmer highlighted this issue. David instructed the class on farmers market displays, stating, "All of you have flat displays. You need to elevate produce. You need to have potatoes spilling out of tipped over buckets!" A Black urban farmer sitting near me whispered to those of us sitting near her, "I can't get abundance. I have two raised beds, and in each I have twelve plants. I can't grow enough to spill out of buckets." While abundant farmers market displays may seem easy to achieve, creating this abundance—and sometimes leaving with all of it, now wilted and unsellable, on slow days at low-traffic markets—involves costly infrastructural investment.

Value-added products sell well at farmers markets and can set a farmer apart in a market setting, but certifications and safety regulations make this an unaffordable route of entrepreneurship for many Black urban farmers. If, for example, a farmer—or, really, any urban resident—wanted to sell canned jams and jellies at market, they would have to write down the recipe exactly as they plan to use it and send it to Kansas State University for safety testing and certification. This certification costs $300 dollars per recipe. Additionally, Kansas City, Missouri, laws require any value-added product sold at market to be cooked in a certified kitchen—meaning that cooks will either have to pay to have their home kitchens brought up to code and certified, or they will need to travel to, and rent out (the average rate for a daily rental in Kansas City is $100 dollars), commercially available certified kitchens. A 2016 one-day workshop on crafting safely canned acidified foods to sell at farmers markets, offered by the University of Missouri, had a registration cost of $375 dollars—a special discounted rate offered to urban growers in Kansas City. Sometimes, David told us at a SPIN farming class, depending on what you're selling—for example, cookies might be considered low-risk—your farmers market manager might let you sell value-added products that have not been prepared in a certi-fied kitchen. He told us, however, that this is something you undertake at your own risk and shared a story about one of his vendors—who sold cookies and donuts—who was caught by a surprise inspector visit and forced to throw out all of her baked goods. I spoke with a number of African American women, in particular, who had been told by friends and family that their baked goods would sell well at market and had looked into doing so, only to be discouraged by the high prices of certification involved. These experiences undermine he-gemonic public discourse that portrays small-scale urban food production as a profitable career opportunity available to anyone in the urban core.

Finally, while certainly not necessary, organic production methodologies—and organic certification—are highly valuable for an urban farmer, and a highly expensive designation to earn. Farmers with organic certification can access a more elite consumer base and garner a much higher price for their product. Farmers who can document that they farm with organic practices can sell at the Brookside farmers market, one of the most elite and profitable markets in Kansas City. But to gain organic certification, farmers have to ac-count for land use practices for the past three years, demonstrate, and keep records showing, that every input in their farm—even straw—is certified or-ganic, perform lab tests on water used on their farm, and pay around $350 dol-lars for an organic certifier to come and inspect their farm. Farming organi-cally offers a huge market advantage for urban farmers, but is financially out of reach for a majority of the Black and brown urban growers.

Networking Events, Civil Rights, and Intersectional Farmer Identity Politics

Black food producers encounter more than just economic barriers in the lo-cal food economy; social networks, and racialized access to specific, profitable networks, are an unacknowledged aspect of urban farm business success in Kansas City. Urban farmers who attend social events and workshops hosted by powerful foodie-led organizations, such as Grow KC, the Hunger Coali-tion, and Healthy Communities KC, gain access to discounted or special rate farm equipment, opportunities for collaboration with other farmers, and ac-cess to potential sales networks. For example, one urban grower, who operates a small urban garden consultancy business, told me how when she first started out, she had a hard time affording starter plants for the gardens she was hired to design. Her friends, however, at Grow KC, shared extra transplants left over from spring production at the refugee agricultural training program with her.

The next year, her friend at Grow KC told her to come by their greenhouse near the end of winter and pick out exactly what she wanted, for free. "It can be so expensive, but when things are donated like that, it's really nice," the grower told me. Donations such as this one can make or break an urban farm business in its first few years and are predicated entirely off of a farmers ability to cultivate relationships with white, upper-middle class foodies.

Grow KC's yearly Farmers and Friends meeting—dubbed the "white farmers and friends meeting" by many Black urban growers in Kansas City—is where many of these valuable connections are made. While many foodie-created and occupied spaces can provide valuable connections, I focus here on the Farmers and Friends meeting because it is spoken about often by farmers of color in KC and is particularly racially divisive. Farmers and Friends is a one-day conference, held at a church in the wealthy Brookside neighborhood, that attracts urban growers, local chefs, foodies who have connections with local chefs and food distributors, and foodie-led nonprofits. In the morning, attendees are invited to present information pertinent to local growers, distributors, and purchasers. I have witnessed the advertisement of classes, discounted farm equipment rental, and farmers market managers notifying growers of new regulations. For example, a new, small-scale, high-quality organic compost producer advertised their products at Farmers and Friends in the spring of 2018 and offered steep discounts for those who mentioned Grow KC when they called to place an order. Also, small-scale transplant producers, who grow organic, heirloom produce varieties that have been acclimated to the local growing climate, advertise their products at discounted rates, products which are highly valuable in a local market that demands unique varieties of vegetables. These producers grow specialized transplants in a greenhouse or under grow lights, a costly and skilled labor many small-scale growers do not invest in, and are difficult to cultivate connections with if you do not meet them in person at events such as Farmers and Friends.

In informal ways as well, this event is valuable: for example, farmers or foodies who own expensive equipment, such as chainsaws and soil excavators, often agree to share or loan these items with farmers they meet at Farmers and Friends. Farmers can also make connections that lead to collaborative ventures, increasing their competitiveness on the market (for example, farmers who aren't able to offer much produce variety can—and have—met other farmers at the event, who they've decided to partner with in offering a Community Supported Agriculture (CSA) program. CSAs are a valuable sales strategy for farmers for a number of reasons (consistent income stream, often offers an influx of funds at the beginning of the farming season, etc.), but customers expect a consistent, diverse array of products in each weekly produce delivery—an expectation often hard for small-scale farmers to meet, in which customers pay a lump sum for a weekly offering of produce, and a large variety of product is expected. One Black farmer who runs a small community garden in the Northeast, for example, told me that she had been trying to acquire compost for her low-income neighbors. They were trying to grow food in their backyards, but it was not growing well: "They needed good quality compost that would make their gardens grow better." She attended Farmers and Friends a couple years ago, one of only three Black farmers in attendance, and sat in on a discussion on soil health moderated by a woman who owns an organic compost company in Kansas City: "I sat through her session, learned some things, and stayed after. We got to talking, and by the time I was done telling her about my neighborhood she was almost in tears, saying 'Oh, we gotta help out!' So that's how it started. She was my liaison and made it happen. Now we have this free compost day every year, and they provide it all." Connections like these are valuable for urban farm businesses, or in the case of this farmer, in supporting low-income neighborhood activities and goals.

As the term in circulation "white farmers and friends" implies, many Black urban growers I spoke with did not want to, and/or did not feel welcome to, attend foodie networking events such as this one. This is for a number of reasons—for one, numerous foodies have themselves voiced to me discomfort in speaking about agriculture with African American growers. This is evident, for example, in Nancy's statements about how uncomfortable her Black farmer friend made her when he shared that not too long ago, he would have been lynched for talking to her (see chapter 2). White upper-middle class foodies feel more comfort with those who have unequivocally positive associations with agriculture and actively seek out conversation and connection with these individuals, avoiding conversation with those who might have painful or mixed associations with farming. Similarly, other scholars have argued that farmer support organizations in the United States, such as Grow KC, along with agricultural development agents, draw on a narrow, whitened understanding of entrepreneurialism when supporting beginning farmers— necessarily narrowing the scope of their assistance and shaping a particular kind of normative farmer (cf. Van Sant 2016).

Several Black urban growers told me that white foodie discomfort and inability—or unwillingness—to speak about broader structural inequalities made it difficult to network in these circles. One Black grower told me he did not like attending these events because "they're liars. There's no organization in this city that deals with Black hunger, yet they all say they do." Another

Black urban grower, Marcus, who runs a small peri-urban farm and considers himself on friendly terms with several white foodies, told me how painful it was to engage with them in more than surface-level conversation: "They ['foodie' friends] tell me when they buy a house, and they've all bought houses east of Troost. And it hurts me, literally. It's like ouch—'I can capitalize on the fact that all these Black folks pushed down property values enough to make it accessible to me. And purchasing this house and farming in its backyard will ensure my equity and probably push out neighbors in the process. You wanna come to my new house?' And I've kind of learned to limit my exposure and not react in rage, because it's not healthy."

Marcus indicates how Black geographies—meaning, the materiality of white violence on the landscape, here, via the suppression of value in Black neighborhoods (McKittrick 2006; 2011)—inform his interactions with white local foodies. These geographies are invisible to them, while ever-present for him. For Marcus, their uncritical capitalization on Black dispossession creates an unbridgeable divide—even though they do share values about the importance of organic food production and diverse urban ecologies.

Another issue for some Black urban growers is that an overwhelming majority of prominent foodies who host and attend networking events are women, and a sizable number of them identify as lesbian or queer. Marcus once shared with me that he considered one of the most dangerous people in the world to be a "kind white woman," whom he said had historically inflicted the most violence on Black people. These tensions were exacerbated, locally, after the 2016 U.S. presidential election, in which more than half of white women in America voted Donald Trump into office.

Black farmers often told me that white foodie silence about "Black issues" was unforgiveable. Several Black urban farmers told me that these foodies—in person at networking events, and online, via Facebook and Instagram—speak vocally and assertively about women's rights and LGBTQIA rights, while rarely speaking about racialized police violence, housing inequity affecting Black urban communities, or any other civil rights discussion that affects people of color. Bob, a middle-aged African American aquaponics farmer who sells at several East Side farmers markets, spoke to this issue as we drove together to the seed supply store one spring morning. I had asked him if he would be attending a Grow KC happy hour that evening, an event that provides a good opportunity to network with other farmers and local food advocates. In response, referencing the fact that Grow KC is run by several self-identified queer, feminist women, Bob replied, "Feminists and the gay community have *never* cared about our issues. The thing is, the Civil Rights movement, Dr.

King's push for civil rights, that got take up by so many people—the gay movement, the feminist movement, whatever—that it took attention away from the
plight of Black people in America. That's just not right. That's not right."

Bob highlights a disjuncture voiced at national levels (cf. Kearl 2015). For
some African Americans, the comparison of the gay rights movement to the
civil rights movement is felt as an unfair one that minimizes the struggles
faced by Black Americans. As several Black growers pointed out to me, this
is felt as even more frustrating when those making the comparison are drawing on white privilege, are upper-middle class, and hold leadership positions.
These intersectional tensions highlight debates about the interlocking forces
of class, race, and gender, debates that have been argued within the context
of the women's movement, for example, as women of color have pushed back
against purely gendered understandings of women's oppression (hooks 1981;
Ware 2015).

This issue is highlighted in local discussions among Black urban growers
about Pigford v. Glickman and USDA treatment of "minority" farmers over the
past several decades. Numerous Black urban farmers voiced frustration to me
that farming grants often classify white women as minorities, eligible for minority farmer support. The USDA Farm Service Agency offers a number of mi-
cro loans for those who identify as minority farmers; meaning, for the USDA,
they self-identify as women, African Americans, Alaskan Natives, American
Indians, Hispanic, Asian, or Native Hawaiians. Neferet, the Black woman who
founded Sacred Life Urban Farm, once told me in response to being told that a
local white woman—an upper-middle class retiree—had received one of these
loans, "She thinks she's disadvantaged, huh?," drawing on and referencing her
own double-racialized and gendered discrimination (cf. Collins 2000). Another Black urban grower, Arnold, who farms in his backyard and sells within
his neighborhood, told me, in response to me asking why he did not attend
Farmers and Friends that year, "Well, I'm gonna answer that like this: you
know the Pigford v. USDA? Black people won that. Money was set aside to increase their ability to farm. Because of USDA discrimination against us. Now,
because of inclusion, also included in 'disadvantaged' populations are white
women. Also included is sexual orientation. So four hundred years of discrimination on Black people, now that money gets filtered out. We have to com-
pete on an open playing field with other 'minorities' for attention. That's why
I don't want to go to their [Grow KC's] event."

While his understanding of how Pigford settlement money is disbursed is
inaccurate (money set aside for this settlement is disbursed through a highly
specific and strict compensatory process, described earlier, for Black farmers

alone), that is not the main point Arnold is trying to make with his statement. Arnold feels that the specific violence enacted upon Black U.S. citizens is dismissed when he is lumped together into the category of minority along with other groups that have faced discrimination. As a result, it is painful for him to attend networking events with people he considers to be more privileged than him, but who are nevertheless eligible for minority farmer assistance. This disjuncture between understandings of history, civil rights, and intersectional identity (Collins 2009) combines to create "white public space" (Page 1994) at networking events for urban farmers in Kansas City, spaces that makes some Black farmers feel unwelcome. One Black farmer told me, "I want to get my information out to other people, but I don't want to talk to those people [white 'foodies']. When I didn't have tomatoes or onions for my CSA, it would have been nice to know a farmer who I could get surplus from. We're so isolated and cut off."

These contradictory understandings of privilege, oppression, and intersectional identity cannot, and should not, be compared—it is neither possible nor useful to analyze who has been discriminated against most. Rather, these debates are important because they point toward the fraught process of rights-claims for systemically disadvantaged populations. They help highlight histories of those in power suppressing class consciousness and uprising through the pitting of minority groups against one another (for example, this is evident in the ways wealthy white slave-owners worked to create hierarchies of difference between captive Africans and poor whites, cf. Hartigan 2005).

Selling to Chefs:
White Privilege in Restaurant Labor and Farmer Sales

Restaurant contracts are highly lucrative for urban farmers. Farmers growing young specialty greens or microgreens, in particular, can find restaurant sales to be their most profitable outlet. A half-pound bag of arugula, for example, might sell at a farmers market for around three to five dollars, but can be sold to a restaurant for sixteen to eighteen dollars a pound. Because high-end restaurants often prefer young greens for salads and plate decoration, urban farmers who exclusively grow greens for restaurants can also see a quicker turnaround on their profits; the crop can be planted successively throughout the season, and there is less waiting time for it to come to full growth. These sales can also, but not always, be more consistent than farmers market sales—if a farmer cultivates a good relationship with a chef, that chef will collaborate with the farmer to grow specific produce as their menu changes seasonally and will give the farmer a good idea of how much produce they can expect to sell per week in each season. This sort of reliability is nonexistent in farmers market sales. Farmers who sell to high end restaurants also, often, have their farm name prominently displayed on the menu; some restaurants also host "meet our farmer" dinners, in which diners are invited to mingle with farmers over cocktails—an arrangement that often leads to diners later seeking out these farmers at farmers markets, or signing on to be CSA members. If a farmer is successful in arranging a sales contract with one high-end farm-to-table restaurant, it is likely that this reputation will make it easier for them to sign another contract with another restaurant. For all of these reasons, restaurant sales are one of the most highly regarded, stable, and lucrative marketing avenues for urban farmers in Kansas City.

Accessing this market, however, is a highly racialized process. To begin with, many chefs at high-end restaurants prefer certified organic produce, which, as discussed earlier, is an expensive certification to earn. While many farmers of color are farming with organic practices, they are far less likely than upper-middle-class white farmers to afford the costs of certification. Further, without a personal connection to the chef, it is nearly impossible for a farmer to create a sales contract with a restaurant. Often, these personal connections are created by applying for, and working in, server positions in high-end restaurants. In Kansas City, numerous young urban farmers work front-of-the house positions at these farm-to-table restaurants for several years while setting up their farms, then approach the chef or restaurant owner, with whom they are often collegial at that point, to create a market outlet for their produce. Restaurant labor, however, is often racially segregated. Servers in Kansas City have told me that white men are more likely to earn server positions, and people of color are more likely to end up working in the back of the house, or as bussers. Marcus, a young Black urban grower who has sales contracts with several brunch cafes in Kansas City, told me about his experience waiting tables at high-end restaurants:

> I worked at this [high-end farm-to-table restaurant on the Country Club Plaza]. It's the bourgeoisie for sure. And I applied to be a server—most of the restaurant jobs I've had have been front of the house. I waited tables at [a mid-range farm-to-table restaurant] for a little bit. But somehow, there, they didn't want me to be the front of the house. They had a lot of French items on the menu—mussels, and frites, and some other stuff. I took a few French classes in college, so I could correctly pronounce this stuff. And in my interview I was like "hey, your menu has some French stuff. I can pronounce all that." And one

of the managers interviewing me kind of laughed. I didn't get the feeling that they believed me. And then I realized that they really didn't believe me, because I was hired for the back of the house, and all the white servers up front were like "hey, can you tell me how to pronounce this?"

Cultivating relationships with chefs and restaurant owners often requires a more prestigious front-of-the-house position. However, regardless of previous serving experience, these positions are more often given to white applicants. In addition, an overwhelming majority of the chefs and owners of farm to table restaurants in Kansas City are white, upper-middle class or wealthy, men. Philip, a Black man in his thirties who apprenticed with Grow KC and was currently apprenticing with a highly profitable white male microgreen farmer at his greenhouse, spoke to this issue and explained to me further why he could not, and did not, create sales contracts with chefs at these restaurants:

At [the farm business I am apprenticing in] they have about seventy-five contracts with area top-notch restaurants. So on harvest day, we harvest and package stuff and, and they have a big table where [the farm owners] lay out all the orders, and I see all these restaurants. And the fact that they have these accounts is because they're on a first name basis with the chef at one of these restaurants. And they're texting the chef at these restaurants—is opal basil okay, or do you need the Genovese? And so they're on a very personal relationship with these chefs. I would already always assume that these aren't particularly the kind of people that know two Black people, much less know one that they're in business with. Much less know one that they're on a first name basis with, that they can text with. And I've worked fine dining, and I guess I could have tried to make an effort to get my local organic produce in there—all those restaurants buy parsley, oregano, basil, and thyme several times a week. I can do that for them. But the dynamics of fine dining are the dynamics of the United States—the hierarchy is color coded and is reinforced through violence. There's no blood, but there's lost hours, there's verbal abuse, sexual abuse, all of this. Being on a first name basis with those folks is not something that I'm interested in, much less feeding their clientele.

Philip highlights how personal connections are vital to the cultivation of secure, profitable, restaurant contracts for urban farmers—being comfortable enough with a chef to text back and forth inquiries about basil varieties is vital to this business relationship. Moreover, Philip does not want to cultivate close relationships with chefs at these lucrative markets in Kansas City, some of whom vocally self-identify as Republicans. For Philip, a self-identified Black liberation farmer, it would be ideologically at odds with his social justice concerns and commitments to sell to white local foodies.

White upper-middle-class farmers who are able to create close relationships with white upper-middle-class chefs are privy to vital market information. One white farmer told me he knew to grow and sell three rounds of arugula cuttings before pulling out the plant, because arugula gets spicier with each cutting and his friend, a chef at a high-end restaurant, told him he liked spicier salads with new greens. Another farmer, who holds contracts at several farm-to-table restaurants, told me that he knew which greens to grow and offer to chefs at new American restaurants, because his time working as a server at these establishments taught him which types of greens were favored because they held salad dressing the best. A white woman farmer told me once that her friend, executive chef at a high-end farm-to-table restaurant, gave her a sales contract as they met over coffee one day, during which he asked, "Grow me something weird for this salad I'm planning," giving her the freedom and security to experiment with vegetable production as she knew she had a market for the item no matter what. In these ways, entrepreneurship in Kansas City's local food economy is intimately linked to the ability, and desire, to cultivate close relationships with white, upper-middle-class foodie men. Success as an entrepreneur within this green urban economy is thus intimately interwoven with the racial and class- based identities of growers and distributors.

Restaurant contracts are even somewhat difficult for white, upper-middle-class farmers to secure—a fact that is drawn on by foodies to elide the racialized barriers that exist to effectively exclude Black farmers from this market. Without friendships, or social obligation, many chefs even at high-end restaurants are unwilling, or unable, to pay the high price per pound requested by small-scale urban farmers. I asked Anna, a white woman in her fifties, who owns and operates a peri-urban farm with her husband, and who helped teach the SPIN farmer classes, if she thought there were any specific racial barriers for Black farmers in the local food economy. She responded, "No. I think it's all about the produce, not the color of the people. I mean, if you have amazing produce, I don't think people care what color you are. I mean, it's hard for any of us to sell to chefs—they just don't get the value of what we do. It's not about your color."

While it is difficult for farmers, white and Black, to reach out to and create social networks and sales networks with chefs—who face financial and infrastructural constraints that make accepting local produce an extra chore—there are specific barriers in place making this process nearly impossible for Black farmers. In Kansas City's local food economy, a farmers identity is part of their sales package. Foodies are drawn to purchase local food because of a desire to "know where their food comes from" and by ethical imperatives that are informed by specific whitened understandings of agriculture and U.S. history (Alkon and McCullen 2011). White bodies, and white farmers, accompany a marketing pitch and sales narrative that draws on romantic imagery of the white yeoman farmer and resonates with specific whitened understandings of history. Black bodies, and Black farmers, do not index this idyllic picture. Sean, a young, Black, small-scale farmer who manages a garden program at East High School, highlighted this discrepancy, in a verbal disruption of white public space at a SPIN farming class. Interrupting a white urban farmer, who was discussing how he and his partner schedule restaurant deliveries throughout the week, Sean snapped, "You keep telling people on the East Side that you and your partner make $10,000 dollars every summer selling vegetables and that we can too. I'm gonna need you to stop doing that because we're not white, and we can't just go into a restaurant and be like 'buy my beets, buy my carrots, buy my onions,' like you."

Here, Sean highlights that the perception of bodies that create locally-grown produce is an undivorceable aspect of the value of that produce. His body, a Black body, does not carry the same value or currency that a white farmer's body would. The narrative that accompanies his body, one that indexes an economic system predicated on the forced exploitation of agricultural slave labor, imbues his produce with a different, less favored, value than a white farmer's would—a "white farm imaginary," of white homesteaders and Westward expansion (Alkon and McCullen 2011). Sean's statement echoes the experience Adrienne shared with me as well—while both she and the white farmer Sean interrupted often wear overalls, have hands crusted with dirt at the end of a workday, and presented chefs with high quality, locally, organically, grown produce, the white farmer's positionality added a value to his product that her blackness did not. This idea that their undeniable blackness made it more difficult to sell produce to white chefs was commonly voiced to me by Black urban farmers in Kansas City.

Black Sales Networks in Kansas City

In this chapter I have argued that despite claims that green urbanism creates healthy cities and myriad equitable opportunities for entrepreneurs, systemic racism profoundly affects the ability of Black urban growers to make a living in Kansas City. While racism in the urban local food movement is often analyzed from a customers' perspective—as interpersonal discomfort at local food spaces (see Slocum 2007; Guthman 2008; Guthman 2011; Alkon 2009; Alkon and McCullen 2011)—I've argued that urban producers of color are, in many ways, disadvantaged within this economic system that is often considered to be more equitable than the conventional food system. This is because shoppers and distributors in this alternative economy are swayed to purchase local food based on the perceived worth of the product's maker, the narrative associated with the produce. Black bodies, Black narratives, and Black produce are actively devalued in Kansas City—unless, as Adrienne's experience at the beginning of this chapter illustrated, their narratives are mobilized in ways that reproduce popular ideology (in this case, neoliberal self-sufficiency).

While Black farmers face systemic, institutionalized, and interpersonal racism in Kansas City's local food economy that make scaling up their farm businesses difficult, they are often selling in expansive networks that are unrecognized in hegemonic discourse painting the urban core as a food desert. These social networks and systems of support have developed—much like the social networks used to access food, discussed in the previous chapter—within an economic system that marginalizes nonwhite food producers. Black urban growers sell often in farm stands—set up on their own front lawns, in front of gas stations and local cell-phone shops, through church networks and on Sunday service, and often via Facebook (growers will post when they have, or expect to have, a crop ready, and will ask Facebook friends to name their own price and delivery time and place). Marcus operates what he calls a BSA—Black supported agriculture—in which he sells solely to Black friends and relatives, delivering weekly baskets of produce from his farm on an income-dependent sliding scale. One Black urban professional told me that his grandfather owned and operated a farm south of Kansas City for nearly a decade, selling produce to neighbors and taking meat orders for hogs and chicken that he would raise and butcher himself. When his grandfather grew too old to care for the large farm himself, he started a small game-meat business in Kansas City, off the radar of the health department. His grandfather would hunt for game on the outskirts of the city, collecting raccoons, pheasant, pigeon, and rabbit and would drive up and down Paseo in his truck with a sign that displayed his number and advertised the fresh meat. His grandfather would receive countless orders daily; he drove around the metropolitan area delivering game meat until his health no longer permitted it.

In innovative ways—even as they have been excluded from formal sales networks—Black entrepreneurs have flourished in the local food economy. This work is not celebrated in dominant discourse around green urbanism in Kansas City—rather, discussions focus on how to increase food production in "food deserts," where it is assumed this is a novel concept. Black entrepreneur-ship existed long before white local foodies developed an interest in know-ing where their food came from. There are numerous Black urban residents who buy produce on a semiregular or regular basis from small-scale Black growers, specifically; in this way, vast amounts of urban-grown produce circu-lates in Kansas City food deserts through the entrepreneurship and commu-nity engagement of Black farmers. These forms of entrepreneurship are unrec-ognized contributions to the local food economy and creative responses to a white economy that through policy and discrimination works to exclude Black growers and Black-owned businesses. The following chapters explore more deeply the acts of creativity and resistance Black urban residents enact within green urban infrastructure development in Kansas City.

CHAPTER 6

"Apparently We Grow Culturally Appropriate Food in That"

Green Urban Citizenship and the Strategic Utilization of
Urban Agriculture Policy to Meet Community Needs

One spring morning, I joined two life-long residents of Rose Hill (pseudonym, a Jackson County, Missouri, neighborhood) in taking a break from weeding our community garden plots. My fellow gardeners, Agnes and Martha, were both Black, in their sixties, and had been growing food and flowers at the community garden for several years, selling excess produce to their neighbors and family and sometimes selling at the Rose Hill farmers market, which had been founded and was managed by the Rose Hill Neighborhood Council (RHNC). Martha, a retiree, spends her free time with her grandchildren; Agnes supplements a part-time janitorial job with income from her produce sales. We sat on a sun-warmed metal park bench in a small park right across the street from our community garden—a space two-city blocks long, where dozens of neatly arranged raised garden beds are surrounded by a hip-height metal fence. The park includes a brightly colored swing set, surrounded by manicured garden beds. As we watched several children playing in the small park, I commented on how nice it is to have this amenity in the neighborhood, to which Agnes responded, "We had to beg for everything you see around us, and we're very proud of that." A young mother of one of the children jogged up to us with an empty water bottle and asked if there was a water fountain nearby. "No," Martha sighed, "unfortunately not." I asked, is the city not willing to put a fountain in? And Martha replied, "No, they aren't required to because this is a private lot that [RHNC] built themselves. It would cost $90,000 dollars to install one on our own." She added, cheerfully, "It's nice though, isn't it? This park looks like it's in Overland Park." Here, Martha is referencing a wealthy, overwhelmingly white, city located in the southern, Kansas side of the Kansas City metropolitan area. This statement launched Agnes into a quiet recollection. "One time I was here and a white man in an SUV drove by and said to me 'This park looks too nice to be here.' I responded, 'Now what does that mean?' and I kept asking it, and he flustered." She laughed, "He sure won't ask anyone a question like that again." Agnes laughed and shared her own story. "Some white people came by the other day, to look at the house next to mine—you know, there's that vacant lot there too and they wanna farm it. This guy comes to me and says, 'You need to paint your house.' And I said 'Excuse me? Will you pay for it?'" Martha gasped: "I hope they don't move in."

RHNC has been highly successful in garnering city and private support for infrastructural development projects such as the park, swing set, and community garden, largely due to their promotion of themselves as a green neighborhood, committed to projects that encourage "healthy" urban living. In 2007, cognizant of the fact that embracing green urban development would be viewed positively by Kansas City policy makers, RHNC founded a community garden for Rose Hill residents, started offering monthly gardener/farmer training classes in their community center, and established their own farmers market. Rose Hill's farmers market, community garden program, and gardener training classes are often mentioned—in the media, in opinions shared by city council members, and in hegemonic discourse in Kansas City—as proof that the neighborhood is *different* from other urban neighborhoods. This discourse proclaims that Rose Hill is trying to make do with what they have; Rose Hill takes pride in its community; and Rose Hill deserves support because they try to take care of themselves.

RHNC does work diligently to improve the neighborhood and is one of the most active neighborhood councils in the metropolitan area. The council is faced with the difficult task, however, of listening and responding to a diversity of "community" perspectives, as Rose Hill's promotion of itself as a green neighborhood has resulted in the slow gentrification of the area. In 2010 the Kansas City Land Bank, created in consultation with the nonprofit organization Healthy Communities KC, began offering up low-cost "fixer uppers" and vacant lots, explicitly marketing this opportunity to prospective urban farmers. A vast majority of this land is located east of Troost, much of it in Rose Hill, where hypersegregation, racialized lending practices, and systemic disinvestment have created a great deal of vacancy. This has led to speculative development—land-grabs by wealthy urban developers—and an influx of primarily young, white, middle- to upper-middle-class individuals, many hoping to start urban farming businesses, who can here afford to acquire a larger property than would be financially feasible anywhere else in the urban core. All of these groups are drawn specifically to Rose Hill because of its vocal promotion of green urban infrastructure. As a result, Rose Hill, a historically Black neighborhood, is changing. The African American population here, originally concentrated in this area east of Troost Avenue through purposeful city and real estate segregation tactics, has dropped from 96 percent in 2000, to 86 percent in 2010, and 82 percent in 2016. Still, nearly a quarter of Rose Hill's population lives on less than $10,000 dollars a year; 30 percent are classified as living in poverty.

Green urban development discourse, promoted and shaped by city government and third-sector foodies, has so powerfully influenced understandings of productive urban citizenship that neighborhoods in Kansas City are forced to adopt the movement's goals in order to receive city and private support. Neighborhoods that start, and promote, urban garden programs are much more likely to be viewed positively and offered funding for neighborhood development projects. But while these green urban amenities—such as Rose Hill Park and community garden—are desired by and utilized by neighborhood residents, they also invite outside investment, the in-migration of those whose very presence might raise rents, and racialized critique about who actually deserves such development, as evidenced in the comment made to Agnes: "This park looks too nice to be here." Rose Hill's boundaries are already large—the neighborhood encompasses five different zip codes and includes nearly six thousand residents—and the in-migration of white urban farmers makes it even more difficult for RHNC to listen and respond to a diversity of community opinions and needs.

A burgeoning body of scholarship explores how low-income communities of color are impacted by, and work to resist, green gentrification. Chiefly, this work has examined political struggles between activists and urban elites as environmental amenities—in service of luxury development—are established in formerly "blighted" communities (cf. Checker 2011; Gould and Lewis 2017; Curran and Hamilton 2018). One approach, "just green enough," has emerged within this process—as communities fight gentrification while working to create environmentally safe spaces (Curran and Hamilton 2018). This case study of RHNC builds on extant theories of "just green enough," demonstrating how communities strategically utilize green development projects to receive funding for urban farms and gardens, while also advocating for other pressing needs.

In this chapter I explore how RHNC creatively navigates a city environment that privileges green urban development above other urban necessities. I outline how RHNC balances neighborhood desires for green amenities with concerns about green gentrification, and how they work to listen to a diversity of opinions in a gentrifying neighborhood, where it is acknowledged that the influx of white residents brings both development and displacement.

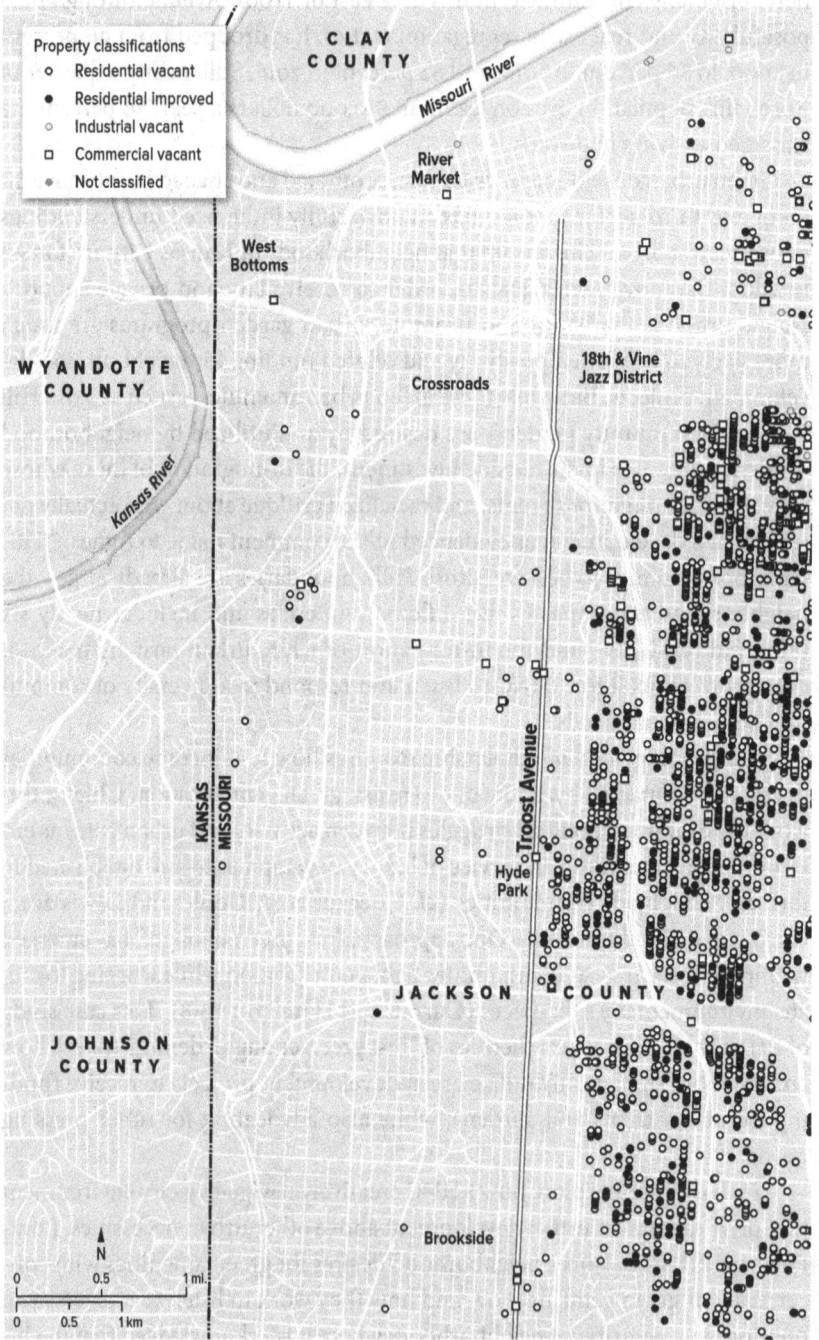

Property classifications
- ○ Residential vacant
- ● Residential improved
- ○ Industrial vacant
- ☐ Commercial vacant
- ● Not classified

CLAY COUNTY

Missouri River

River Market

West Bottoms

WYANDOTTE COUNTY

Kansas River

Crossroads

18th & Vine Jazz District

KANSAS
MISSOURI

Troost Avenue

Hyde Park

JACKSON COUNTY

JOHNSON COUNTY

Brookside

N

0   0.5   1 mi.

0   0.5   1 km

Kansas City Land Bank Properties

A listing from Zillow.com for a property east of Troost. The listing advertises: "Urban Farmers this could be your dream come true!" Screenshot captured by author, 2019.

City Beautiful:
Black Resistance to "Beautification" Policy in KC

RHNC takes great pains to resist the displacement that accompanies their green urban development projects, since Kansas City has a storied history of violently displacing Black residents for parks and other green urban amenities. The displacement that accompanies green urban development in the twenty-first century is hardly a new process—as discussed in chapter 1, the City Beautiful movement at the turn of the twentieth century functioned in much the same way, as beautification was used as justification for displacing Black and brown urban residents.[1] While parks and urban greenspace have served myriad policy agendas, many Black and brown communities associate these amenities with displacement.

These acts of urban violence enacted via the creation, and/or withholding of, greenspace, have a history of being contested by African American Kansas City residents. In 1924 Kansas City's Board of Parks and Boulevards set aside certain tennis courts, picnic grounds, and baseball diamonds specifically for use by African Americans—Black Kansas Citians protested this segregation, and the municipal court sided with them, only with the result that KC Parks and Boulevards worked surreptitiously, arranging for non–city affiliated white Kansas City residents to hang unofficial "whites only" signs in Kansas City parks (Schirmer 2002, 150). In Swope Park, African Americans were restricted to "Watermelon Hill," a section of the park located adjacent to the Kansas City

Photo of an annual picnic at what white Kansas Citians called "Watermelon Hill," 1933. A policeman stands on the far right. Photo courtesy of the Missouri State Archives.

Zoo entrance. Long-term Kansas City residents shared with me that white zoo visitors would often gawk at Watermelon Hill as if it were another zoo exhibit.

In 1927 a group of Black Girl Scouts wandered out of Watermelon Hill and were threatened by white park attendants. Black Kansas Citians protested and petitioned the park board, protests that resulted in only nominal change. In 1951 the NAAACP backed three Black Kansas City residents who were denied entrance into Swope Park's whites-only pool, a case that was won in the U.S. District Court (Griffin 2015). In response, the city shut down Swope Park Pool for three years. When they finally reopened in 1954, now open to white and Black patrons, many whites stayed away—attendance dropped by more than 60 percent(Griffin 2015). These protests, in which Black Kansas Citians asserted their right to greenspace, continued well into the twentieth century. In 1963 sixteen activists marched into racially restricted Fairyland Park at Seventy-Fifth and Prospect and refused to leave; the activists were arrested and jailed (Griffin 2015). Today as well, Black Kansas City residents assert their right to green amenities, as Agnes evidenced in her push back against the white visitor to Rose Hill. "What do you mean this park looks too nice to be here?"

Aerial photo of segregated, whites-only Swope Park Pool, 1945. Photo Courtesy of Missouri Valley Special Collections, Kansas City Public Library.

The kiddie pool at Nelson C. Crews Square Park, circa 1950s. The pool was one of the only public pools available for African American Kansas Citians to use during segregation. Photo courtesy of the Missouri State Archives.

Boys swimming in one of Kansas City's fountains, unknown date. Because of strictly enforced Jim Crow laws and segregation, Kansas City's African American residents have had to strategically work to access greenspace and outdoor recreation opportunities readily available to white residents. Photo courtesy of Missouri Valley Special Collections, Kansas City Public Library.

In recent years, the impact of supposedly apolitical green urban development infrastructures has been no less violent than these early, blatant, acts of segregation and displacement enacted via the creation of greenspace. As Gould and Lewis (2017, 1) argue, "greening whitens." Environmental and food justice efforts have often been at odds with the stated needs of marginalized communities, as "sustainable" development planners have ignored the role that their work can play in gentrification (Curran and Hamilton 2018).

Recently, scholars have explored how low-income, marginalized communities have resisted green gentrification. Central to many communities' concerns is the question: "Must they reject environmental amenities in their neighborhoods in order to resist the gentrification that tends to follow such amenities?" (Checker 2011, 211). Curran and Hamilton (2018, 16) document, in the context of Greenpoint, New York, how the conjoined struggle of long-term residents and recent gentrifiers around environmental cleanup created an equitable process of change within the neighborhood. This process, termed "just green enough," involves a strategy explicitly focused on resisting speculative development and solely on environmental remediation for existing residents (Curran and Hamilton 2018). RHNC is unique within these case studies, as they purposefully utilize green development projects such as urban farms and gardens to receive development funding and to profit from the influx of capital-

rich new urban residents, while concurrently working to mitigate the antici-
pated effects of gentrification.

In Kansas City third-sector urban governance dovetails with green development initiatives to create new kinds of green citizenship (cf. Maskovsky
2014). When market-based models of urban "uplift" and renewal intersect
with urban greening and sustainability strategies, they have impacts on how
citizenship is understood within Kansas City. Citizenship becomes inter-
locked with "greenness," and in this context, "green" often involves consumption. For example, Jung and Newman (2014, 24), in their pilot research on a
new "ethical capitalist" venture—a Whole Foods in Detroit—illustrate how
these this private-sector policy mediators ask citizens to "informally govern
themselves through a range of practices such as civic involvement, consumer-
ism, and even the act of eating well." In this way, "green" corporate actors may
seek to blur the boundary between global corporation and social movement,
taking part in regimes of urban governance (2014). Likewise, Sheller has argued that the promotion of eco-mobility creates a visible hierarchy of "green"
citizenship on city streets (2014). Sheller argues that "the rejection of automo-
bility becomes a structured story about a kind of (white) urban citizenship
that represents 'good' mobility for a whole generation" and ignores racialized
transport inequality (2014, 75).

This scholarship on green urban governance has important implications
for understanding how gentrification works, as a process, and how it intersects
with urban citizenship. In Kansas City, specifically, this process is particularly
fraught, as green citizenship has become recognized as one of the most productive, and rewarded, forms of urban citizenship—yet enacting green urban
development projects often leads to gentrification and displacement.

"Rose Hill Grown":
Cultivating Perceptions of Personal "Green" Responsibility
and "Productive" Urban Citizenship

In 2016 I volunteered to help staff the welcome desk, along with several long-
time Rose Hill residents and community gardeners, at the Rose Hill Community Garden for Grow KC's biannual "Urban Grown" tour. This experience shed light on the dichotomy between how Rose Hill "green" amenities are
viewed and utilized by Rose Hill residents and how they are presented to visitors and policy makers. Grow KC's biannual "Urban Grown" tour is an opportunity for Kansas City metropolitan area urban farmers and gardeners to show
off their unique strategies for growing food in the city. Farmers and gardeners

open their growing spaces up for public tours during one weekend in the summer; foodies and urban residents meet new urban growers, learn "where their food comes from," and celebrate urban food production in Kansas City. Importantly, Grow KC also arranges for city officials and influential Kansas City residents to tour a select number of these gardens, in an effort to further convince policy makers of the importance of supporting urban food production as part of green urbanism. Because of its high profile in Kansas City, this event serves, for some neighborhoods, as an opportunity to demonstrate their self-sufficiency and beautification efforts in the urban core. Urban Grown tour visitors, most years, are often white local foodies who live in Kansas City suburbs.

In 2016 the event was held in June, and I joined two African American Rose Hill community gardeners in staffing our welcome desk on an already hot summer morning. We sat under a white tent, waiting to lead any interested visitors on tours of the garden. Stacks of the "Urban Grown Guidebook," printed by Grow KC were piled on our registration table, ready to be disbursed. The guidebook contained biographies and photos submitted from participant farms and gardens; it described Rose Hill Community Garden as follows:

> [Rose Hill Community Garden] is a grassroots community initiative that aims to empower residents of the [Rose Hill] community of Kansas City, Missouri to grow healthy fruits and vegetables [Rose Hill Community Garden] combines education and resources for growers as well as coordinating community garden locations, facilitating a network of residents selling foods through farm stands, and running a farmers' market. The [Rose Hill] Children's Garden and Scouts Sprouts consists of seven raised beds in which [Rose Hill] youth are learning to grow. The [Rose Hill] Boys and Cub Scouts are involved from the beginning and they are taught, not just about the benefits of good, healthy food, but they are encouraged to share the information with their friends, families and neighbors. The [Rose Hill Community] Garden continues to serves this urban-core neighborhood by demonstrating fruit and vegetable production on an old vacant lot. The plots have been adopted out by residents of the neighborhood. Growers are growing for market, community and for families. The Lena & Nina Memory Garden is a unique hybrid of a rain garden that also provides culturally relevant produce, cutting flowers for to be sold at market and is utilized as neighborhood beautification.

The text is accompanied by a photo of young Black girls wearing high top sneakers and tending greens in an urban garden plot; from what I can tell, the photo was not taken in Rose Hill's Community Garden. This narrative, one that draws heavily on neoliberal rhetoric of personal responsibility, guided the interactions the welcome-table staffers had with garden visitors. For example, one of my fellow tour guides and community gardeners, Betty, an African American woman in her sixties, started every tour interaction with, "These are community plots where we grow food to feed our hungry neighbors." This rhetoric, however, was not personally reflective of how they themselves, lifelong residents of Rose Hill, interacted with the garden. At the start of our shift staffing the welcome table I asked Richard, a forty-year-old African American man who had started growing in the community garden several years ago (primarily with the goal of growing produce to make salsa) to give me an example of how to lead a tour. Even though I had been growing in the garden with Richard for several garden seasons, I wanted to make sure that I was describing the garden in a way that a Rose Hill native would approve. Richard walked me through the raised garden beds dotting the two city blocks that make up Rose Hill Community Garden and discussed aspects of the site as we passed them; walking past the "Scouts Sprouts" garden, two long wooden and cement-block raised beds, Richard said flippantly. "I think the Boy Scouts take care of these, but who knows. I think they made omelets with this stuff [vegetables] once." As we neared a small U-shaped native plant garden—the Lena and Nina Memory Garden—at the corner of one of the lots, Richard told me, sarcastically, "Apparently we grow *culturally appropriate* food in that, not sure what that means, but there's some onions there I think." I asked Richard who dedicated the garden—which is named in honor of Lena Horne and Nina Simone, influential African American women—and he said, "I have no idea who those people are." Richard's description of the garden is more reflective of other Rose Hill Community members' perceptions than Betty's was. A majority of the urban gardeners I spoke with at the Rose Hill Community garden were food-secure, simply gardening as a fun retirement activity, and were unconcerned with the sociopolitical aims of the garden laid out in the Urban Grown description of the site.

Rose Hill Community Garden was founded in 2010 after RHNC applied for, and received, a federal grant aimed at supporting "healthy community projects" in food insecure urban areas. While RHNC had not heard from any community members interested in urban food production, there was great focus on urban agriculture within the city—foodie-led nonprofits such as the Kansas City Grower's Club, Our Daily Bread, and Grow KC could offer them infrastructural support in building a community garden and staffed educators who could come teach urban farming classes. The choice to use grant funding in support of urban food production, distribution, and consumption seemed easy—other neighborhoods that created community gardens were being covered in the news and were spoken of highly. The farmers market, held weekly May through September, was founded soon after the garden was built. "Rose Hill Grown," a series of monthly gardener/farmer training classes, open to the public, began a year later, hosted for free by instructors from the Kansas City Grower's Club and Grow KC.

For a majority of Rose Hill Community members, the community garden does not function as it is advertised. It is not an overwhelmingly positive force in their lives, and it is not solving urban food insecurity in the neighborhood. It's not even on many community members' radars. A RHNC staff member who founded the garden program told me that her initial excitement dissipated when she began to try to recruit Rose Hill residents for the garden programs: "We canvassed the neighborhood, we put fliers out, and we had less than ten people show up at the first meeting. They were all over the age of eighty. And they did not want to grow food, they just wanted to get food." She continued, telling me that she learned that a lot of this reticence stemmed from racial politics: "The old folks said, 'Been there, done that, don't wanna do it again.' With the twenty, thirty, forty-year-olds it was 'I'm not a slave, I'm not a share cropper, I don't do that kind of work, I can go out and buy my own food thank you very much.' And a whole lot of others were like 'It's hot, its dirty, its buggy, I don't want to do that.'"

For many in Rose Hill's historically African American neighborhood, urban food production indexes painful geographies of land dispossession, exploited labor, and violence (cf. Guthman 2008). Many residents do not want to grow their own food, rather, they want access to affordable locations to buy their own food. RHNC did find some individuals, however, interested in growing food. In their first year, the community garden drew sixteen growers, only three of whom were residents of Rose Hill. RHNC staff tell me that individuals—upper-middle class, a majority of them white—come from "as far as North Kansas City to as far south as Olathe," both areas that would necessitate a thirty-minute drive, to grow food in the Rose Hill Community Garden. In recent years this has changed; a majority of the gardeners in the community garden are now African American Rose Hill residents. None, however, would self-identify as food insecure—as they are described in RHNC grant applications—and those who sell extra produce at market do so as a hobby, to supplement full-time salaries or retirement savings. Similar demographics are seen at "Rose Hill Grown" classes—white suburbanites drive into the urban core to take classes on season extension and garden planning with Black urban residents. One suburban visitor to Rose Hill told me, as we walked out of a pest management class held at Rose Hill Community Center, "I just love coming here to learn, it's so inspiring to see people make do with what they have!" Painful racialized histories keep many Black Rose Hill residents from participating in Rose Hill Grown programs. These same histories, however— and perceptions of Rose Hill residents as self-sufficient, successful neoliberal subjects—are a draw for white upper-middle class suburban Kansas Citians.

The discrepancy between how Rose Hill Grown programs are advertised and actually utilized is most evident in RHNC's farmers market. The market is quite small—comprising around six or seven vendors per week, around half of whom are growing produce within Rose Hill. Other vendors represent wealthier, whiter, larger-scale urban farms from outside of the neighborhood. A market DJ is hired weekly for the event and often plays R&B music; some weeks, RHNC funds a cookout, offering free hamburgers and hot dogs. An RHNC staff member told me, "The neighborhood is not supporting it like we thought." This is evident in SNAP dollar data for the market. While Grow KC's SNAP doubling incentive is available at the Rose Hill farmers market, low-income customers are not utilizing it. There have been several years in which, over five months of operation, the market has only received around $10 to $20 dollars in SNAP money. Foot traffic increased even more after RHNC received a grant to put up a billboard, advertising the market on highway U.S. 71—but not among Rose Hill residents themselves. "We've had a lot of outside folk come in. Getting people from [Rose Hill] to start wanting to shop here on a regular basis is still an obstacle," an RHNC staff member told me.

The absence of Rose Hill community members may be explained by several factors—for one, many have told me they cannot afford the produce sold there, regardless of whether or not their SNAP-dollars (if they have them) are doubled. One Black Rose Hill resident and market vendor told me that her friends have expressed interest in shopping at the market but say they cannot afford the produce, and finding transportation there is tricky, as they do not have cars. Additionally, some RHNC staff members have speculated that there is an element of embarrassment. At such a small market, SNAP usage will be made visible to ones' neighbors, and many SNAP recipients are ashamed of the fact that they receive assistance. As a result, the Rose Hill farmers market's customer base is largely middle to upper-middle class, a sizable proportion of whom are outsiders to the area, who drive in with the intention of "supporting" Rose Hill residents by circulating their food dollars in the urban core.

RHNC staff members are not oblivious to the fact that the Rose Hill Community Garden, farmers market, and training classes have a limited, and somewhat critiqued, role within the neighborhood; rather, they strategically utilize and deploy these programs to receive city praise and support. As an

RHNC staff member told me, "Our market is in the red year after year, so as a *market*, strictly defined, it is absolutely failing." He continued, telling me that the market serves a larger purpose:

> It's a bargaining chip, it's a farce. It's used as leverage. We get all these pol-icy makers and city officials coming through here—you remember, I told you I was giving a tour to the state health commissioner last week?—they come down here because they think we're *really* fixing things, you know. And I say, "Oh yeah, we have these health programs and free health screenings," and they go, "But what else?" and I say, "Well, we have this farmers market that feeds the poor in our community, and we have these community green spaces," and oh they *love* it. So yes, it functions as a source of community pride and co-hesion, but the market isn't a *market*. And the training program doesn't help people make money, or feed their families. It isn't doing what we say it does. But it's really meaningful for people in some other senses.

So while RHNC staff recognize the limitations of Rose Hill Grown garden programming, and a majority of Rose Hill residents do not utilize or benefit from it, these green programs serve as bargaining chips. For example, since the inception of its garden programs, Rose Hill has received recognition and sup-port from a number of private and public sources. Several large philanthropic organizations in the city have gifted Rose Hill development funds and infra-structural support to expand their community center and staff offices. Rose Hill was nominated for, and received, a KC Green Neighborhood Award—which accompanies free access to city clinics and workshops, new green street signage heralding the accomplishments of the neighborhood, funding for a neighborhood sustainability project, and recognition in city and media dis-course. Rose Hill representatives have been invited to speak at city events, as an example of productive green urban citizenship and self-sufficiency, and the neighborhood has been featured in national urban farming magazines as a "transformational community." Rose Hill received a grant from the Missouri Department of Agriculture for community garden expansions; when the grant inspector heard about the green developments in the neighborhood, he told RHNC to encourage Rose Hill residents to apply for their grants—they would love to fund people in this community, they said. Similarly, the NRCS match-ing grants for high-tunnel implementation are given, I am told, with prefer-ence to Rose Hill applicants, as the USDA representative in charge of the pro-gram has been so impressed with the neighborhood. In these ways, public demonstration of "green productivity" through vocal promotion of their urban food production and distribution programs has garnered Rose Hill quite a bit of state and private support.

Rose Hill's promotion of itself as a green community has led to its image as a new frontier for urban farming, and an influx of a high number of young, white foodies hoping to start farming businesses. Growing food in Rose Hill, and including that in your marketing—as many of these farmers do—is a valuable currency that helps sell your product; proclaiming that your business is part of "urban revitalization," ending "food desertification," and urban "beautification" is highly regarded in Kansas City. As of 2018, at least ten white, middle-to-upper-middle class, urban farmers have bought land within Rose Hill intending to start farm businesses. These farmers benefit from racialized home repair and mortgage lending that disinvested in Black neighborhoods like Rose Hill, pushing down housing values and leading to a large number of low-cost homes for purchase. The close proximity of Highway 71—the placement of which displaced low-income Black families and geographically isolated Black Kansas Citians to the East Side of the city—has been cited by many of these urban farmers as a boon. The highway's proximity means that customers can potentially drop by to pick up farm-fresh groceries on their way home from work.

In 2017 a young white couple came to RHNC with a proposal for a native wildflower nursery that would involve purchasing several city lots within the neighborhood. Their discussions with RHNC exemplify many of the issues highlighted above. Those who wish to purchase land in Rose Hill are required to come make a presentation to the Rose Hill Housing Council; the council comprises RHNC staff members and is open to neighborhood residents as well. The council includes mostly long-term Rose Hill residents who hold a number of diverse identities, including urban farmers. The council is not diverse, however, in terms of class status; a majority of the council members are middle to upper-middle class. I listened in as Tracy pitched their business plans:

> We're looking to start our own native wildflower nursery, and we're looking for about an acre and a half to three acres. Getting that much land is a challenge, so we have one potential site within your neighborhood and the others we're considering are more rural. But we're attracted to [Rose Hill] and want to be located in [Rose Hill] because of the food initiatives you guys have going on, and the fact that you have put so much work in already in cleaning up the neighborhood. We really like the idea of being in the city, and just trying to expand this urban agriculture idea that [Rose Hill] is passionate about. We

know that a lot of our customers would be coming from the Brookside area, and also Johnson County, Kansas—those are the people who are buying natives currently, and some of them might not want to drive through the 'hood, if you will. I feel like being right along 71 helps that issue—they can just, if they're not comfortable driving through inner city, Kansas City, they can just get right off the highway. There's a lot of bad rep [about the inner city], and I know some of it is real, but I'm hoping that some of it is not, too. It sounds like [Rose Hill] is really starting to clean up and we're really attracted to that. We hope you guys would be interested in having us in your neighborhood!

Tracy's statements illustrate that Rose Hill's prominence as a neighborhood that supports green urban development has a direct relationship to the in-migration of white urban farmers. Several of Tracy's comments—about safety and her wealthy, white customers not wanting to drive through the "hood"—were met with side-glances among the council members, and several rolled eyes. While the council approved Tracy and her husband's preliminary request for land, in private conversations they told me they disagreed with her racially discriminatory understandings of the urban core, yet knew that her presence in the neighborhood could possibly bring more foot traffic and revenue to the Rose Hill farmers market and other local businesses. Some RHNC staff shared with me that much of their job was taken up by the stress of constantly working to mitigate the damage caused by Tracy, who they consider to be a gentrifier, while simultaneously utilizing the influx of green urban development funding to reach more urgent community-stated needs and goals. While Tracy, as an individual, contributes little to the overall raise in rents and cost of living that price out long-term residents, RHNC is deeply concerned that their green development focus will lead to enough concerted development that gentrification will occur.

"I've Been to Detroit and I Don't Want [Rose Hill] to Look Like That": Strategically Leveraging Green Urban Development Funds

Because RHNC staff—the majority of whom live within Rose Hill—worry about letting green urban development interests "overtake" the neighborhood, they have instituted several mechanisms for Rose Hill–resident feedback and input in their neighborhood development decisions. Monthly neighborhood meetings are heavily attended and offer a chance for resident feedback and requests for assistance. This chance to speak up is utilized by many attendees, whom I have seen voice concerns about trash on their block, illegal dumping, and inadequate sidewalks and street lights and pose questions about home repair assistance. RHNC committees—beautification, crime and safety, youth, and housing—are organized and run by RHNC staff members and attended, regularly, by a large number of Rose Hill residents. RHNC implements, every few years, large-scale neighborhood feedback surveys—going door to door, mailing questionnaires, and incentivizing residents to come in to the community center for interviews—in order to better understand neighborhood concerns. A recent set of focus group interviews with Rose Hill residents, facilitated by RHNC, found that while several residents cited the farmers market as a boon to the community, they stated that the "greatest issues" facing the neighborhood were not food insecurity but rather affordable housing, "slumlords, "lack of jobs, and control over neighborhood development, as indicated by several participants' concern over "new businesses moving into our community." Thus, one of RHNC's main programmatic foci is the creation of affordable, quality rental housing and the promotion of home ownership within Rose Hill.

RHNC staff are vocal about their concerns that urban agriculture, and those who promote it, will eclipse these other stated, more pressing, community needs. An interaction between white foodie farmers and Black long-term Rose Hill residents exemplifies this tension and concern. I missed attending the monthly RHNC housing committee meeting in May 2017. One morning, in the Rose Hill Community Garden, two fellow gardeners—white, urban farmers who each run their own farm-business within Rose Hill—caught me up on the discussion that they had had there the previous night. One farmer, Trey, told me, "Oh man, I wish you had been at the housing meeting last night—it was a watershed moment. Three people came in with ag. proposals, and after they had presented, the committee just went: 'Is this really the way we want to go?'" Trey continued, telling me that one of the committee members had recently visited Detroit for a conference and was adamant that she did not want similar development in Rose Hill: "She said, 'I've been to Detroit and I don't want [Rose Hill] to look like that.'"

Postindustrial Detroit has recently witnessed the rise of several large-scale urban agriculture projects, as outside investors—and some Detroit residents—draw on vacancy and disinvestment to create farms and agricultural distribution centers. While such projects often have stated goals of addressing food insecurity and urban poverty, RHNC staff members have privately critiqued them, stating that they distract from the creation of affordable housing and the influx of businesses that could offer jobs with a livable wage. And, historically and currently, green developments have been built specifically to displace

Black residents. Mason, the second white urban farmer who joined Trey in narrating the housing committee events to me added, "Some people just don't get it. They don't know what urban agriculture can do. I mean, I guess let's not even talk about social justice, eco-security or food insecurity!" Mason's comments exemplify why RHNC works so concertedly to contain and control the spread of urban agriculture initiatives in their neighborhood. While Trey and Mason unequivocally view urban food production as a positive addition to cities, and a resource for urban residents, RHNC staff worry, as do long-term Rose Hill residents, that these developments accompany outside investment, lack of control over neighborhood development, and the eclipsing of major neighborhood issues such as lack of housing and jobs.

To both draw on the increased attention and revenue that the influx of white urban farmers affords them, and to mitigate their influence on decision-making processes in the neighborhood, RHNC staff place extensive focus on housing policy in their programmatic efforts. One major way that Rose Hill accomplishes this is through discretion over land use within their neighborhood, which they gained after petitioning the Land Bank for assistance. Rose Hill was able to purchase hundreds of Land Bank properties and vacant lots, located within the bounds of their neighborhood, for a reduced price. Rose Hill was also successful in negotiating discretion over land use on lots and homes that they did not purchase; those interested in purchasing Land Bank properties must first come and present their business or home plan to the RHNC housing committee, at which point the committee—and any present community members—will vote to accept, dismiss, or modify the proposed plan and will present their decision to the Land Bank. While the Land Bank is not required to follow RHNC's recommendations, in practice they often do—sometimes denying applications for home purchases that RHNC has flagged as potential irresponsible landlord situations.

RHNC has used city favor and support to acquire funding for the development of affordable housing projects and senior living, based on the stated needs of long-term Rose Hill residents. A combination of city grants and loans facilitated the creation of numerous affordable housing projects and low-income senior homes within RHNC over the past ten years. Additionally, through collaboration with Legal Aid of Kansas City, RHNC brings a housing lawyer to their monthly neighborhood and housing committee meetings who offers free assistance to those hoping to purchase housing within the neighborhood, housing stock which often has complicated title history and legal complications. RHNC offers a minor home repair program that provides low-cost and sliding-scale assistance to low-income Rose Hill homeowners needing to repaint their homes, replace roofs, or accomplish other costly tasks; this program works to provide support to those historically disadvantaged through racialized lending.

RHNC works to educate low-income homeowners within the neighborhood about opportunities widely known within foodie circles—such as the fact that Rose Hill is designated as an Urban Renewal area, where home and landowners are eligible for ten years of tax abatement. At one RHNC monthly meeting, staff passed out tax abatement applications and told those who could not afford the application fee that they would figure out how to help them pay it, stating, "Outside investors and flippers *do* know about these opportunities, and you should too. Because they *will* take advantage of it."

This fear of, and protection against, outside urban agricultural investment interests was made very apparent at a RHNC monthly meeting in January 2018. At the meeting, attended by roughly fifty, primarily African American, Rose Hill residents, two presenters had given presentations about potential developments and businesses they wanted to start within the neighborhood, one of which was a small urban farm. At the end of the meeting, an RHNC staff member spoke about these developments to the residents:

> Recently I've been getting a lot, a lot, of calls inquiring about properties in [Rose Hill], wanting to do projects like this. Calls from those who live outside of our neighborhood. I want you all to know that this is because of the hard work you have put into our community over the years. But to keep this neighborhood in line with how we'd like it to grow, we need to do several things: if you do not have a will passing on your home to your children, call me and I will help you write one. Otherwise, your property can pass on to anyone, not just someone from the neighborhood. If you have a vacant lot next to your home, buy it. That is important. Buy it. I can help you figure out how to do that as well. If we do these things we can shape how the neighborhood grows.

Here, the RHNC staff member emphasizes for long-term residents how valuable local property is, as gentrification and speculative investment begins within the neighborhood. Make sure you have control over your property and make sure you acquire any vacant land near your property, he cautions, because if you do not, somebody else will, and you won't have any control over what they do with that asset. In these ways, RHNC staff work to increase neighborhood investment and control over urban space, as an increasing number of white urban farmers and green developers begin to recognize value in Rose Hill's land.

Debates and contestations over appropriate land use are apparent at a larger scale as well, as RHNC staff vet new development proposals in housing committee meetings. For example, while white prospective urban farmers are usually welcomed into the neighborhood—as Tracy was, earlier, despite her racialized rhetoric about urban space—their land acquisition is strictly controlled and monitored. One white urban farmer, who approached the housing committee with a plan to purchase two houses and eleven vacant lots, has been strictly supervised, likely because he plans to acquire a greater volume of land than any other urban farmer in Rose Hill so far. After the farmer presented his plans to the committee—which include a personal farm, and land he hopes to develop into space available for co-operative farming with other Rose Hill residents—the committee insisted he attend monthly RHNC community meetings and other events, such as block parties and cookouts, so that he "gets a feel for what the community is like and what they want." Later, at another housing committee meeting, this farmer attempted to volunteer for a subcommittee to help a land bank lawyer on title-work for neighborhood homes, a position he was denied, sharply and quickly. While white urban farmers are in some senses welcomed into Rose Hill and invited to be involved in community events, in other ways their presence is strictly contained and regarded warily by long-term residents.

This curtailment of urban agriculture projects and investment in Rose Hill is illustrated in RHNC's reception of a large philanthropic gift and development proposal from a local philanthropist and architecture firm, in 2017. The proposal was made at a housing committee meeting in October—a middle-aged white man wearing a dark blue suit carried in a tube of rolled architectural mock-ups, and presented, out of the blue, a philanthropic gift to RHNC. He told the committee and the ten gathered neighborhood residents in attendance that night that he came on behalf of an executive director of a local nonprofit. This ED had purchased an abandoned church within the boundaries of Rose Hill and wanted to offer it free of charge, along with five years of paid utilities, to RHNC. The ED had heard what a great job Rose Hill was doing, and how they had a "thriving" community garden, and decided he wanted to help. "We're envisioning a space for a food pantry and health screenings," he said, "and there's land in the back for a garden and another farmers market." As the man continued, telling the committee that they were undergoing renovations right now, updating the bathrooms and kitchen, one RHNC staff member interjected: "A lot of those services you're offering, we already provide. We have a food pantry. We offer health screenings. We don't need another garden. We give people enough of that stuff." Another RHNC staff member added, "What about a computer cafe or a coffee shop? We don't have a lot of computers in homes in this neighborhood, and that could be a really useful service." All of those in attendance murmured in support of that idea, and residents nodded their heads, but the man in the suit retorted, "Well, the zoning for that would be different. The [ED] wants it to be a community space, because otherwise it would cost quite a bit more to get it rezoned for the purposes you're discussing." RHNC staff responded, "Well, how about you suggest to your ED that he can come to the next community meeting and the next housing meeting as well, so he can actually hear what the neighborhood wants. We need other amenities, we need internet cafes and the next level of services, not handouts." Even though green urban development is encouraged and enforced through hegemonic discourse, grant funding streams, and philanthropic interests, Rose Hill advocates for other, more urgent community needs—here, internet access, so that residents can search for and apply for jobs. In this instance, the ED's philanthropic donation was rejected and RHNC denied the right of outside investors and donors to identify and serve neighborhood needs.

Representing a "Community": Narratives of Unrepresented Rose Hill Residents

While RHNC works quite hard to advocate for community needs, many voices and perspectives are left out of their decision-making processes. Rose Hill's expansive boundary—five zip codes and six thousand residents—complicates any clear understanding of "community," an already problematic term that implies homogeneity in an extremely heterogeneous group (cf. Thomas-Houston 2005, Kato 2015; McKinney and Kato 2017). Data from a recent resident survey illustrated that nearly 60 percent of those living within Rose Hill neighborhood boundaries had no idea they were part of the Rose Hill community. Rose Hill experiences high rates of transience, as low-income renters relying on unreliable or nonexistent paychecks become caught in cycles of eviction and migration. This transience likely contributes to a lack of neighborhood identification; RHNC believes that Rose Hill residents need to identify as a community in order for them to effectively protect land use and future decision making about the neighborhood's development. Further, as one Black East Side resident pointed out to me, it is difficult for residents to identify as a community when they have been forcibly—through racialized lending, redlining, and block busting—pushed into an area of the city they never purposefully chose to live in. "It's not a community, it's a state-regulated ghetto," this resident told me, speaking about his East Side neighborhood. "How can you call it a community when people are forced to live there?"

The concept of community development is fraught with assumptions about who exactly is included in the community; often, in Rose Hill, neoliberal ideas about productive citizenship are reconstituted at the local scale, and in the dismissal of the neighborhood's "undeserving poor" (Katz 1989). This concept of undeserving poor draws on racist and sexist stereotypes of welfare recipients and marketizes the idea of social worth—meaning, individuals are valued primarily for the economic value they generate (cf. Neubeck and Cazenave 2001; Goode and Maskovsky 2001; Morgen and Gonzales 2008). While RHNC is more cognizant of, and more proactive against, speculative land grabs resulting from green urban development than other neighborhood councils, they rely on a strategy promoting home ownership, "broken windows" policing, and neoliberal self-help rhetoric in order to do so. This strategy marginalizes those experiencing the most acute poverty in Rose Hill, for whom home ownership is out of reach and for whom even the affordable housing developed within the neighborhood is economically out of reach. One Rose Hill resident told me, during a conversation at the bus stop, "[Rose Hill] sucks for renters. They do not like renters here." Instead of any concerted effort to develop programming for this most economically disadvantaged population, Rose Hill works to displace them from their ranks (cf. Maskovsky 2014), with many people moving into historically Latinx neighborhoods in North Kansas City or farther east to find low-income rental housing. This adoption of personal responsibility rhetoric—evidenced through its urban garden programs and classes aimed at teaching the poor to grow their own food, and through discourse promoting home ownership—is what garners Rose Hill citywide praise and support.

Regardless of lack of programmatic support for the most economically disadvantaged Rose Hill residents, even those excluded from RHNC's community planning processes still strategically utilize green urban development within the neighborhood, much like RHNC does. In 2016 a new, glass-walled two-story community center and gym opened in Rose Hill. I attended festivities held for its opening celebration: a step troupe from a local high school performed, city councilmen cut a ribbon tied across the community center doors, and Rose Hill residents ate catered barbecue and cake. RHNC staff played a role in bringing the new community center into the area, bidding for the construction by drawing on examples of their neighborhood's commitment to healthy eating and urban beautification. The community center and gym fits in well with Rose Hill's branding of itself as a green healthy community; the landscaping around the new development reflects this as well, including several raised garden beds and a community orchard.

On my way out of the opening day celebration, I walked alongside Marcy, a young Black woman. She wore a dark blue hoodie and was attempting to carry six stacked paper plates—piled with barbecue and cake from the catered lunch—under her chin. I offered to help her carry her food, and she thanked me—she lived right across the street, so it would not be too much to ask, she said. I commented on how nice the new facility was, but how I was disappointed that I could not afford a gym membership there—the sliding scale rate would still be more than $60 dollars a month. Marcy responded while shaking her head, "Yeah I can't afford that either. But, I hope these other Black folk don't mess it [the community center] up." She added, "they're always messing things up. I've been watching them build this place for three years, waiting patiently." I asked her what she meant, and in her response, she illustrated how diverse actors, many of them often depicted without agency—who historically were subjected to displacement and violence through the creation of greenspace—are capitalizing on green urban development: "See that brown house? That's mine. My mom bought that for $20,000. As soon as this community center and garden raise [housing] prices in my neighborhood, I'm selling this damn house and moving to Florida."

CHAPTER 7

"We Can Change the Landscape"

Reinscribing Black Geographies into
City Space via Urban Agriculture

Darian wore a bright green and yellow handwoven African-fabric tunic. On his feet, crocodile-skin cowboy boots; a ten-gallon cowboy hat sat atop his shoulder-length dreads. He held a microphone and bellowed out to a school gymnasium packed with Black and brown Kansas City residents, who had come out on a Sunday evening in July to hear about a new initiative, the Troost Co-op. The co-op proposed to buy large swaths of vacant property on the East Side of Kansas City on which to farm. The property they proposed to buy was in an area of the city that experiences high rates of vacancy and poverty and is predominantly occupied by African American residents. Darian yelled to the crowd of around two hundred, "We haven't had space for our community since they tore down Black Wall Street, and it is time to take that space back again." Darian pointed a laser clicker at the screen behind him, pulling up a PowerPoint slide with data on vacant properties in Kansas City: "This city has over five thousand vacant properties and lots. We have roots as a food hub. Y'all used to work in the stockyards. Y'all used to make all the food for this city. We taught America agriculture—cotton, tobacco—we taught them that, and we can take it back." The crowd cheered as Darian finished, clapping sharply to emphasize each word: "If we plan on playing in this country, we need to play by the rules that are here. And right now, we don't own nothin'. We buy all these lots, and we can change the landscape of Kansas City. Own and control. Own and Control!"

As white upper-middle-class farmers and speculative developers move to acquire land and take advantage of increased funding for urban food projects, an increasing number of Black Kansas Citians are purchasing and farming on land themselves—simply to retain control over urban space, as numerous policies work to divest this control from them. Further, many are using this as an opportunity to make racialized geographies visible in Kansas City, counteracting dominant spatialized whiteness.

Scholarship on Black-led urban farming initiatives has grown in recent years. For a burgeoning movement of Black farmers, farming is an act of resistance (cf. White 2011a; 2011b). Cultivating urban space can be a way of crafting ownership and demonstrating agency and self-reliance within a society that has worked to deny Black communities all three (Reese 2018; 2019). The narratives shared in this chapter complement this work; I uplift the ways that Black urban farmers in Kansas City reclaim spaces of historic importance and violence, reshaping them through the cultivation of food.

Specifically, in this chapter I explore oft-marginalized understandings of city space by highlighting the narratives of some Black urban farmers—like Darian—who are purposefully using urban agriculture to draw attention to, and contest, how racism has been historically spatialized in Kansas City. Specifically, I document the work of Black farmers who developed their urban food initiatives in direct response to white-led land grabs and speculative development resulting from Kansas City's green urbanism initiatives.

Insurgent Citizenship:
Countering Geographies of Dispossession

Whiteness is implicated spatially in Kansas City in myriad ways, often through urban greening initiatives. Black bodies that move through the same city are racially coded as belonging in certain spaces and not others (Brahinsky et al. 2014; Thomas-Houston 2004). Racialized narratives of "ghetto" and "blight" discursively enforce these spatial norms, mask historical processes of spatial creation, and imbue the urban landscape with racial ideology (Anderson 1987; Wacquant 1997). "Cartographic whiteness," wherein nonwhite bodies and behavior are pinpointed as abnormal, is surveilled and enforced in U.S. cities, not just by agents of the state but also by urban citizens who define and enforce these invisible norms (Fiske 1998; Anderson 2014). In these ways, white behavior, dress, and appearance come to define urban space. Black urban residents of Kansas City encounter cartographic whiteness in the privatization of downtown neighborhood streets—where, historically, newly freed captive Africans tended small urban farms; in the commercialization of places of historic Black entrepreneurship, such as the Jazz District; in the whitewashing in dominant discourse of the urban food movement, which denies their historical participation; and in narratives of food desertification, which paints urban spaces as sites of lack (cf. Reese 2019). Black Kansas Citians today involved in growing food—urban farmers and gardeners—are acutely affected by this dominant whiteness, as their racialized experiences are marginalized and denied both citywide and within the urban food movement.

It is important to highlight how spatialized white privilege affects urban residents of color. However, as McKittrick (2006, 4) has noted, this focus on cartographic whiteness means that within the academy, the geography of Black subjects is discussed solely in relation to dispossession, segregation, and violence. Most of the time when we talk about how power circulates geographically within cities, we are discussing the power and influence of whiteness (cf. Wilson 2012, 940). In contrast, the work of Black urban farmers in Kansas City highlights how people of color are also powerful agents in shaping urban space. As their narratives here will illustrate, Black urban residents work to create city space that bears the power of *their* racial influence.

Activism at the local, city level, in particular, has the power to spur meaningful political change. Scholars argue that this is because in the United States, neoliberalism has created privatized and globalized systems of governance. Today, it is much easier to engage with those with power at the local level than it is at the national level (cf. Sassen 2004b, 64; Sassen 2004a; Holston and Appadurai 2009). This sort of work has been called "street level politics" (Sassen 2004b); the everyday political protestations that resulted in the Civil Rights Act of the 1960s, for example, can be theorized within this framework. These powerful acts of claim-making, enacted often by marginalized subjects, are how new understandings of citizen rights, and citizenship, are built; they are most visible, and powerful, at the city level, where extremes between poverty and affluence are starkly juxtaposed (Sassen 2004b).

More broadly, scholars have theorized these acts of claim-making as "insurgent citizenship,"—a process that occurs, in the context of extreme urban poverty and peripheral urbanization, when marginalized urban citizens expose entrenched inequalities and claim their right to city space (Holston 2009). In this framework, everyday actions such as land cultivation can be seen as politically meaningful acts; the "insurgent citizenship" perspective makes clear how everyday demands for dignity, recognition, and rights are vastly important actions that help continually redefine the relationship between marginalized subjects and the state (cf. Ghannam 2002; Zhang 2008). Many Black urban farmers in Kansas City see their work through this lens: as political acts of resistance to whiteness as written on city space within the urban food movement, an understanding that offers new insight into how people of color respond to spatially hegemonic whiteness in U.S. cities.

Contestations of Spatialized Whiteness in
Kansas City's Urban Food Movement

For many of the Black urban farmers I spoke with, agricultural production on historically Black owned land was an important and meaningful consideration when choosing sites to farm. Greg, a marketing executive and father of two, took up farming as a way to honor his avid-gardener grandmother's legacy and to spend time with his sons. Around 2010 he began taking urban farmer training classes offered by area nonprofits, researched companion planting and water catchment systems, and bought four vacant city plots in the historic Jazz District, at Eighteenth and Vine Street. In addition to its fame for birthing Jazz legends such as Charlie Parker, the area between Twelfth and Eighteenth on Vine was a hub for Black businesses, known locally as "Black Wall Street." But blockbusting and redlining pushed African Americans to the east of the city in the 1950s, and a city-led revitalization project—which demolished and rebuilt the area in service of tourism—led to a mass exodus of African American residents from the Jazz District during the second half of the twentieth century (Schirmer 2002). The Jazz District, which formerly encompassed six city blocks, is now confined to one block on Vine, where new museums and murals commemorate the Black industry that has since been displaced. Greg explained the history of the area to me, as we walked the perimeter of his land at Eighteenth and Vine, which borders a low-income senior housing complex: "At Twelfth and Vine, you had that vast quantity of flower shops and dress shops and restaurants—all the amenities of residential high life. That was destroyed. Now you've got the strip and these museums—the Negro Baseball League, and the Jazz Museum. Those are the major businesses down here. That mural? There's nothing behind that façade. It's a long billboard that shows an impression of old musicians and restaurants and things that used to be, and they've given us just one block now."

Greg is developing what he hopes will be a more meaningful mural for a wall bordering his farm plots. To that end, he has been distributing questionnaires about its design to nearby residents (some of whom have remained at Eighteenth and Vine throughout the changes the area has experienced), and the fourth, fifth, and sixth graders whose school sits across the street from his land. He told me that just the fact that he owns land, that he has increased the amount of Black-owned land in the Jazz District, is important to him, whether or not his farm is monetarily successful.

Likewise, Hank, the eighty-year-old farmer whom Nancy critiqued for his increasingly "polarized" views of racial inequality, attaches meaning to the history of land and the very act of owning land. Hank grew up in a small town south of Houston, where his family sharecropped, and moved to Kansas City as a young adult to teach grade school, a job he held for thirty-five years. From a young age, Hank told me, he had liked the idea of cultivating soil and growing his own food. When he retired from teaching in 1990, the school told him they would keep him on the substitute teachers list, but Hank had decided to farm: "I said don't ever call me. I'm gonna start digging in the ground." Today, Hank owns eight and a half acres in North Kansas City, a site he chose because he had been told that historically, a stop on the Underground Railroad had been stationed there. The land also sits near the site where Western University once stood, a historically Black college established in 1865 that struggled during the Great Depression and closed in 1943 (Schirmer 2002). The farm overlooks Quindaro Townsite, a settlement established by abolitionists in 1857 as part of the resistance aimed at stopping the westward spread of slavery; escaped slaves from Missouri were often linked into the Underground Railroad through Quindaro Townsite (Schirmer 2002).

Apart from the history of the land, it matters to Hank simply that he owns it. I visited Hank on his farm on a hot June morning—he had already been up for hours, tilling several acres to put in a couple hundred peach tree saplings. As he walked me around his land and showed me how he had pruned his trees to make the fruit easy to pick, Hank told me about how he had decided he wanted to own a farm after watching his father manage one: "I grew up on a farm. And when I finished high school I found that the love of farming maintained everywhere I stopped—everywhere I ever stopped I had a garden." Hank linked his desire to own land to racism he had experienced in his childhood, telling me he "grew up in segregation, where they said, 'get back, shut up, we don't do that for y'all,' and what have you. I was twelve, and I told my daddy, 'If it ain't but two jobs out there, I'm gonna have one of 'em. If it ain't but two houses in America, I'm gonna own one.' So as of that day I've done that. I've owned at least twelve houses. I buy land with my money. I've bought over seven hundred acres of land in my life."

After putting in a bid at auction on his eight and a half acres in Kansas City in 1972, his bank—which had agreed to loan conditions—went up in flames. Unable to secure another loan, the title company told Hank "Oh, no, we can't help" and informed him he had thirty-six hours to raise the $35,000 dollars for the land. Clive called his friends and family for loans and showed up at the title office the next day: "That lady, she said 'What can I do you?' I said well I came to sign those papers. She said, 'You mean to tell me you raised $35,000 dollars?' I said, 'Black dollars.' She turned bright red. I said it again, 'Black dollars bought your land.'"

Hank's statements are powerful locally but also on a national scale—his words resonate with a long lineage of Black intellectual and activist arguments for self-reliance (cf. Reese 2018). Many prominent Black intellectuals have advocated for self-reliance and the development of communities independent of white philanthropy, as a means of Black liberation—W. E. B. DuBois, Booker T. Washington, and activists such as Fannie Lou Hamer and leaders of the Southern Cooperative Movement, to name a few (Reese 2018; McCutcheon 2011; White 2018). Crucially, this "self"-reliance refers not to individuals but to a "community made up of blacks" (McCutcheon 2011, 186). More recently, Hank's statements find common ground with the ideologies of the Buy Black Movement, and FUBU—For Us, by Us—which push back against the economic extraction and exploitation of Black cultures and communities by advocating for Black entrepreneurship and circulation of Black dollars within Black communities as a means of political autonomy (cf. McCutcheon 2011). Black Nationalist movements and religions, such as the Pan-African Orthodox Christian Church (PAOCC) and the Nation of Islam (NOI), have also, for example, long argued that control of food and land are central to Black self-sufficiency and autonomy (McCutcheon 2011, see also Safransky 2017a). Both the PAOCC and the NOI have purchased thousands of acres of farmland, each with distinct goals, but with the overlapping interest of building Black Nationhood and community. In 1999, PAOCC purchased over fifteen hundred acres of farmland in Georgia and South Carolina to build Beulah Land Farms; in the years since, the working farm has grown to encompass more than four thousand acres. Beulah (taken from the Book of Isaiah, meaning "married to the land") Land Farms was founded with the intent of creating a spiritual community—a place where church members can connect with the land (McCutcheon 2011, 184). Fannie Lou Hamer's Freedom Farm Cooperative, a 680-acre communal farm founded in 1967 in the Mississippi Delta, is another similar enactment of Black autonomy and liberation via land acquisition and stewardship (White 2017).

For another Black urban farmer in Kansas City, the cultivation of soil health on her farm is deeply entwined with Blackness and artifacts of Black presence in Kansas City's urban landscape. Neferet—who chose early in her twenties to take a Kemetic name, a move that ties her to ancestors in Egypt—grew up in St. Louis, Missouri, in a family heavily involved with the Black Panther Party. While the Black Panthers has been depicted by the U.S. government and media as violently militant, solely concerned with white supremacy and police brutality, the organization was, and is, largely preoccupied with developing social programs and providing basic community needs for Black U.S. citizens who have been dismissed, and unprovided for, by the state (cf. Heynen 2009; Sbicca 2012). Most notably, for example, this occurred with the Panthers' Free Breakfast for Children Program. Her family's association with the Panthers, Neferet shared, instilled in her the cultural and political significance of food in efforts for Black autonomy.

Neferet's understanding of Black land ownership and dispossession in the United States factors heavily into her decision to farm in Kansas City. Black individuals who have owned and farmed land, in her understanding, have historically been able to better resist economic downturn and racism:

> Those people who were Black farmers, that have land, they recovered very nicely from the reconstruction period in America. It was not just sharecroppers—the stereotype of what people think of when they think of Black farmers. They didn't know that there was a depression. They had their hogs, their animals. They went out hunting. They always had their farm resources and lived prosperously. But there is this history of trying to destroy African American people that have land—if I were a Black shop owner, or Black grocery owner, I would be lynched, they burnt down their farms. There have been a lot of prosperous African Americans that were destroyed.

Neferet's understanding of the importance of her farmland echoes Fannie Lou Hamer's statements on the necessity of Black farmland ownership; Hamer famously stated that if she had a pig and a garden, "she might be harassed and physically harmed but at least she would not starve to death" (White 2017, 21). Neferet farms on the African American majority East Side of Kansas City, on one city block named Sacred Life Urban Farm. When I visited her, she was growing herbs, peppers, kale, cabbages, and squash in her front yard and farming corn and beans intensively on the large lot adjacent to her home. Neferet told me that the health of her soil meant everything to her: "It's a strictly natural organic compost that I use. There are worms, coffee grounds, leaves, grass cuttings, barbershop hair, kitchen scraps from my neighbors and Black-owned restaurants, lawn care clippings, and other kinds of community contributions from the Black urban landscape." Neferet, quite literally, nourishes her soil and land with the contributions of Black neighbors and Black industries.

Growing historically significant crops on Black-owned space, and selling them in hegemonic white spaces, was a powerful act of resistance for many of the Black farmers I met in Kansas City. On his land at Seventeenth and

Vine, Greg grows African tree collards, mustard greens, African sugar cane, and red foliated cotton, which he displays decoratively in vases when he sells at farmers markets. Customers buy it from him for novelty, or for cosmetic purposes—many women buy it, he told me, as an organic makeup remover. Darla, a thirty-five-year-old woman who grows food in her backyard to supply her organic vegan catering business, held up a fistful of collards when I first visited her home, in the middle of a discussion about the recent ruling that no charges would be filed against the police officers who shot Alton Sterling: "This is the true form of resistance. Took a long time to realize that the anger and hatred I felt gave them my power. Now I see, hear, release, then head to the garden. My way of protesting."

Twenty of the thirty-five Black urban farmers I interviewed in Kansas City have grown cotton—though each of them grew it for different reasons, many did so as a means of identifying and publicly asserting the role of African Americans in U.S. agriculture. Hank, for example, chose cotton as his first crop during his first year of production on his land in Northeast Kansas City. When I visited his home, he had proudly hung a large, framed photograph of himself and his brother, both leaning against a freshly picked bale of cotton, on the wall of his kitchen. For comparison, I only met one white farmer in Kansas City who had grown the crop.

Sean, an aquaponic urban farmer, grew up in Johnson County, an affluent suburb of Kansas City, where his family worked cleaning houses and repairing cars for white neighbors. His family migrated to Kansas from Mississippi, and often talked openly, Sean told me, about their agricultural history—his grandfather sharecropping, his great-grandfather's death while working on a plantation in Kentucky. After becoming heavily involved with the Kansas City Green Party, Sean started farming aquaponically in his basement and growing food in raised beds in his backyard. When I met him, Sean was working as urban farm manager for East High School—a historically Black high school on the East Side of Kansas City—encouraging minority students to pursue careers in agriculture. At East High school's greenhouse, Sean grows several varieties of cotton, African Moringa tree, and tobacco: "For me, it's preservation of culture. We've been so involved, it might be a painful history, but I think a lot of times our history gets whitewashed, and it gets exploited. I wanna grow tobacco, I wanna grow a lot of cotton, just to show this is what it looks like. Just to connect, to show this is ours. Cotton—we grew that. That's one of the hugest, biggest commodities in America."

Cotton, produced and harvested with captive African labor, was historically central to the U.S. economy—between 1803 and 1937, it was the leading American export (Baptist 2014). Captive African cotton production, on lands forcibly taken from Indigenous inhabitants, was a key mechanism used by U.S. cities to accumulate wealth (Baptist 2014). Donna Morris, owner of Salt of the Earth farm in Northeast Kansas City—a market garden and garden training site for area teens—lines the perimeter of her urban farm with cotton plants. "When we started growing cotton that was a bit of a controversy; of course, the stigma attached to cotton. But I told the kids—nobody is lashing your back on this, so you should feel proud about growing and picking the cotton you grow." Donna and her teen volunteers sell the cotton at the Zona Rosa farmers market, located in an exclusive shopping district in an upper-middle class, largely white, gated community in North Kansas City. "We took our cotton transplants to market and it was just a hit—you wouldn't believe what they'll pay for 'em," Donna laughed.

Other Black urban farmers choose to verbally assert their historical presence in Kansas City's agricultural landscape while in white public spaces, discursively disrupting them. A notable example of this occurred at Grow KC's annual Farmers and Friends Meeting—an event referred to by some Black urban farmers, as noted earlier, as the "White Farmers and Friends Meeting." The first time I attended a meeting, held in February 2017 in a Presbyterian church in the affluent Brookside neighborhood, there were only around ten Black and brown participants, including myself. The rest of the two hundred or so attendees were white and upper-middle-class; farmers, local food advocates, or avid farm-to-table diners. Most were dressed in Birkenstocks, brightly colored shawls, Lulu Lemon-fitted athletic jackets, and bandanas. After attending a morning panel on food waste in the local food movement, I joined the rest of the conference attendees in eating our potluck lunch. I filled my plate and joined a table that included four employees of Grow KC, all thirtysomething white women, a woman in her fifties who does not farm but enjoys and advocates for farm-to-table dining, and Arthur Davis—a sixty-year-old Black urban farmer, who owns land in Northeast Kansas City. One of the Grow KC employees remarked happily on the pickled quail eggs, which one of the conference attendees had brought to share. The giver had placed a sign in front of the eggs with his name and number, stating that more eggs could be bought for fifteen dollars a dozen. I laughed at that and remarked to the group that a dozen of those eggs is not even as big as one chicken egg, so it is a high price to pay. The local food advocate reacted sharply to my laughter. She told me that raising those quails had taken a lot of time, and that the eggs were a delicacy. She asked the other women at the table if they had eaten the quail egg salad at the Antler Room, a relatively new upscale restaurant that sources from a select few organic urban farms in Kansas City. As the women began to praise their spring menu offerings, Arthur interrupted angrily, "All these restaurants you're talking about—people like me were not allowed in those restaurants. We couldn't eat there. But back in the day we were supplying them with what they sold. They made us come around the back door. They used to ask us boys to climb the Chouteau Bridge to grab them young pigeons for their French food. They wanted young ones, but just when they were getting heavy chests, and we were to bring them down to their back doors. At the base of the bridge, we could collect quail eggs and sell those too. We didn't get fifteen dollars a dozen for those, I'll tell you that."

Conversation at the table stopped abruptly after Arthur's statement. By voicing his historical contributions to the high-end farm to table dining scene, Arthur disrupted white public space: he insisted upon the consistent contributions of African Americans to the local food economy in Kansas City, and contested his, and others', erasure within this space by white local foodies. Arthur's assertion "We didn't get fifteen dollars a dozen for those" highlights that Black Kansas Citians have been engaging in activities and industries currently promoted by foodies and green urban development agendas for years and have not received fair pay or recognition for their labor.

Reclaiming Dispossessed Space

Troost Co-op—whose first recruitment meeting I described at the beginning of this chapter—was organized by five Afro-centrist farmers and activists in the summer of 2016, as a result, one of its founding members told me, of "all this discussion on Black lives matter." Marcus, a thirty-five-year-old son of Arkansas sharecroppers, is well respected on the East Side of Kansas City. In addition to helping found the co-op, Marcus runs an after-school program for local boys, which focuses on science and leadership education through aquaponic farming. Marcus also runs Nile River, a community greenhouse and aquaponics system at Twenty-Seventh and Prospect, situated squarely in one of Kansas City's most economically depressed neighborhoods. Nile River is named to reference the fertile areas on the Nile River banks, farmed, as Afrocentrists like Marcus argue, by Africans, not Egyptians (cf. Harrison 2018). Marcus opens his streetside gardens to his neighbors, who frequently harvest the fruits, greens, tomatoes, and peppers as they pass by.

Marcus was trained by Growing Power's Will Allen, a well-known former basketball player who runs a large-scale aquaponic farm in Milwaukee. Much of Allen's work centers on community infrastructure development. Marcus brings a similar focus to his own projects. During my discussions with him, he always emphasized how both traditional agriculture and aquaponic farming can be vehicles to improve cities in ways beyond just food security.

For Marcus and the other Co-op founding members, the inception of Troost Co-op is intimately linked to racialized police violence in U.S. cities. After being introduced at their first recruitment meeting, I reached out to Marcus, and the other founding members Adama, Lisa, and Darian. The next week, we got together at a local Black-owned organic juice restaurant, and I asked them to tell me about the inception of the project and their goals for it in the future. Marcus told me that after reading some Black Lives Matter discussions on twitter, he approached his friends with the idea for the Co-op: "I just felt like this energy was not being used correctly. People here needed to be doing something. And one of the most abundant resources we have here in Kansas City is land, so why not use it? Urban agriculture reduces our dependency upon outside sources. So the Co-op helps us shift away from protesting and move into action."

In 2006 there were 5000 vacant and deteriorating houses in Kansas City; by 2010 there were 10,900—almost all of them located east of Troost Avenue (Shortridge 2012, 177). The USDA identifies nearly all of the land between Troost and Woodland Avenues (the East Side of Kansas City) as a food desert (USDA 2015). This classification facilitates grant funding for individuals hoping to buy land for agricultural use—locally (as discussed in chapter 3), Kansas City's tax incentives, such as the Urban Agriculture Zone ordinance, encourage settler-colonials to farm or raise livestock on "blighted" urban space. Vacant land on the East Side of the city is easy to come by and given away relatively cheaply; many lots can be bought from the Kansas City Land Bank or Homesteading Authority for less than $100 dollars; it is important to note that the Land Bank was established in 2012 in Kansas City through city collaboration with the foodie-led Hunger Coalition, supposedly to help facilitate urban food production for food-insecure residents east of Troost. In conjunction, however, these two incentives have resulted in a high number of upper-middle class, white-led urban agriculture projects situated in low-income, African-American majority neighborhoods. This sort of "urban pioneer"–led gentrification (Smith 1996) was acutely felt by many of the Black East Side residents I spoke with and spurred numerous Black urban farmers to buy land before white, upper-middle class farmers could acquire it.

Lisa, a young, twentysomething woman who often wears large wooden Ankh-shaped earrings, spoke to this frustration with land loss on the East Side of Kansas City: "I'm here [participating in the Co-op] because I believe in the liberation of my people. There is a mission to get our people, our land, our bodies—a deliberate mission, and I'm here for our autonomy." Adama, a tall man in harem pants, who in addition to helping run Troost Co-op operates a yoga studio with his wife, nodded in agreement, saying, "A city that controls my food, my land—that city controls me." Adama directly addressed city policy that incentivizes white land grabs on Black-majority East Side land, stating:

> The Urban Agriculture Zone Initiative—on the surface it's used to fix these land problems, but at the end of the day it's more like a plan where someone said: "okay, how do people who classify themselves as white acquire more wealth and power within communities inhabited by people who classify themselves as nonwhite?" So we see the end result being the same thing that's been propagated over the past four hundred years. That's how *they* use "blight." When *we* use the word blight, specifically when I use the word blight, I use it to describe areas that, to our community, have no "value"—areas we don't see any value in. Troost Co-op *makes* the community see value in the land. In America, that's all we're taught to value—forty acres and a mule. And we're a people, like other melanated people around the world, who are inextricably tied to the land. We want to use that. That's what we're addressing.

Here, Adama touches on several issues: for many Black East Side residents, green urban development policies such as the Urban Agriculture Zone Ordinance are seen as merely a continuation of urban projects that work to preserve white public space and displace and marginalize people of color. Adama argues that such development uses "blight" as a designation to facilitate easy access to Black owned or occupied land. Troost Co-op addresses this violent city policy by acquiring land through city-supported incentives, for city-sanctioned use, but for the purposes of Black autonomy and resistance. Adama and the Co-op members draw on logic that argues if land is made most accessible for agricultural use, then they will acquire land for agricultural use before others can do the same and extract value out of their communities.

Acquiring land in this way does not mean that the Co-op imagines providing for the welfare of Black Kansas Citians through food alone; Troost Co-op founding members envision myriad ways this project could contribute to community health and autonomy. For example, founding members are discussing how to arrange for Co-op members to be covered under group insurance—a conscious effort to find ways to offer health insurance to those who cannot afford it.

Wallace, an African American urban farmer in his sixties and member of the Nation of Islam, told me more about how his work enacts NOI's political and religious goals of land acquisition and Black liberation. Wallace farms on the East Side of Kansas City on three consecutive city lots; he told me that he originally started doing so because the Prophet Muhammad "told us to take our mouths out of the white man's kitchen." Drawing on years of donations from Nation of Islam members, the group purchased 1,556 acres in Southwest Georgia in 1994 to found Muhammad Farms; they have plans to purchase more land in the Mississippi Delta (McCutcheon 2011, 178). Wallace told me they are just taking back what should have been theirs, land on which captive African labor was extracted for decades. Watermelon and cotton are two of the main crops grown on Muhammad Farm, an act that indexes the post-emancipation liberation of captive Africans who ran watermelon farms (Black 2018). Ultimately, the NOI hopes to be able to develop a sustainable agriculture system on Muhammad Farms that has the capacity to provide at least one meal a day for forty million Black people (McCutcheon 2011, 181).

In Kansas City, the Troost Co-op hopes to enact resistance to a state-controlled landscape and food system by farming large swaths of land in the urban core of Kansas City—partly for market sales, partly for redistribution within Co-op membership, and partly for public consumption and grazing. Adama showed me their preliminary mock-ups of several urban lots; they are still waiting for approval from the Land Bank to go ahead with their plans but are securing membership fees, tools, and transplants in the meantime. For one farm location—labeled Orchard A—they are hoping to grab three adjacent lots, located right behind a bus station. The plans involve an open "neighborhood grazing orchard" directly adjacent the bus stop seating, with apples, pears, peaches, bush cherries, figs, raspberries, and blackberries. Behind that will be a fenced garden to raise produce to sell at market; the plan is to plant figs, jujubes, hazelnuts, and chestnut trees. Adama flipped through their plan book, showing me similar orchard layouts at different locations all along the East Side, many near bus stops or strip malls, places where primarily low-income public transit users can enjoy shade trees and free produce. Co-op members will be required to contribute a small amount monetarily or put in a specified number of labor hours on one of the farm lots; in return, they will receive produce and a share of the market sales. "Black restaurants will buy our produce. They'll be forced to," Lisa added. "That's why the Black Panther movement was so successful—because they said you do not have a business in our area if you are not going to give back to the community." Adama chimed in, "We can just tell them [restaurant owners]—'We're buying food. Might as well be buying our own damn food."

At first glance, many of Troost Co-op's plans for the city sound similar to foodie-led green urban development agendas: Troost Co-op envisions an East Side populated with fruit-bearing trees and greenspace. Our Daily Bread, for example, also plants orchards across the metropolitan area—primarily in Black and brown neighborhoods—but was often derided by the Black East Side residents I spoke with, who saw the orchards as a paternalistic hand out. Intentionality, optics, and models of community-organization and ownership separate the two visions (see also Newtown Florist Collective's discussion of Direct Action Growing; NFCWC 2013). I sat down with Keisha, a Troost Co-op member who contributes a portion of her monthly paycheck to infrastructure building for the nonprofit, to discuss why the Co-op's orchards are so much better-received than Our Daily Bread's: "I think it has a lot to do with the presenter. When you have somebody who probably doesn't look like them, going in there, trying to tell them this is what you need to do—that's shutting it down immediately. I can very much say, in our minds it's like . . . you're an overseer. It may seem like, 'oh who would really think that way?' But coming from where we have been, you know, as people of color, that's just how it is. So when they come in and try to 'offer' us stuff, it's like 'no thank you.'"

Keisha's comments highlight, importantly, that East-Sider derision of white-led green urban development policies is *not* a rejection of their attendant ecological principles. Many low-income Black East Side residents spoke thoughtfully to me about how they privilege holistic understandings of health and land stewardship. And, both chapter 4 and this current chapter illustrate that there are a diversity of Black-led community food security projects occurring in Kansas City. However, city and foodie-led green urban development infrastructures index centuries of state-led control of Black bodies, diets, and communities, and draw upon pathologies of the Black urban residents as deficient, as incapable of understanding or enacting the best use of their land. Troost Co-op speaks to the wealth of Black urban residents who care about urban ecological health, greenspace, and increasing food security for their community but desire these changes uncoupled from white public space and white racial hegemony; it also draws those passionate about Black liberation and creating "Black geographies" in the city.

The Street Level Politics of Cotton Production: Disrupting Hegemonic Spatialized Whiteness

This chapter contributed to extant understandings of racialized urban space by exploring the ways Black urban residents in Kansas City contest dominant whitened understandings of city space. Fisk (1998, 69) writes that city space is cut through with lines that "blacks cannot cross and whites cannot see"; the farmers highlighted in this chapter work to highlight these lines of racial violence through the everyday act of cultivating food. Black urban farmers enact street-level politics in Kansas City in a number of ways—centrally, these farmers undertake the political work of making histories of violence visible. Though typical understandings of civic action and rights claiming are envisioned as participation in protests, formal petitions to law-makers, and ballot-casting, this work of highlighting state-sponsored violence against Black urban residents can, and should, be seen as civic action as well (see also White 2011a; White 2011b; Reese 2018; Reynolds and Cohen 2016). By using urban agriculture to highlight areas of city-led disinvestment, histories of exploited captive African labor, and racialized segregation and violence, Black urban farmers draw on a currently favored medium—green urban development—to critique and protest their unequal treatment as urban citizens. Growing cotton in the urban core, for example, is a powerful political statement that demands: see me, remember what the state has done to me, and see that I have a right to this city, too. In these ways, Black urban farmers in Kansas City undertake the important work of creating "counter-geographies" to hegemonic spatialized whiteness that "disrupt the sanitized landscape of national forgetting" (Razack 2002).

In other ways, as the Troost Co-op's work illustrates, Black Kansas City residents use established and condoned methods of urban development—green urban infrastructure—to enact Black liberation and Afro-centrists' goals for urban space. While one could theorize the Co-op's land acquisition as simply part of typical urban growth, I argue that this should also be seen as street-level politics. As Darian noted, if "we plan on playing in this country, we need to play by the rules that are here," which, he points out, means land and capital ownership. In this way, the Troost Co-op utilizes the capitalist logic that dominates in U.S. cities to further their own political goals of Black liberation. It is also a powerful refutation of what many Black urban farmers described to me as the white settler colonial urban agriculture movement—claiming land, themselves, before white "settlers" can, is an important political statement.

However, not every Black urban farmer in Kansas City would identify with Black liberation politics or would identify their work, or the act of growing cotton, as street-level politics. People do not automatically share a political project simply because they have experienced shared histories of violence (as Thomas-Houston 2005 discusses well). This chapter has focused on shared moments of public, political disruption in the urban food "movement" in

Kansas City, but it is important to note that there is intense heterogeneity of thought among Black urban farmers.

There were strong generational and class divides among my interviewees—these different positionalities deeply informed their views, especially about political strategies for bringing about social change. Despite those differences, Black urban farmers often shared critiques of white privilege and urban development. For example, while I once listened to Philip (a young Black liberation farmer, introduced in chapter 5) and Alfred (a fiftysomething retired corporate lawyer who bought vast swaths of land west of Kansas City to grow soybeans) arguing over their differing opinions on Black Lives Matter activism, they ultimately found common ground when discussing how they "always have to protect their land from white folks." In this chapter I focused on these shared contestations, though it would be incorrect to call them collective or cohesive, in order to highlight how Black farmers are undertaking the work of disrupting the whiteness of the food movement and Kansas City's green urban development.

The street-level politics shared here are happening nationally, as well, on a number of scales. The histories of urban land dispossession, urbicide, in Kansas City that affected the Black urban farmers in this study can be understood as a small part of national, historical efforts to displace, and erase, Black presence in the American landscape. As highlighted earlier, Black nationalist religions and social movements have been undertaking the work of disrupting white public space for quite some time—reclaiming land and drawing attention to histories of purposive state-led violence against Black Americans. This work of drawing attention to and disrupting the ways white supremacy has constructed history and city space is enacted in smaller ways, as well, in myriad social movements across the United States. Black urban farmers in Kansas City disrupt spatialized hegemonic whiteness along with protestors in southern cities who tear down monuments to slavery and in concert with protesters against racialized police violence in urban space, all of whom claim their roles in constructing U.S. space and their right to define its path forward.

CHAPTER 8

Imagining Another Way
to Live in the City

Confronting Spatialized Whiteness in
Urban Greening Initiatives

In the fall of 2017, I joined a group of young, diverse urban farmers in planning and hosting a panel titled "Critical Conversations on KC's Local Food Scene." We hosted the event with the goal of disrupting the dominant narrative, constructed by white voices, surrounding urban sustainability, agriculture, and history in Kansas City. The panel was borne out of shared frustration and collective experiences of marginalization, and with the hopes of elevating different, more diverse, narratives of sustainability and urban food production—of a more inclusive green urban future.

The event drew a large crowd of around fifty foodies, many representing the influential nonprofits discussed in this book. The panelists worried about this almost entirely white audience; one commented before the event began, "Shit, it is white in here." During planning for this event, the organizers and I had experienced difficulty in recruiting panelists because of the potential whiteness of the audience—farmers of color whom we approached told us they were worried about the repercussions of sharing their perspectives honestly in front of influential foodies.

Our speakers included a young urban planner (a first-generation Mexican immigrant to Kansas City), a young Black farmer and activist, an African American woman who runs an urban garden at a homeless shelter, and the owner of the oldest (dating from the turn of the last century) African American owned farm in KC. I moderated the discussion, during which the panelists discussed what "blight" meant to them, talked about the history of Black and brown land dispossession, shared thoughtful considerations about how to address food insecurity, and discussed their concerns about capitalism and the role of nonprofits in city welfare provision. A throughline in this conversation: panelists' assertion that that discussion of food, diets, and urban green-

space should be tied to larger issues—systemic poverty and inequality, racialized violence, disinvestment in specific communities.

Our panelists were correct to worry about disrupting white public space.
When we opened up to questions from the audience, influential foodies began
to attack the perspectives that had been shared. Nancy, the director of Grow
KC, spoke angrily:

> So I'm looking at the history of the local food movement, I think that there's
> a lot of work that's happened that hasn't been recognized here. I'm thinking
> specifically around [a Latinx-focused healthcare nonprofit] organizing their
> own folks, educating their own folks, I'm thinking about some of the Hmong
> growers I know who are educating their own folks. Those kinds of engage-
> ments in specific grounded communities is what's ultimately going to change
> our food system. I wanna offer that there is more than just this group in the
> local food movement. So characterizing the local food movement as just this
> group is diminishing of other people, who in fact are working quite hard in
> their own communities, and who didn't show up to this event because they're
> working in their own communities. I agree, our meetings are white. You look
> at any group of social community activists and it's either white women, or its
> African American women, or it's Latina women. And that's just the character-
> istics of who gets involved, by and large, I would say. And so in this movement
> we've got mostly white women. I don't look out and see a purely white local
> food system in Kansas City. I see, as I move through my world, a very diverse,
> constantly mixed group of people, all engaging in a whole variety of ways. And
> some of them are recognized by the mainstream, and some of them aren't.

Nancy minimizes and inappropriately reframes several of the concerns the
panelists voiced about racialized and class-based inequality in Kansas City's
urban food movement. First, she turns the onus of (mis)representation back
onto the panelists: in their statements about feeling marginalized by the whiteness of the urban food movement, these panelists, Nancy argues, are themselves ignoring the "diversity" of farmers involved in urban food production.
The whiteness of food movement leadership, Nancy argues, stems from the
fact that white women are the ones who get involved—a statement that elides
historical leadership of Black and brown U.S. citizens in food movements,
such as in La Via Campesina and the Black Panther Party's food program.
Nancy displaces responsibility for inclusivity and equity by arguing that minority communities helping out "their own folks" is how our food system will
change. One panelist, the young Black farmer, responded,

I think you made a good point about recognizing work that's already been done, and it made me think of the Black Panthers in Kansas City. I mean, they started the food program at St. Mary's on Twelfth and Brooklyn. The church is still there, but they're gone. They're actually in jail or killed by the state. So me thinking personally about Black people in this areas' efforts to transform their realities, their food system—we run into violence. We run into radical politics. We run into oppositional politics. We run into the limits of electoral politics. So it broadens out all of a sudden into imagining another way to live in the city—what does that mean? It broadens out into a revolutionary project, like we can't just grow food. Food was a major part of what the Panthers were doing—so was education, so was housing, so was access to health care. But they recognized that none of these programs can actually work if we have an oppressive system that seems to be intent on killing us . . . through our diet, through numerous ways. That's kind of what your comment brought up for me.

Here, Nancy's microconcerns about the food system, and people of color working to support their own communities, are placed in the context of macro forces. The farmer reminds Nancy: Black people who have attempted self-determination and self-sufficiency have been targeted and jailed or killed by the state. Soon after this comment was made, another panelist raised concern that Grow KC's upcoming Farmers and Friends meeting would now cost five dollars to attend, stating, "I can't help but think that makes it less inclusive, and really restricts who has access to that information and those networking opportunities, because so much of the work we do is based on who you know." A Grow KC member stood and snapped, sarcastically, in response, "I am thrilled to be here, and thank you for this conversation. There is a big table of [Grow KC staff] here. Put your feet underneath it for a minute. I think it's awesome that you're bringing this up, I'm all for tension and drama. I think you have some vendetta for [Grow KC]. I think you have all have had opportunities to engage with people positively, and you're not putting your feet underneath that table."

Here, critiques of structural inequalities are read as personal attacks, requests for white foodies to acknowledge privilege are read as denigrations of an individual's hard work, and demands for change are met with allegations of incivility. The audience member's response is illustrative of Dr. Martin Luther King Jr.'s famous statements about the danger of the "white moderate" who stands in the way of racial justice by being "more devoted to 'order' than to justice" and who is unwilling to recognize that activists are not creators of "tension and drama" but rather "bring to the surface the hidden tension that is already alive" (King 1963).

The panel and its aftermath offer useful insight into how those with power and influence react when their whiteness, and structural white privilege, is challenged. In the months following the event, several foodie nonprofits— Grow KC, Our Daily Bread, and Healthy Communities KC—responded to these critiques by increasing institutional diversity on their boards of directors and in promotional advertising and fundraising events. Paradoxically, these kinds of efforts end up reinforcing racial hierarchies and "otherizing" practices (cf. Dominguez 1994), as groups of color are categorized and ordered. Often, singular representatives are chosen to represent diverse, heterogenous groups, and the underlying power structure of the organization is fundamentally unchanged (see also Kolavalli 2020).

Increased tokenism of farmers of color has followed this event as well; at several charity fundraisers, Black farmers have been called on stage in front of white donors to "share their struggle." Events, such as one hosted by a foodie-led nonprofit at a local distillery, feature "farm fresh tamales, Kansas City soul food, and locally-sourced Choctaw corn mush," and advertisements proclaim, "All it takes to discover Kansas City's diverse cultures and rich food traditions is finding a dinner table!" These acts draw on the idea that increased *visibility* of Black and brown KC residents is all it takes to create equity. As Sara Ahmed (2012) has argued, this performativity of "diversity" work often serves to obscure institutional racism. Surface level representational diversity is not socially transformative; it does nothing to disrupt extant hierarchies of privilege.

Several foodies have approached me, following the panel, with requests for help diversifying their organizations—requests that illustrate, combined with this increased tokenism, a profound misunderstanding of the issues presented by the panelists during "Critical Conversations on KC's Local Food Scene." Foodies have asked me to provide feedback on their websites, the language their organizations use, and to offer insight on why more food insecure people of color do not attend opportunities they host for collaboration and feedback. Such requests, well-meant, miss the point: instead of asking how to better include people at the table, the question should be—why are we discussing this specific issue at the table in the first place? Rather than using community feedback to redefine their goals and projects, foodies have asked: how do we get you to support the areas of focus we have already identified?

This is perhaps most evident in the 2018 bankruptcy of a local foodie-led business, a mobile grocery store. At a working group meeting hosted by Healthy Communities KC, the grocery store's founder spoke about the failure of her business, a truck filled with groceries that she parked at various spots throughout the city each week. "We've just gotta teach people to shop with us," she said. "You know, it's like people have their routines and however inconvenient they are they don't want to change them—even if they have to take this bus and transfer to that bus line, or whatever, it's their routine and they don't want to change it. People are like 'I already have my shopping habits.' Well we just need to teach people how to shop with us."

Comments shared with me by food-insecure Feast! participants would indicate that shoppers choose to shop elsewhere because of the mobile grocer's high prices and low variety. But rather than asking why low-income, food-insecure customers would rather take a more inconvenient route to purchase groceries than shop at her truck, the foodie places the onus of blame on them: they do not know how to shop; we need to teach them to shop with us.

The panel conversation, and its aftermath, illustrates some of the challenges we face when thinking about how to dismantle white privilege within green urban development. White structural privilege is not merely a relational problem and cannot be addressed through the techniques outlined above: nominally diversifying organizations; celebrating ethnic others in print materials; and tweaking website language. A true accounting of how whiteness and green urban development intersect requires us to critically interrogate the power structures that shape whose voices have the power to impact city space.

Conclusions and Policy Recommendations

When local and national news sources celebrate the rise of green urban development projects in Kansas City for promoting food security, improving the health and quality of city life, and creating "dynamic aesthetically pleasing cityscapes" (Crupper 2008), they ignore the historical contributions—and exploitations—of minority groups in urban food production. So-called food deserts in Kansas City have long been occupied by ecologically resourceful urban residents, who have contributed in myriad ways to urban greenspace: cultivating hog farms in Kansas City's marshy swamps; tending, harvesting, and distributing products from urban fruit and nut trees; making use of storm water runoff to tend urban kitchen gardens; and hunting and selling urban game meat when racially excluded from conventional food distribution markets.

In Kansas City, urban policy mediators, such as "foodies," who develop green infrastructure, are not informed by this history. They draw on misunderstandings of urban space that ignore the Black laborers who built city infrastructure and were pushed out of desirable real estate; that see poverty-related illnesses as a result of ignorance, undereducation, and poorly spent food dollars; and that contend that urban disinvestment is the result of people simply not caring for their environment. The foodie lens suggests urban food production and distribution as a solution to these problems: grow food in formerly occupied lots that purposeful racialized development turned into vacancy; "teach" Black urban residents how to cook food that is "good" for them; invest in urban orchards to make people want to invest in their communities again. Massive funding and energy are mobilized to support these seemingly innocuous solutions to major urban problems. It is easier, and more profitable, for all parties involved to imagine that urban orchards will address urban poverty than to question and work to address racialized violence enacted through the police state, real estate industry, and global urban growth machine.

It matters that those in charge of urban development—an increasingly broad group, as welfare rollback makes space for third-sector governance—are held accountable to our violent history of racialized violence and settler colonialism. In this book, I have not attempted to make a case for whether or not these policies are purposefully or inadvertently harmful. Arguably, intent is irrelevant—what matters is holding our policy makers accountable to outcomes of their actions. Policy makers should be held accountable to, and encouraged to act on, the fact that the history of urban space they draw on was constructed and informed entirely by white voices. Policy makers should be held accountable to the histories, and current, racial violence that is enacted in U.S. cities. Holding our policy makers accountable to these facts could be the difference between policy that describes "blight" as a tool the state has used to displace populations and extract value from land, and policy that describes "blight" as an aesthetic problem, a way to pinpoint an area of the city that needs more trees. This accountability matters to low-income people of color—who wish not only to have their histories acknowledged but to have a voice in decision-making processes for urban development.

Green urban development projects today in Kansas City are predicated on white settler colonial understandings of "productive" land use and vacancy. These understandings primarily see value in land when Black and brown residents are removed from it, displacements that are naturalized with neoliberal discourse about productive investment and capital accumulation (see also Stoval and Hill 2016). This process—the erasure of subaltern subjectivities, stories, and land—should be theorized as spatial colonization with the goal of profit (cf. McKitrrick 2006; 2011). This book illustrated how actors in green urban development profit from this erasure of landed history, in promoting and drawing on an apolitical understanding of urban space.

The decision to utilize urban food production and distribution as a chief means of addressing food insecurity and urban vacancy was never a ballot measure. East Side residents were never given the opportunity to tell policy makers whether or not they approved of this use of urban space, or to voice feedback on whether or not this method of improving food security would work for them. No one voted Nancy, David, or any other foodie into office, yet these individuals are effectively involved in urban governance and in utilizing urban food projects as a key mechanism of welfare distribution. Neoliberal welfare rollback and the space it creates for third-sector governance is dangerous precisely because seemingly apolitical means of shaping city space—such as urban greening—are allowed to take hold, to serve the interests of an elite few, without oversight or research into their effects. For instance, the fact that hunger has risen, concurrently, with the rise of urban food production and distribution projects on the East Side of Kansas City should concern policy makers. But foodie insistence on the efficacy and necessity of urban food production, combined with national public and private support for green urban development, masks these programmatic failures.

Structural whiteness and white privilege upholds urban food projects with important effects on not just welfare provisioning but also on racialized urban economies. In Kansas City, white public space is created through green urban development projects and has racialized implications for who can participate in (re)development plans for city space and city economy. Small-scale urban food production is a significant, meaningful practice for many foodies because it addresses capitalist alienation from labor; by hyper-focusing on the methods of production, the essence and labor of the "maker" is imbued in the product and provides it with value (Gagne 2011; Paxson 2012). This economic reenvisioning does not exist in a color-blind vacuum. In fact, racialized and class-based understandings about the worth of a product's "maker" might be even more pronounced in a local-food economy. Using urban food production to address urban disinvestment then, becomes a highly racialized affair in which the raced and classed positionality of urban food producers has profound implications for their success in the green economy. While organizations like Grow KC herald the diversity of the local food movement and prominently display photos of Black and brown growers on their advertisements and grant applications, growers of color in Kansas City consistently make less than white growers. Several Black growers in KC have told me they have lost money during farmers market days, as they made so few sales, yet their presence at the market is celebrated and capitalized on by white foodie-led organizations as an indicator of diversity and inclusivity.

Those subjected to white public space in Kansas city's emerging green infrastructure creatively maneuver to make this city agenda work in their favor. Neighborhood councils strategically use the enforced language of green urban development to demonstrate urban citizenship and acquire urgently needed support. Myriad marginalized actors in Kansas City undertake the work of disrupting white public space and asserting alternate, corrected, histories of urban space—this is evident in the way Feast! participants educate their instructors about poverty and racialized urban history, and in the work of Black urban farmers, who remind Kansas Citians that they taught America how to farm. I shared these moments not in order to blindly celebrate human agency (Abu-Lughod 1990), but rather as illustrative of how marginalized urban residents can make bad policies work for them—as a diagnostic of how power works and is navigated.

By discussing and critiquing white public space in urban greening initiatives I do not mean to disregard the benefits urban residents garner from urban food production, distribution, and consumption. Many people I spoke with in Kansas City found working in their gardens, selling occasionally at farmers markets, and eating local, fresh food to be incredibly fulfilling activities. Urban garden space made available to low-income people of color, via Kansas City Grower's Club, provided a space for some—who were unable to afford mental healthcare—to practice mindfulness and spend time in nature. These opportunities are rare in segregated city space that limits the availability of greenspace in low-income communities (Heynen 2003). For others, gardening in a community garden was simply pleasurable because it allowed them to carry on family traditions of growing food. It allowed some growers to connect with religious traditions and mandates, such as calls to agrarianism within the Nation of Islam, and to enact political commitments, like the statement made by growing cotton and the importance of food production for some Black Nationalist farmers in Kansas City. The Troost Co-op's proposed urban gardens are a source of pride for many of those involved in it; and Black urban residents who run charity programs that use urban gardens to provide for the hungry find their work to be locally important and meaningful. For these reasons, it would be inaccurate to paint any binary conception or understanding of "good" and "bad" urban food projects. Urban residents can find value in some aspects of urban food projects that in other ways, such as green gentrification, might inflict violence on urban space.

What I do mean to suggest is that urban food projects do not function as adequate or useful long-term measures against food insecurity, and that when used as a key component of green urban development infrastructures they further racialized urban inequality. Greenspace, available for community decision-making and use, is a necessary component of cities—but it must be created with racial and class-based equity in mind. As scholars of green gentrification have argued, sustainable urban development can be enacted, but practitioners must "hardwire social equity into the design of a project" and institute policy mechanisms that limit speculative investment (Curran and Hamilton 2018, 228). Urban development cannot be enacted equitably through the use of race-avoidant discourse (Bonilla-Silva 2006). Racial inequities need to be acknowledged and placed at the forefront of urban policy.

Positive efforts to address food insecurity in Kansas City should be supported but should be accompanied by attempts to provide a livable wage to urban residents. Healthy Communities KC occasionally undertakes the work of lobbying for and supporting bills that would better the lives of those experiencing hunger—such as those which would expand the Kansas TANF safety net, decrease the Kansas food sales tax from 7 to 5.5 percent, and offer income tax credits to incentivize grocery store development in food deserts. This work—which importantly understands the value of safety net programs in the lives of the urban poor—should be expanded. Activists, who advocate for the states' responsibility in providing for the poor, often run up against national-level conservatism and neoliberal pushback. For example, Kansas City, in 2017, passed a voter-approved measure to raise the minimum wage to $10, and eventually $15, dollars an hour. Missouri House Bill 1194, however, overturned this decision and ruled that cities cannot force businesses to offer more than $7.70 an hour to low-wage laborers—a move that resonates nationally, as tens of other states have overturned local voters' decisions to provide livable wages. While social movements to raise the minimum wage and move toward a living wage are relatively strong in Kansas City—the Fight for $15, for example, has a long local history of activism—foodies largely stand apart from this discourse supporting a living wage. Rather than falling back on neoliberal strategies of self-help to combat food insecurity, foodie-organizations involved in urban development could support Fight for $15 and other efforts of those who are vocal against the right of conservative state governments to roll back local rights. It is not naive to think that foodie support of such issues could result in change. In Kansas City, third-sector foodie organizations operate as an effective arm of city government. Foodies devote considerable time, energy, and discourse in support of urban food projects, with the result that they have been incorporated into local development schemes; similar support, lent to the cause of a livable wage, could result in meaningful outcomes (see, for example, Sbicca 2015).

Radical reenvisionings of food charity schemes are possible. As I argued in chapter 4, cash transfer programs are significantly cheaper, easier to administer, and offer the same or better results in terms of health outcomes than paternalistic foodie nutrition education courses (cf. Hidrobo et al. 2014; Cunha 2014). The research I undertook in Kansas City indicated that urban gardens do not significantly improve food security; promoting them as if they do is inaccurate and ineffective urban policy. While food charity services are important stopgap measures in the lives of the urban poor, paternalistic decision making about what foods they receive adds another level of unnecessary oversight on the diets of the food insecure, who are already surveilled and constrained by federal welfare programs. As studies show, cash transfer recipients often spend food dollars on "healthy" food choices and on improving the diets of their children (cf. Peas-Sousa et al. 2010). Envisioning a city in which food charity takes the form of strings-free cash transfer, with potential urban garden space and infrastructure offered to those who want it, paints a picture of a more just urban environment.

Importantly, Kansas City could institute greater oversight and accountability on measures such as the Urban Agriculture Zone. If third-sector actors are going to be utilized as an extension of the state, local governments can institute community advisory councils and other increased accountability measures—an important measure, as nationally, at the federal level, accountability and transparency are decreasing drastically. Local actions such as these can be powerful criticisms against national trends toward privatization, concentrated monopolies of wealth, and decreased state accountability to the public. Urban Agriculture Zone recipients receive tax breaks for providing jobs and urban food security. They should be required to document these contributions. The UAZ advisory commission, which currently consists solely of foodies, should include neighborhood residents of the proposed development site. Furthermore, UAZ's should be required to create more than one job—UAZ investors could even be encouraged to offer higher than minimum wage for the labor opportunities they create. If UAZ recipients purport to provide food to food-insecure residents, their efforts to do so should be documented. Sliding scale food fees could make it possible for land and capital-divested urban residents to afford the food produced in their neighborhoods, meaning that in small measure, the value from their land would not be completely extracted. By increasing oversight in these ways, city officials could combat speculative investment in the guise of "community" building, with the ultimate outcome of increased involvement and commitment of oft-marginalized urban citizens in civic government.

City residents could petition the local government to instate rent/and or property tax controls, which would act as a measure against eco-gentrification. Rent control, circuit breaker programs, assessment limits, and property tax referrals are all tools that would allow low-income neighborhood residents some measure of control as urban (re)development works to price them out of their homes. These are measures unlikely to be implemented without citizen pressure—as this book has illustrated, rising rents and property values, in previously devalued Black neighborhoods, are incredibly valuable for city governments. The increasing unaffordability of the East Side—as speculative development has led to skyrocketing property values—illustrates the importance of these measures.

One step forward that would potentially increase urban residents' control of city space is city and nonprofit adoption of the community land trust model. Community Land Trusts can take many forms—state or third-sector led—and ensure that low-income community member needs are accounted for through the promotion and creation of affordable housing, often alongside the creation of community gardens and greenspace. Civil rights leaders introduced community land trusts, as a model, to the United States in the 1960s (Davis 2014). Envisioned as a way to assist Black share croppers, resist the eviction and discrimination against Black southerners who fought for civil rights and to provide high quality affordable housing, community land trusts began with the purchase of thousands of acres of land in Georgia and have been copied in small diverse models throughout the country (Davis 2014). Other case studies (notably, those situated in Minneapolis) illustrate that this process can result in both sustainable development and affordable housing (cf. Trudeau 2018). Land Trusts can take myriad forms—from a nonprofit urban land trust in Chicago that manages urban land and farming infrastructure for low-income urban residents, to a defunct privately held land-trust in Kansas City's Vine Street corridor that has been locally disparaged for misleading urban residents.

Land Trusts would still require great amounts of oversight and continual reassessment of whose voices are being heard, who constitutes the "community" of advisors, and whose needs are being represented and addressed. Rose Hill Neighborhood Council, for example, operates somewhat like a land trust but could be more effective with more comprehensive neighborhood involvement. In Kansas City, a community land trust with broad resident participation could have a say in what urban agricultural projects are started in their neighborhoods and could ensure that all urban development accompanies the creation of affordable housing, so that agricultural projects enhance urban space, rather than displace urban residents. Thinking about urban development through the lens of community land trusts helps us re-envision the process of urban decision making and expands the boundaries of who is and is not included in plans for city space.

In many ways, these suggestions for equitable "green" development are applicable to other mid-size cities.[1] An increasing number of cities across the United States—including but not limited to Detroit, where racialized green discourse has been extensively researched and theorized—are adopting green urban infrastructure and urban agriculture zoning ordinances similar to those in Kansas City. In some of these cities, proactive community organizers have been effective in advocating for equitable measures as green urban policy is implemented. In St. Louis, for example, a coalition of nonprofit leaders and community members organized to ensure that community voices were represented in city development of an urban agriculture zone advisory board (personal communication). As a result, a pilot urban agriculture program spearheaded by the Missouri Coalition for the Environment ensured that "previous engagement in a neighborhood" is a prerequisite for anyone seeking to purchase a vacant lot to farm (Lippman 2020), an important measure against green gentrification.

In other cities, similar inequities to those we see in Kansas City are playing out. Cincinnati, for example, offers urban agriculture mini-grants for growers utilizing the city's Vacant Lot Reutilization Program and is currently working on expanding this program to "invest in ways to develop blighted properties" with urban farming (Kahle 2018). In Milwaukee—currently the most segregated metropolitan area in the United States and site of so much police violence that it is statistically one of the most dangerous cities for African Americans to live in—the current urban-ag proponent city council is addressing urban disinvestment through an urban orchard program and policies that make vacant land more accessible to urban farmers (Mazur 2017). Minneapolis has instituted various urban agriculture zoning incentives over the past decade, with a city urban agriculture plan that promises municipal prioritization of local food production in urban development projects. In all of these highly segregated rust-belt cities, similar racialized discourse to that in Kansas City surrounds urban greening efforts—regarding Milwaukee, a CivilEats article proclaims, "The city is taking on hunger, poverty, and blight through a vibrant network of urban ag efforts" (Mazur 2017). A common thread in these initiatives, across geographic contexts, is that they are taking place in cities where third-sector entities play significant roles in urban welfare provision. And, similarly to the KC context, few of these cities are measuring the impact of these public/private partnerships in concrete ways—Tim McCollow, director of HOME Gr/own Milwaukee (a city initiative that encourages urban food production as a means of addressing food insecurity and obesity) stated, regarding project outcomes, that they are "too busy doing to measure" (Mazur 2017). As urban greening, via urban agriculture incentivization, takes hold across U.S. cities, it is important to pay keen attention to the ways these programs function, in comparison to the discourse that animates them. My contention in this book has been that often, foodie enthusiasm for these solutions to urban disinvestment has resulted in policy that accepts green urban development as an unequivocal good. Uncritical implementation of land-use policy that prioritizes urban food production is not innocuous, or harmless—without purposeful attention to racial equity in policy planning and implementation, it actively contributes to making urban space unaffordable and inhospitable to low-income people of color and actively enmeshes actors involved in "green" urban development in processes of settler colonialism.

Ultimately, however, even my policy suggestions here are myopic—a constrained version of the politics of the possible. Why? Because my perspective, alone, is not enough. No individual's perspective, alone, is enough to envision the possibilities of what green, sustainable, equitable and just cities would look like. Leah Penniman, farmer and food sovereignty activist, began her book *Farming While Black* (2018, 10) with the following: "As a multiracial, light-skinned, raised-rural, northeastern, college-educated, cisgender, able-bodied, Jewish-Vodun-practicing biological mother who grew up working class, this author will invariably introduce bias into the text and invisibilize crucial experiences of members of our Black farming community."

Likewise, the identities I hold, the background I've experienced, fundamentally shape how I traverse the city and inform and constrain the recommendations for change I make. As someone who is white-passing, I had a unique opportunity to bear witness to a lot of the insidious ways whiteness operates in private spaces. But, my background and perspective, as Leah Penniman notes, have invariably invisiblized some experiences, subdued some voices, and highlighted some pathways over others. For example, as someone formally educated it's probably no surprise my suggestions for green urban development reform are primarily suggestions for policy change, rather than collective grassroots action.

The real work of equitable development comes through conflict, connection, and the work of actively seeking out and listening to perspectives unlike one's own. Recent scholar/activist coalitions and engagement are good examples of this in practice (cf. Hammelman et al. 2020; Levkoe et al. 2020).

These participatory engagements, which work to develop inclusive demo-cratic decision-making into food policy councils, are difficult to establish and maintain, but they show promise in creating systems that are more responsive to a diversity of urban residents (cf. Sbicca et al 2020; Gilbert and Williams 2020).

My contention in this book has been that uncritical adoption of "green" policy is not harmless—in Kansas City, it has had far-reaching effects. It cre-ates urban spaces and economies that are safe for some and unsafe for oth-ers; profitable for some and out of reach for others. That's because the world-view through which green urban policy is developed is often informed solely by white ideologies, voices, and histories. This case study of Kansas City has il-lustrated that (often well-intentioned progressives) individuals are instrumen-tal in creating and (re)enforcing whiteness in our cities, which has had deeply violent impacts on communities of color. I've argued that our everyday ideol-ogies, even in seemingly policy-distant social movements such as urban agri-culture and local food, matter. The process of constructing a dominant story about a city is both individual and collective; collectively, ideologies support certain policy agendas over others. They allow some of us to lay claim to our city space; to make our presence here visible, while others are invisible. How would we imagine a different city—and a different urban sustainability? We ask: Whose mark is legible on our cities? Whose voices informed our under-standings of what an ideal city looks like? Who stands to profit in that space? Who feels safe there? Whose perspectives are absent? All local foodies know that in a garden, diversity breeds plants that are strong, resilient, healthy, beau-tiful. It's not too much of a leap to think that listening to these diverse perspec-tives can do the same for our cities.

NOTES

1. Engaged anthropologists have highlighted the messy work of collaboration in field-work (Anderson-Lazo 2016; Rose Johnson 2010; Low and Merry 2010). While conducting the research that informs this book, I engaged in partnerships and collaboration with multitudes of research participants, in sometimes shared, and often times contradictory, objectives—in these partnerships, congruence existed in that there were often shared questions about how culture and power operate (Anderson-Lazo 2016). Partnerships and engaged anthropological research took form in ways such as the sharing of research findings with area nonprofits, helping friends write grants and garner city support, and driving friends experiencing "food insecurity" to the grocery store.

2. Reading and listening to the work of Michael Twitty, Psyche Williams-Forson, and Andi Murphy (host of Toasted Sister podcast) is a good place to start.

3. Following a number of other critical race scholars, I capitalize Black (in reference to Blackness as a cultural identification, rather than a phenotypic marker) and refer to white people, whiteness, and brown people in lowercase. Interview participants who identified as white were referencing phenotypic difference, rather than cultural identification; and whiteness, as used in this manuscript references a structural system rather than an ethnic group. Similarly, those who refer to themselves as "brown" are often making a tongue-in-cheek reference to phenotypic difference and are not denoting a cultural identification.

CHAPTER 1. Green Urbicide

1. I avoid using the term "slave" in historical discussions because many Black Kansas Citians I interviewed avoided using the term themselves and found other ways to refer to slavery. This, I was told, is because they did not want this enforced role to define their historical narratives. While certainly not all Black Kansas City residents would agree with this position, I avoid using the term "slave" in order to respect those who voiced their aversion to the term. Additionally, the use of the term "slave" erases the role of whiteness; for that reason, I follow Battle-Baptiste's (2011) terminology of "captive African," or "enslaved person" (as some U.S. historians have argued for, cf. Miller 2012; Gal-

tung 1969) to maintain focus and emphasis on the structural violence inherent to this role.

2. Public discourse against the development of this unaffordable housing is strong; a recent panel discussion—which included prominent KC landlords—on the high rate of evictions and unaffordable housing in the urban core drew around three hundred urban residents, many of whom used the question-and-answer portion of the event to publicly shame and heckle the developers.

CHAPTER 2. Creating White Public Space in the Urban Food System

1. Although, of course, focusing on common themes within foodie language does mean we miss the opportunity to fully explore the nuance and difference in white voices. This sort of linguistic analysis is beyond the scope of this book; Suzuki (2017), Sbicca (2015), and Hartigan (2005), to name a few, have explored this topic well.

CHAPTER 4. "Don't You Know You Live in a Food Desert?"

1. Once disassociated from Black liberation, the Black Panthers' free breakfast for children program would provide the model for all federally funded school breakfast programs nationally, and within Kansas City, today (Heynen 2009).

2. See Jones 2019 for discussion of how a narrow focus on nutrition and "healthy food access" elides the multifaceted meaning corner stores can hold in Black and brown communities.

3. I am aligned with a body of critical scholarship that argues that concerns over body size are rooted in dubious science (cf. Julier 2008; Kirkland 2010; Brown 2016). Further, terminology like "obese" and "overweight" can be harmful in that they help perpetuate linkages between body size and health and contribute to weight stigma. I reproduce those words here, however, as quotes from Feast! curriculum.

CHAPTER 5. "We Know We're Being Treated Like Tokens"

1. The Trump administration's response to the coronavirus pandemic exacerbated these existing inequities in U.S. agriculture. Unsurprisingly, Black farmers received only $20.8 million of the $26 billion in aid distributed via the Coronavirus Food Assistance Program. Ninety-nine percent of this funding went to white farmers (Reiley 2021, see also Alkon et al 2020).

2. This apprenticeship model, and the inequities it can engender, is not unique to Kansas City. Nationwide, the dominant model of farm internships privileges white, middle-class young people and creates barriers for racialized people (cf. Levkoe and Offeh-Gyimah 2019).

CHAPTER 6. "Apparently We Grow Culturally Appropriate Food in That"

1. Conversely, other movements, such as the Parks Movement, functioned in different ways: one goal of this national movement during the nineteenth century was to pro-

vide space for immigrants and lower-class U.S. citizens to assimilate, by rubbing shoulders with the wealthy (Cranz 1982).

CHAPTER 8. Imagining Another Way to Live in the City

1. Other scholars have analyzed green urban development as it unfolds in larger
U.S. cities (cf. Curran and Hamilton 2012; Reynolds 2014; Reynolds and Cohen 2016;
Checker 2011).

BIBLIOGRAPHY

Abujidi, Nurhan. 2014. *Urbicide in Palestine: Space of Oppression and Resilience.* New York: Routledge.

Abu-Lughod, Lila. 1990. "The Romance of Resistance: Tracing Transformations of Power through Bedouin Women." *American Ethnologist* 17, no. 1: 41–55.

Aistara, Guntra A. 2011. "Seeds of Kin, Kin of Seeds: The Commodification of Organic Seeds and Social Relations in Costa Rica and Latvia." *Ethnography* 12, no. 4: 490–517.

Albritton, Robert. 2013. "Between Obesity and Hunger: The Capitalist Food Industry." In *Food and Culture: A Reader,* edited by Carol Counihan and Penny Van Esterick, 342–54. New York: Routledge.

Alkon, Alison Hope. 2012. *Black, White, and Green: Farmer's Markets, Race, and the Green Economy.* Athens: University of Georgia Press.

———. 2013. "The Socio-Nature of Local Organic Food." *Antipode* 45, no. 3: 663–80.

———. 2018a. "Entrepreneurship as Activism? Resisting Gentrification in Oakland California." *Journal of Business Management* 58, no. 3: 279–90.

———. 2018b. "Looking Back to Look Forward." *Local Environment* 23, no. 11: 1090–93.

Alkon, Alison Hope, and Julian Agyeman. 2011. "Introduction: The Food Movement as Polyculture." In *Cultivating Food Justice: Race, Class, and Sustainability,* edited by Alison Hope Alkon and Julian Agyeman. Cambridge: MIT Press.

Alkon, Alison Hope, Sarah Bowen, Yuki Kato, and Kara Alexis Young. 2020. "Unequally Vulnerable: A Food Justice Approach to Racial Disparities in COVID-19 Cases." *Agriculture and Human Values* 37: 535–36.

Alkon, Alison Hope, and Josh Cadji. 2018. "Sowing Seeds of Displacement: Gentrification and Food Justice in Oakland, CA." *International Journal of Urban and Regional Research:* 1–16.

Alkon, Alison Hope, Yuki Kato, and Joshua Sbicca, eds. 2020. *A Recipe for Gentrification: Food, Power, and Resistance in the City.* New York: New York University Press.

Alkon, Alison Hope, and Christie Grace McCullen. 2011. "Whiteness and Farmers Markets: Performances, Perpetuations . . . Contestations?" *Antipode* 43, no. 4: 937–59.

Alkon, Alison Hope, Marisol Cortez, and Julie Sze. 2013. "What Is in a Name? Language, Framing and Environmental Justice Activism in California's Central Valley." *Local Environment* 18, no. 10: 1167–83.

Alkon, Alison Hope, and Teresa Marie Mares. 2012. "Food Sovereignty in US Food Movements: Radical Visions and Neoliberal Constraints." *Agriculture and Human Values* 29, no. 3: 347–59.

Alkon, Alison Hope, Daniel Block, Kelly Moore, Catherine Gillis, Nicole DiNuccio, and Noel Chavez. 2013. "Foodways of the Urban Poor." *Geoforum* 48: 126–35.

Anderson, Kay J. 1987. "The Idea of Chinatown: The Power of Place and Institutional Practice in the Making of a Racial Category." *Annals of the Association of American Geographers* 77, no. 4: 580–98.

Anderson-Lazo, A. L. 2016. "Ethnography as Aprendizaje: Growing and Using Collaborative Knowledge with the People's Produce Project in San Diego." In *The Routledge Companion to Contemporary Anthropology*, edited by Simon Coleman, Susan Brin Hyatt, and Ann Kingsolver, 475–94. London: Routledge.

Austin, Brad. 2017. "The Prudhomme Farm." *Flatland: KCPT's Digital Magazine*. https://www.flatlandkc.org/people-places/founders-prudhomme-farm/.

Bachaud, Nicole. 2022. "Black Mortgage Applicants Denied 84% More Often than White Borrowers." *Zillow Research*. https://www.zillow.com/research/black-denial-rate-hmda-2020-30510/.

Baker, Lee D. 2010. *Anthropology and the Racial Politics of Culture*. Durham: Duke University Press.

Balko, Radley. 2013. *Rise of the Warrior Cop: The Militarization of America's Police Forces*. New York: PublicAffairs.

Baptist, Edward E. 2014 *The Half Has Never Been Told: Slavery and the Making of American Capitalism*. New York: Basic Books.

Barnes, Sandra L. 2005. *The Cost of Being Poor: A Comparative Study of Life in Poor Urban Neighborhoods in Gary, Indiana*. Albany, Ind.: State University of New York Press.

Battle-Baptiste, Whitney. 2011. *Black Feminist Archaeology*. Walnut Creek, Calif.: Left Coast.

Bayat, Asef. 2012. "Politics in the City-Inside-Out." *City & Society* 24, no. 2: 110–28.

Becker, Geoffrey S. 1993. "Food Marketing in the Inner City: Trends and Options." *Congressional Research Service Report for Congress 92-731 ENR*. Washington, D.C.: U.S. Library of Congress.

Bedore, Melanie. 2014. "Food Desertification: Situating Choice and Class Relations within an Urban Political Economy of Declining Food Access." *Studies in Social Justice* 8, no. 2: 207–28.

Benson, Peter. 2012. *Tobacco Capitalism: Growers, Migrant Workers, and the Changing Face of a Global Industry*. Princeton: Princeton University Press.

Berman, Marshall. 1987. "Among the Ruins," *New Internationalist* 178: 8–9.

Berube, Alan. 2014. "All Cities Are Not Created Unequal." *Brookings Institute Report*. https://www.brookings.edu/research/all-cities-are-not-created-unequal/.

Bielo, James S. 2013. "Promises of Place: A Future of Comparative U.S. Ethnography." *North American Dialogue* 16: 1–11.

Black, William R. 2018. "How Watermelons Became Black: Emancipation and the Origins of a Racist Trope." *Journal of the Civil War Era* 8, no. 1: 64–86.

Bonilla-Silva, Eduardo. 2006. *Racism without Racists: Color-Blind Racism and the Persistence of Racial Inequality in America*. Oxford: Rowman & Littlefield.

Bourdieu, Pierre. 1984. *Distinction: A Social Critique of the Judgement of Taste*. Oxford: Routledge.

Boytte, Michael, and Randi Boyette. 2013. *Let It Burn: MOVE, the Philadelphia Police Department, and the Confrontation That Changed a City*. San Diego: Quadrant.

Bradley, Katharine, and Ryan E. Galt. 2014. "Practicing Food Justice at Dig Deep Farms & Produce, East Bay Area, California: Self-Determination as a Guiding Value and Intersections with Foodie Logics." *Local Environment* 19, no. 2: 172–86.

Brahinsky, Rachel, Jade Sasser, and Laura-Anne Minkoff-Zern. 2014. "Race, Space, and Nature: An Introduction and Critique." *Antipode* 46, no. 5: 1135–52.

Brodkin, Karen, Sandra Morgen, and Janis Hutchinson. 2011. "Anthropology as White Public Space?" *American Anthropologist* 113, no. 4: 545–56.

Brown, Harriet. 2016. *Body of Truth: How Science, History, and Culture Drive Our Obsession with Weight—And What We Can Do About It*. Boston: Da Capo.

Brown, Jacqueline Nassy. 2000. "Enslaving History: Narratives on Local Whiteness in a Black Atlantic Port." *American Ethnologist* 27, no. 2: 340–70.

Bubinas, Kathleen. 2011. "Farmers Markets in the Post-Industrial City" 23, no. 2: 154–72.

Burgess, Ernest. 1925. "The Growth of the City: An Introduction to the Research Project." In *The City*, edited by Robert E. Park, Ernest W. Burgess, and Roderick D. Mackenzie, 47–62. Chicago: University of Chicago Press.

Burton, Orisanmi. 2015. "To Protect and Serve Whiteness." *North American Dialogue* 18, no. 2: 38–50.

Bush, Melanie E. L. 2011. *Everyday Forms of Whiteness: Understanding Race in a "Post-Racial" World*. Langham, Md.: Rowman & Littlefield.

Cadji, Josh, and Alison Hope Alkon. 2015. "'One Day, the White People Are Going to Want These Houses Again': Understanding Gentrification through the North Oakland Farmers Market." In *Incomplete Streets: Processes, Practices, and Possibilities*, edited by Stephen Zavestoski and Julian Agyeman, 154–75. London: Routledge.

Caldeira, Teresa. 2005. "Fortified Enclaves: The New Urban Segregation." In *Theorizing the City: The New Urban Anthropology Reader*, edited by Setha M. Low, 83–107. London: Rutgers University Press.

Campbell, Matt. 2014. "History of the Stockyards Is Saved from the Trash and Now on Display." *Kansas City Star*, April 29, 2014.

Carney, Megan. 2014. "'La Lucha Diaria': Migrant Women in the Fight for Healthy Food." In *Women Redefining the Experience of Food Insecurity: Life off the Edge of the Table*, edited by Janet Page Reeves. Lanham, Md.: Lexington.

Carter, Robert T. 1997. "Is White a Race? Expressions of White Racial Identity." In *Off White: Readings on Race, Power, and Society*, edited by Michelle Fine, Lois Weis, Linda Powell, and L. Mun Wong. New York: Routledge.

Charity Navigator. 2010. "The Most Charity-Conscious Cities in America." *Charity Navigator*, June 1, 2010.

Checker, Melissa. 2011. "Wiped Out by the 'Greenwave': Environmental Gentrification and the Paradoxical Politics of Urban Sustainability." *City and Society* 23, no. 2: 210–29.

Chin, Elizabeth. 2006. "Confessions of a Negrophile." *Transforming Anthropology* 14, no. 1: 44–52.

Clendenning, Jessica, Wolfram H. Dressler, and Carol Richards. 2015. "Food Justice or Food Sovereignty? Understanding the Rise of Urban Food Movements in the USA." *Agriculture and Human Values* 33, no. 1: 165–77.

Colby, Tanner. 2012. *Some of My Best Friends Are Black: The Strange Story of Integration in America*. New York: Penguin.

Collins, Patricia Hill. 2000. *Black Feminist Thought: Knowledge, Consciousness, and the Politics of Empowerment*. New York: Routledge.

Collins, Patricia Hill. 2009. "Race, Class, and Gender as Categories of Analysis and Connection." In *Inequality and Society: Social Science Perspectives on Social Stratification*, edited by Jeff Manza and Michael Sauder. New York: W. W. Norton.

Collison, Kevin. 2011. "Zhou Brothers Plan to Convert Empty School into A Kansas City Arts Hub." *KCUR*, October 11, 2017.

Connor, Michael. 2005. *The Invention of Terra Nullius: Historical and Legal Fictions on the Foundation of Australia*. Paddington, New South Wales: Macleay.

Corrigan, M. 2011. "Growing What You Eat: Developing Community Gardens in Baltimore, Maryland." *Applied Geography* 31, no. 4: 1232–41.

Crane, Sheila. 2017. "Housing as Battleground: Targeting the City in the Battles of Algiers." *City & Society* 29, no. 1: 187–212.

Cranz, Galen. 1982. *The Politics of Park Design: A History of Urban Parks in America*. Cambridge, Mass.: MIT Press.

Crupper, Carol. 2008. "Urban Farms Open Doors." *GRIT*, January/February issue, 2008.

Cunha, Jesse M. 2014. "Testing Paternalism: Cash Versus In-kind Transfers in Rural Mexico." *American Economic Journal: Applied Economics* 6, no. 2: 195–230.

Curran, Winifred, and Trina Hamilton. 2012. "Just Green Enough: Contesting Environmental Gentrification in Greenpoint, Brooklyn." *Local Environment* 17, no. 9: 1027–42.

Curran, Winifred, and Trina Hamilton, eds. 2018. *Just Green Enough: Urban Development and Environmental Gentrification*. New York: Routledge.

Daniel, Pete. 2013. *Dispossession: Discrimination against African American Farmers in the Age of Civil Rights*. Chapel Hill: University of North Carolina Press.

Davila, Arlene. 2004. *Barrio Dreams: Puerto Ricans, Latinos, and the Neoliberal City*. Berkeley: University of California Press.

Davis, Allison, Gardner, Burleigh B., and Mary R. Gardner. 1941. *Deep South: A Social Anthropological Study of Caste and Class*. Chicago: University of Chicago Press.

Davis, Angela. *Are Prisons Obsolete?* New York: Seven Stories, 2006.

Davis, John Emmeus. *Origins and Evolution of the Community Land Trust in the United States*. Lincoln, Nebr.: Lincoln Institute of Land Policy, 2014.

Davis, Mike. *City of Quartz: Excavating the Future in Los Angeles*. Chicago: Haymarket, 1990.

———. 1986. *Prisoners of the American Dream: Politics and Economy in the History of the US Working Class*. New York: Verso.

De Genova, Nicholas. 2007. "The Stakes of an Anthropology of the United States." *CR: The New Centennial Review* 7, no. 2: 231–77.

DeLind, Laura. 2014. "Where Have All the Houses (Among Other Things) Gone? Some

Critical Reflections on Urban Agriculture." *Renewable Agriculture and Food Systems* 30, no. 1: 3–7.

———. 2011. "Are Local Food and the Local Food Movement Taking Us Where We Want to Go? Or Are We Hitching Our Wagons to the Wrong Stars?" *Agriculture and Human Values* 28, no. 2: 273–83.

de Souza, Rebecca T. 2019. *Feeding the Other: Whiteness, Privilege, and Neoliberal Stigma in Food Pantries.* Cambridge, Mass.: MIT Press.

Dimitri, Carolyn, Lydia Oberholtzer, and Andy Pressman. 2016. "Urban Agriculture: Connecting Producers with Consumers." *British Food Journal* 118, no. 3: 603–17.

Dominguez, Virginia R. 1994. "A Taste for 'the Other': Intellectual Complicity in Racializing Practices." *Current Anthropology* 35, no. 4: 333–48.

———. 1986. *White by Definition: Social Classification in Creole Louisiana.* New Brunswick, N. J.: Rutgers University Press.

Drake, Luke. 2014. "Governmentality in Urban Food Production? Following 'Community' from Intentions to Outcomes." *Urban Geography* 35, no. 2: 37–41.

Drake, St. Clair, and Horace R. Cayton. 1945. *Black Metropolis: A Study of Negro Life in a Northern City.* Chicago: University of Chicago Press.

Dressler, William W. 1993. "Health in the African American Community: Accounting for Health Inequalities." *Medical Anthropology Quarterly* 7, no. 4: 325–45.

Driggs, Frank, and Chuck Haddix. 2005. *Kansas City Jazz: From Ragtime to Bebop—A History.* Oxford: Oxford University Press.

DuBois, W. E. B. 1994. *The Souls of Black Folk.* Mineola, N. Y.: Yale University Press.

DuPuis, E. Melanie. 2002. *Nature's Perfect Food: How Milk Became America's Drink.* New York: New York University Press.

Durington, Matthew. 2009. "Introduction: The Stakes of Whiteness Studies." *Transforming Anthropology* 17, no. 1 (2009): 2–3.

EDCKC. 2015. "Chapter 353 Board Meeting Minutes, March 25, 2015." *Economic Development Corporation of Kansas City.* March 25, 2015. https://s3.amazonaws.com/353 -Minutes/353%20MINUTES%20-%202015.pdf.

———. 2014. "How the Land Clearance for Redevelopment Authority Helps Urban Renewal in Kansas City." *Economic Development Corporation of Kansas City.*

Edgar, Iain R., and Andrew Russell, eds. 1998. *The Anthropology of Welfare.* London: Routledge.

Emerson, Robert M., Rachel I. Fretz, and Linda L. Shaw. 1995. *Writing Ethnographic Fieldnotes.* Chicago: University of Chicago Press.

Feagin, Joe R. 2013. *The White Racial Frame: Centuries of Racial Framing and Counter-Framing.* New York: Routledge.

Ferguson, James. 1990. *The Anti-Politics Machine: "Development," Depoliticization, and Bureaucratic Power in Lesotho.* Cambridge, U.K.: Cambridge University Press.

Fielding-Singh, Priya. 2017. "A Taste of Inequality: Food's Symbolic Value across the Socioeconomic Spectrum." *Sociological Science* 4, no. 17: 424–48.

Finney, Carolyn. 2014. *Black Faces, White Spaces: Reimagining the Relationship of African Americans to the Great Outdoors.* Chapel Hill: University of North Carolina Press.

Fisher, William F. 1997. "Doing Good? The Politics and Antipolitics of NGO Practices." *Annual Review of Anthropology* 26: 439–64.

Fiske, John. 1998. "Surveilling the City: Whiteness, the Black Man and Democratic Total-
itarianism." *Theory, Culture & Society* 15, no. 2: 67–88.

Foucault, Michel. 1977. *Discipline & Punish: The Birth of the Prison.* New York: Random
House.

Fox Gotham, Kevin. 2002. *Race, Real Estate, and Uneven Development: The Kansas City
Experience, 1900–2000.* Albany: State University of New York Press.

Fox Piven, Frances, Joan Acker, Margaret Hallock, and Sandra Morgen, eds. 2002. *Work,
Welfare, and Politics: Confronting Poverty in the Wake of Welfare Reform.* Eugene:
University of Oregon Press.

Frankenberg, Ruth. 1993. *The Social Construction of Whiteness: White Women, Race Matters.* Minneapolis: University of Minnesota Press.

Galeano, Eduardo. 1971. *Open Veins of Latin America.* New York: Monthly Review.

Galtung, Johan. 1969. "Violence, Peace, and Peace Research." *Journal of Peace Research* 6,
no. 3: 167–91.

Ghannam, Farha. 2002. *Remaking the Modern: Space, Relocation, and the Politics of Identity in Global Cairo.* Berkeley: University of California Press.

Ghose, Rina, and Margaret Pettygrove. 2018. "Urban Community Gardens as New
Spaces of Living." In *The Routledge Handbook on Spaces of Urban Politics*, edited
by Kevin Ward, Andrew E. G. Jones, Byron Miller, and David Wilson. New York:
Routledge.

———. 2014. "Urban Community Gardens as Spaces of Citizenship." *Antipode* 46 no. 4:
1092–112.

Gibson, Campbell, and Kay Jung. 2005. "Historical Census Statistics on Population To-
tals by Race, 1790 to 1990, and by Hispanic Origin, 1970–1990, for Large Cities and
Other Urban Places in the United States." *U.S. Census Bureau.*

Gilbert, Jessica L., and Rebekah A. Williams. 2020. "Pathways to Reparations: Land and
Healing through Food Justice." *Human Geography* 13, no. 3: 228–41.

Gillis, Delia C. 2007. *Black America Series: Kansas City.* Charleston, S.C.: Arcadia.

Gilt, Jay. 2010. *The Bourgeois Frontier: French Towns, French Traders, and the American
Expansion.* London: Yale University Press.

Gioielli, Robert. 2015. *Environmental Activism and the Urban Crisis: Baltimore, St. Louis,
Chicago.* Philadelphia: Temple University Press.

Glover, Troy D. 2004. "Social Capital in the Lived Experiences of Community Gardeners." *Leisure Sciences* 26, no. 2: 143–62.

Goode, Judith, and Jeff Maskovsky, eds. 2001. "Introduction." In *The New Poverty Stud-
ies: The Ethnography of Power, Politics, and the Impoverished People in the United
States*, edited by Judith Goode and Jeff Maskovsky. New York: New York University
Press.

Goodling, Erin, Jamaal Green, and Nathan McClintock. 2015. "Uneven Development of
the Sustainable City: Shifting Capital in Portland, Oregon." *Urban Geography* 36, no.
4: 504–27.

Gordon, Colin. 2008. *Mapping Decline: St. Louis and the Fate of the American City.* Philadelphia: University of Pennsylvania Press.

Gould, Kenneth A., and Lewis, Tammy L. 2017. *Green Gentrification: Urban Sustainability and the Struggle for Environmental Justice.* New York: Routledge.

———. 2013. "The Environmental Injustice of Green Gentrification: The Case of Brooklyn's Prospect Park." In *The World in Brooklyn: Gentrification, Immigration, and Ethnic Politics in a Global City*, edited by Judith N. DeSena and Timothy Shortell. Lanham, Md.: Rowman & Littlefield.

Gose, Joe. 2014. "Millennials Going to Kansas City, to Live and Work." *New York Times*, August 19, 2014.

Gotham, Kevin Fox. 2002. *Race, Real Estate, and Uneven Development: The Kansas City Experience, 1900–2000*. Albany: State University of New York Press.

Graham, Stephen. 2004. "Postmortem City: Towards an Urban Geopolitics. *City* 8, no. 2: 165–96.

Greenlee, Cynthia. 2019."On Eating Watermelon in Front of White People: 'I'm not as Free as I Thought.'" *Vox*, August 29, 2019.

Griffin, G. S. 2015. *Racism in Kansas City: A Short History*. Traverse City, Mo.: Chandler Lake.

Gundersen, C., A. Dewey, A. Grumbaugh, M. Kato, and E. Engelhard. 2016a. *Map the Meal Gap 2016: Food Insecurity in Kansas by County*. http://www.feedingamerica .org/hunger-in-america/our-research/map-the-meal-gap/2014/KS_AllCounties _CDs_MMG_2014.pdf.

———. 2016b. *Map the Meal Gap 2016: Food Insecurity in Missouri by County*. http:// www.feedingamerica.org/hunger-in-america/our-research/map-the-meal-gap/2014 /MO_AllCounties_CDs_MMG_2014.pdf.

Guthman, Julie. 2012. "Doing Justice to Bodies? Reflections on Food Justice, Race, and Biology." *Antipode* 46, no. 5: 1153–71.

———. 2011a. "'If They Only Knew': The Unbearable Whiteness of Alternative Food." In *Cultivating Food Justice: Race, Class, and Sustainability*, edited by Alison Hope Alkon and Julian Agyeman. Cambridge, Mass.: MIT Press.

———. 2011b. *Weighing In: Obesity, Food Justice, and the Limits of Capitalism*. Los Angeles: University of California Press.

———. 2009. "Teaching the Politics of Obesity: Insights into Neoliberal Embodiment and Contemporary Biopolitics." *Antipode* 41, no. 5: 1110–33.

———. 2008. "Bringing Good Food to Others: Investigating the Subjects of Alternative Food Practice." *Cultural Geographies* 15, no. 4: 431–47.

———. 2003. "Fast Food/Organic Food: Reflexive Tastes and the Making of 'Yuppie Chow.'" *Social & Cultural Geography* 4, no. 1: 45–58.

Guthman, Julie, and Melanie DuPuis. 2006. "Embodying Neoliberalism: Economy, Culture, and the Politics of Fat." *Environment and Planning D: Society and Space* 24, no. 3: 427–48.

Hacking, Ian. 1991. "How Should We Do the History of Statistics?" In *The Foucault Effect: Studies in Governmentality*, edited by Graham Burchell, Colin Fordon, and Peter Miller. Hemel Hempstead: Harvester Wheatsheaf.

Hallett, Lucius F., and Dave McDermott. 2011. "Quantifying the Extent and Cost of Food Deserts in Lawrence, Kansas, USA." *Applied Geography* 31, no. 4: 1210–15.

Hamilton, Trina, and Winifred Curran. 2013. "From 'Five Angry Women' to 'Kick-Ass Community': Gentrification and Environmental Activism in Brooklyn and Beyond." *Urban Studies* 50, no. 8: 1557–74.

Hammelman, Collen, Charles Z. Levkoe, Julian Agyeman, Sanjay Kharod, Ana Moragues Faus, Elisa Munoz, Jose Oliva, and Amanda Wilson. 2020. "Integrated Food

Systems Governance: Scaling Equitable and Transformative Food Initiatives through Scholar-Activist Engagement." *Journal of Agriculture, Food Systems, and Community Development* 9, no. 2: 71–86.

Harrison, Faye V. 2013. "Racial Profiling, Security, and Human Rights." In *At Close Range: The Curious Case of Trayvon Martin*, edited by Katheryn Russell-Brown. Tampa: University of Florida.

———. "The Persistent Power of 'Race' in the Cultural and Political Economy of Racism." 1995. *Annual Review of Anthropology* 24, no. 1: 47–74.

Harrison, Paul. 2018. *Profane Egyptologists: The Modern Revival of Ancient Egyptian Religion*. New York: Routledge.

Harper, A. Breeze. 2011. "Vegans of Color, Racialized Embodiment, and Problematics of the 'Exotic.'" In *Cultivating Food Justice: Race, Class, and Sustainability*, edited by Alison Hope Alkon and Julian Agyeman. Cambridge, Mass.: MIT Press.

Hartigan, John Jr. 2005. *Odd Tribes: Toward a Cultural Analysis of White People*. Durham, N.C.: Duke University Press.

Harvey, David. 2008. "The Right to the City." *New Left Review* 53: 23–40.

———. 1989. *The Urban Experience*. Baltimore, Md.: Johns Hopkins University Press.

Havard, Cassandra Jones. 2001. "African American Farmers and Fair Lending: Racializing Rural Economic Space." *Stanford Law and Policy Review* 12, no. 2: 333–60.

Hendrickson, Mary K, and Mark Porth. 2012. "Urban Agriculture: Best Practices and Possibilities." *University of Missouri Extension*: 1–52.

Herscher, Andrew. 2020. "The Urbanism of Racial Capitalism: Toward a History of 'Blight.'" *Comparative Studies of South Asia, Africa and the Middle East* 40, no. 1: 57–65.

Heynen, Nik. 2009. "Bending the Bars of Empire from Every Ghetto for Survival: The Black Panther Party's Radical Antihunger Politics of Social Reproduction and Scale." *Annals of the Association of American Geographers* 99, no. 2: 406–22.

———. "The Scalar Production of Injustice within the Urban Forest." *Antipode* 35, no. 5 (2003): 980–98.

Hidrobo, Melissa, Hohn Hoddinott, Amber Peterman, Amy Margolies, and Vanessa Moreira. 2014. "Cash, Food, or Vouchers? Evidence from a Randomized Experiment in Northern Ecuador." *Journal of Development Economics* 107: 144–56.

Hoover, Brandon M. 2013. "White Spaces in Black and Latino Places: Urban Agriculture and Food Sovereignty." *Journal of Agriculture, Food Systems, and Community Development* 3, no. 4: 109–16.

Holston, James. 2009. "Insurgent Citizenship in an Era of Global Peripheries." *City and Society* 21, no. 2: 245–67.

Holston, James, and Arjun Appadurai. 1996. "Cities and Citizenship." *Public Culture* 8, no. 2: 187–204.

hooks, bell. 2009. *Belonging: A Culture of Place*. New York: Routledge.

———. 1981. *Ain't I a Woman: Black Women and Feminism*. New York: Routledge.

Horning, Melissa L., and Jayne A. Fulkerson. 2014. "A Systematic Review on the Affordability of a Healthful Diet for Families in the United States. *Public Health Nursing* 32, no. 1: 68–80.

Horst, Megan, Nathan Mcclintock, and Lesli Hoey. 2017."The Intersection of Planning, Urban Agriculture, and Food Justice: A Review of the Literature." *Journal of the American Planning Association* 83, no. 3: 277–95.

Hurston, Zora Neale. 1937. *Their Eyes Were Watching God*. New York: Harper.

———. 1935. *Mules and Men*. New Jersey: Research & Education Association.

Jackson, John L. 2006. "Gentrification, Globalization, and Georaciality." In *Globalization and Race: Transformations in the Cultural Production of Blackness*. Durham, N.C.: Duke University Press.

Jackson, Andrew S., Kenneth J. Ellis, Brian K. McFarlin, Mary H. Sailors, and Molly S. Bray. 2009. "Body Mass Index Bias in Defining Obesity of Diverse Young Adults: The Training Intervention and Genetics of Exercise Response (TIGER) Study." *British Journal of Nutrition* 102, no. 7: 1084–190.

Janovy, C.J. 2016. "Here's How Kansas City Spent $100 Million at 18th and Vine since 1990." *KCUR*, February 11, 2016.

Johnson, Marilynn S. 2003. *Street Justice: A History of Police Violence in New York City*. Boston: Beacon.

Jones, Naya. 2019. "(Re)Visiting the Corner Store: Black Youth, Gentrification, and Food Sovereignty." In *Race in the Marketplace*, edited by Guillaume D. Johnson, Kevin D. Thomas, Anthony Kwame Harrison, and Sonya A. Grier. London: Palgrave.

Julier, Alice. 2008. "The Political Economy of Obesity: The Fat Pay All." In *Food and Culture: A Reader*, edited by Carole Counihan and Penny Van Esterick. London: Routledge.

Jung, Yuson, and Andrew Newman. 2014. "An Edible Moral Economy in the Motor City: Food Politics and Urban Governance in Detroit." *Gastronomica: Journal of Food and Culture* 14, no 1: 22–31.

Kahle, Karen. 2018. "Farm the City." *Edible Ohio Valley*, 2018.

Kansas City Food Hub Working Group. 2014. "Kansas City Food Hub Feasibility Study." https://www.lincolnu.edu/c/document_library/get_file?uuid=fc230a11-68f7-4951 -a366-09f23333d169&groupId=145912.

Kansaspedia. 2012. "Junius G. Groves." Kansas State Historical Society. Updated December 2012. https://www.kshs.org/kansapedia/junius-g-groves/12075.

Kato, Yuki. 2015. "Gardeners, Locavores, Hipsters, and Residents: An Alternative Local Food Market's Potential for 'Community' Building." *Journal of Agriculture, Food Systems, and Community Development* 5, no. 1: 145–59.

———. 2013. "Not Just the Price of Food: Challenges of an Urban Agriculture Organization in Engaging Local Residents." *Sociological Inquiry* 83, no. 3: 369–91.

Kato, Yuki, and Laura McKinney. 2015. "Bringing Food Desert Residents to an Alternative Food Market: A Semi-Experimental Study of Impediments to Food Access." *Agriculture and Human Values* 32, no. 2: 215–27.

Katz, Michael. 1989. *The Undeserving Poor: From the War on Poverty to the War on Welfare*. New York: Pantheon.

Kayak, Anoop. 2006. "After Race: Ethnography, Race, and Post-Race Theory." *Ethnic and Racial Studies* 29, no. 3: 411–30.

Kearl, Michelle Kelsey. 2015. "'Is Gay the New Black?': An Intersectional Perspective on Social Movement Rhetoric in California's Proposition 8 Debate." *Communication and Critical/Cultural Studies* 12, no. 1: 63–82.

Kennedy, Liam. 2000. *Race and Space in Contemporary American Culture*. Edinburgh: Edinburgh University Press.

King, Martin Luther, Jr. 1963. "Letter from Birmingham Jail." Martin Luther King Jr. Papers Project. April 16, 1963.

King, Tiffany Lethabo. 2018. "Racial Ecologies: Black Landscapes in Flux." In *Racial Ecologies*. Seattle: University of Washington Press, 2018.

———. 2016. "The Labor of (Re)Reading Plantation Landscapes Fungible(Ly)." *Antipode* 48, no. 4: 1022–39.

Kingfisher, Catherine. 1996. *Western Welfare in Decline: Globalization and Women's Poverty*. Philadelphia: University of Pennsylvania Press, 2002.

———. *Women in the American Welfare Trap*. Philadelphia: University of Pennsylvania Press.

Kingfisher, Catherine. 2007. "Spatializing Neoliberalism: Articulations, Recapitulations, and (a Very Few) Alternatives." In *Neoliberalization: States, Networks, Peoples*, edited by Kim England and Kevin Ward. Oxford: Blackwell.

Kingsolver, Ann. 2002. "Poverty on Purpose: Life with the Free Marketeers." *Voices* 5, no. 1: 23–26.

Kirkland, Anna. 2010. "The Environmental Account of Obesity: A Case for Feminist Skepticism." *Signs: A Journal of Women in Culture and Society* 35, no. 4: 463–86.

Kobayashi, Audrey, and Linda Peake. 2011. "Racism Out of Place: Thoughts on Whiteness and an Antiracist Geography in the New Millennium." *New York* 90, no. 2: 392–403.

Kohl, Ellen, and Priscilla McCutcheon. 2014. "Kitchen Table Reflexivity: Negotiating Positionality through Everyday Talk." *Gender, Place and Culture*: 1–17.

Kolavalli, Chhaya. 2020. "Confronting Whiteness in Kansas City's Local Food Movement: Diversity Work and Discourse on Privilege and Power." *Gastronomica* 20, no. 1: 59–68.

———. 2019. "Whiteness and Food Charity: Experiences of Food Insecure African-American Kansas City Residents Navigating Nutrition Education Programs." *Human Organization* 78, no. 2: 99–109.

Kremer, Peleg, and Tracy L. DeLiberty. 2011. "Local Food Practices and Growing Potential: Mapping the Case of Philadelphia." *Applied Geography* 31: 1252–61.

Kumar, Sharanya, Bronkesh, Sheryl, and Catherine Loden. 2017. *An Invisible Problem: Food Insecurity: Devastating Consequences Go Far beyond Hunger*. Health Care Foundation of Greater Kansas City. https://healthforward.org/wp-content/uploads/2017/12/Food_Insecurity_White_Paper_2017.pdf

Lanza, Michael L. 1990. *Agrarianism and Reconstruction Politics: The Southern Homestead Act*. Baton Rouge: Louisiana State University Press.

Larchet, Nicolas. 2014. "Learning from the Corner Store: Food Reformers and the Black Urban Poor in a Southern US City." *Food, Culture & Society* 17, no. 3: 395–416.

Levkoe, Charles Z., and Abena Offeh-Gyimah. 2019. "Race, Privilege and the Exclusivity of Farm Internships: Ecological Agricultural Education and the Implications for Food Movements." *Environment and Planning E: Nature and Space*: 1–19.

Levkoe, Charles Z., Hammelman, Colleen, Reynolds, Kristin, Brown, Xavier, Chappell, M. Jahi, Salvador, Ricardo, and Beverly Wheeler. 2019. "Scholar-Activist Perspectives on Radical Food Geography: Collaborating through Food Justice and Food Sovereignty Praxis." *Human Geography*: 1–12.

Lewis, Oscar. 1966. "The Culture of Poverty." *Scientific American* 215, no. 4: 19–25.

Lippman, Rachel. 2020. "St Louis Launches Urban Ag Program in Neighborhoods North of Forest Park." *St. Louis Public Radio*, March 29, 2020. https://news.stlpublicradio .org/politics-issues/2020-03-29/st-louis-launches-urban-ag-program-in -neighborhoods-north-of-forest-park.

Lipsitz, G. 2007. "The Racialization of Space and the Spatialization of Race: Theorizing the Hidden Architecture of Landscape." *Landscape Journal* 26, no. 1: 10–23.

Lloyd, Richard. 2010. *Neo-Bohemia: Art and Commerce in the Postindustrial City*. New York: Routledge.

Logan, John R., and Harvey Molotch. 2007. *Urban Fortunes: The Political Economy of Place*. Berkeley: University of California Press.

Low, Setha. 2009. "Maintaining Whiteness: The Fear of Others and Niceness." *Transforming Anthropology* 17, no. 2: 79–92.

———. 2003. *Behind the Gates: Life, Security, and the Pursuit of Happiness in Fortress America*. London: Routledge.

———. 1996. "The Anthropology of Cities: Imagining and Theorizing the City." *Annual Review of Anthropology* 25, no. 1: 383–409.

Lyon-Callo, Vincent. 2004. *Inequality, Poverty, and Neoliberal Governance: Activist Ethnography in the Homeless Sheltering Industry*. Ontario: University of Toronto Press.

Lyson, Helena C. 2014. "Social Structural Location and Vocabularies of Participation: Fostering a Collective Identity in Urban Agriculture Activism." *Rural Sociology* 79, no. 3: 310–35.

Mancino, Lisa, and Jean Kinsey. 2008. "Is Dietary Knowledge Enough? Hunger, Stress, and Other Roadblocks to Healthy Eating." *USDA Economic Research Report* 62: 1–20.

Mares, Teresa M., and Devon G. Pena. 2010. "Urban Agriculture in the Making of Insurgent Spaces in Los Angeles and Seattle." In *Insurgent Public Space: Guerrilla Urbanism and the Remaking of Contemporary Cities*, edited by Jeffrey Hou. New York: Routledge.

Martin, Asa. 1913. *Our Negro Population: A Sociological Study of the Negroes of Kansas City, Missouri*. Kansas City, Mo.: Franklin Hudson.

Martin, David. 2016. "Once Again, City Leaders Are Trying to Find a Groove at 18th & Vine." *Pitch*, July 5, 2016.

Maskovsky, Jeff. 2014. "The Other War at Home: The Geopolitics of U.S. Poverty." *Urban Anthropology and Studies of Cultural Systems and World Economic Development* 30, no. 2: 215–38.

Massey, Douglass, and Nancy Denton. 1993. *American Apartheid: Segregation and the Making of the Underclass*. Cambridge, Mass.: Harvard University Press.

May, Reuben A. Buford. 2014. "When the Methodological Shoe Is on the Other Foot: African American Interviewer and White Interviewees." *Qualitative Sociology* 37, no. 1: 117–36.

Mazur, Laurie. 2017. "Milwaukee Is Showing How Urban Gardening Can Heal a City." *Civil Eats*, October 2017.

McClintock, Nathan. 2018a. "Cultivating (a) Sustainability Capital: Urban Agriculture, Eco-Gentrification, and the Uneven Valorization of Social Reproduction." *Annals of the American Association of Geographers* 108, no. 2: 579–90.

———. "Urban Agriculture, Racial Capitalism, and Resistance in the Settler-Colonial City." *Geography Compass* 12 (2018b): 1–16.

McClintock, Nathan, Christiana Miewald, and Eugene McCann. 2018. "The Politics of Urban Agriculture: Sustainability, Governance and Contestation." In *The Routledge Handbook on Spaces of Urban Politics*, edited by Andy Jonas, Byron Miller, Kevin Ward, and David Wilson, 361–74. Thousand Oaks, Calif.: SAGE.

McCutcheon, Priscilla. 2011. "Community Food Security 'For Us, by Us': The Nation of Islam and the Pan African Orthodox Christian Church," in *Cultivating Food Justice: Race, Class, and Sustainability*, edited by Alison Hope Alkon and Julian Agyeman, 177–96. Cambridge, Mass.: MIT Press.

McDowell, Sean. 2019. "Jackson County Executive Points to State Laws concerning Large Tax Assessments." *Fox4KC*, July 1, 2019.

McKinney, Laura, and Yuki Kato. 2017. "Community Context of Food Justice: Reflections on a Free Local Produce Program in a New Orleans Food Desert." *American Institute of Mathematical Sciences Agriculture and Food* 2, no. 2: 183–200.

McKittrick, Katherine. 2006. *Demonic Grounds: Black Women and the Cartographies of Struggle*. Minneapolis: University of Minnesota Press.

———. 2011. "On Plantations, Prisons, and a Black Sense of Place." *Social & Cultural Geography* 12, no. 8: 947–63.

McKittrick, Katherine, and Clyde Adrian Woods, eds. 2007. *Black Geographies and the Politics of Place*. Boston: South End.

Meenar, Mahbubur R, and Brandon M. Hoover. 2012. "Community Food Security via Urban Agriculture: Understanding People, Place, Economy, and Accessibility from a Food Justice Perspective." *Journal of Agriculture, Food Systems, and Community Development* 3, no. 1: 143–60.

Melly, Caroline. 2013. "Ethnography on the Road: Infrastructural Vision and the Unruly Present in Contemporary Dakar." *Africa* 83, no. 3: 385–402.

Miewald, Christiana, and Eugene McCann. 2014. "Foodscapes and the Geographies of Poverty: Sustenance, Strategy, and Politics in an Urban Neighborhood." *Antipode* 46, no. 2: 537–56.

Miraftab, Faranak. 2010. "Making Neo-liberal Governance: The Disempowering Work of Empowerment." *International Planning Studies* 9, no. 4: 239–59.

Miller, Cynthia, James Riccio, Nandita Verma, Stephen Nunez, Nadine Dechausay, and Edith Yang. 2015. "Testing a Conditional Cash Transfer Program in the U.S.: The Effects of the Family Rewards Program in New York City." *IZA Journal of Labor Policy* 4: 11.

Miller, Joseph. 2012. *The Problem of Slavery as History: A Global Approach*. New Haven: Yale University Press.

Mills, Charles W. 1997. *The Racial Contract*. Ithaca: Cornell University Press.

Miriani, Ronald. 2015. *Kansas City's City Market*. Kansas City, Mo.: Kansas City Public Library.

Missouri, City of Kansas City. 2015. "Article VI. Urban Agricultural Zone."

Mobley, Jane, and Whitnell Harris, Nancy. 1991. *A City Within a Park: One Hundred Years of Parks and Boulevards in Kansas City, Missouri.* Kansas City: Lowell.

Mohanty, Chandra, Ann Russo, and Lourdes Torres, eds. 1991. *Third World Women and the Politics of Feminism.* Bloomington: Indiana University Press.

Molotch, Harvey. 1976. "The City as a Growth Machine: Toward a Political Economy of Place." *American Journal of Sociology* 82, no. 2: 309–32.

Morgen, S., and L. Gonzales. 2008. "The Neoliberal American Dream as Daydream: Counter-Hegemonic Perspectives on Welfare Restructuring in the United States." *Critique of Anthropology* 28, no. 2: 219–36.

Muhammad, Khalil Gibran. 2010. *The Condemnation of Blackness.* Cambridge: Harvard University Press.

Narayan, Kirin. 2007. "How Native Is a 'Native' Anthropologist." *American Anthropologist* 95, no. 3: 671–86.

Newtown Florist Club Writing Collective (NFCWC). 2013. "Peas and Praxis: Organizing Food Justice through the Direct Action of the Newtown Florist Club." In *Geographies of Race and Food: Fields, Bodies, Markets,* edited by Rachel Slocum and Arun Saldanha, 137–56. New York: Ashgate.

Nuebeck, Kenneth J., and Noel A. Cazenave. 2001. *Welfare Racism: Playing the Race Card Against America's Poor.* New York: Routledge.

Notar, Beth E. 2012. "'Coming Out' to 'Hit the Road': Temporal, Spatial and Affective Mobilities of Taxi Drivers and Day Trippers in Kunming, China." *City and Society* 24, no. 3: 281–301.

Okongwu, Anne Francis, and Joan P. Mencher. 2000. "The Anthropology of Public Policy: Shifting Terrains." *Annual Review Anthropology* 29: 107–24.

Oliver, Melvin L., and Thomas M. Shapiro. 1997. *Black Wealth/White Wealth: A New Perspective on Racial Inequality.* New York: Routledge.

Omi, Michael, and Howard Winant. 1994. *Racial Formation in the United States from the 1960s to the 1990s.* London: Routledge.

Ortner, Sherry B. 2016. "Dark Anthropology and Its Others: Theory since the Eighties." *HAU: Journal of Ethnographic Theory* 6, no. 1: 47–73.

Paddock, Jessica. 2014. "Invoking Simplicity: 'Alternative' Food and the Reinvention of Distinction." *Sociologia Ruralis*: 1–19.

Paes-Sousa, Romulo, Leonor Maria Pacheco Santos, and Edina Shisue Miazaki. 2011. "Effects of a Conditional Cash Transfer Programme on Child Nutrition in Brazil." *Bulletin of the World Health Organization*, April 29, 2011.

Page, Enoch H. 2006."Toward a Unified Paradigm of Race." *American Anthropologist* 108, no. 3: 530–33.

Page-Reeves, Janet, ed. 2014. *Women Redefining the Experience of Food Insecurity: Life off the Edge of the Table.* London: Lexington.

Pager, Devah, Bruce Western, and Bart Bonikowski. 2009. "Discrimination in a Low-Wage Labor Market: A Field Experiment." *American Sociological Review* 74: 777–99.

Peck, Jamie, and Adam Tickell. 2002. "Neoliberalizing Space." *Antipode* 34, no. 3: 380–404.

Pena, Devon G. 2006. "Toward a Critical Political Ecology of Latina/o Urbanism." *Acequia Institute*: 1–25.

Penniman, Leah. 2018.*Farming While Black: Soul Fire Farm's Practical Guide to Libera-tion on the Land*. White River Junction, Vt.: Chelsea Green.

Perez, Jan, Patricia Allen, and Martha Brown. 2003. "Community Supported Agriculture on the Central Coast: The CSA Member Experience." Research Brief Number 1, Cen-ter for Agroecology and Sustainable Food Systems (CASFS), University of California, Santa Cruz.

Pettygrove, Margaret, and Rina Ghose. 2018. "From 'Rust Belt' to 'Fresh Coast': Remak-ing the City through Food Justice and Urban Agriculture." *Annals of the American As-sociation of Geographers* 108, no. 2: 591–603.

———. 2016. "Mapping Urban Geographies of Food and Dietary Health: A Synthesized Framework." *Geography Compass* 10, no. 6: 268–81.

Plake, Sarah. "Outrage Continues over Jackson County Property Tax Assessments." *KSHB Kansas City*, June 26.

Poppendieck, Janet. 1999. *Sweet Charity? Emergency Food and the End of Entitlement*. New York: Penguin.

Pulido, Laura. 2018. "Geographies of Race and Ethnicity III: Settler Colonialism and Nonnative People of Color." *Progress in Human Geography* 42, no. 2: 309–18.

———. 2017. "Geographies of Race and Ethnicity II: Environmental Racism, Racial Cap-italism and State-Sanctioned Violence." *Progress in Human Geography* 41, no. 4: 524–33.

Purifoy, Danielle M. and Louise Seamster. 2020. "Creative Extraction: Black Towns in White Space." *Environment and Planning D: Society and Space* 39, no. 1: 47–66.

Ramírez, Margaret Marietta. 2014. "The Elusive Inclusive: Black Food Geographies and Racialized Food Spaces." *Antipode* 47, no. 3: 748–69.

Randle, Aaron. 2017. "Is KC Social Scene for Whites Only? Young Blacks Say They're 'Tolerated,' Not Welcomed." *Kansas City Star*, September 17, 2017. http://www.kansas-city.com/entertainment/article173616176.html.

Razack, Sherene H., ed. 2002. *Race, Space, and the Law: Unmapping a White Settler Soci-ety*. Toronto: Between the Lines.

Reese, Ashanté M. 2019. *Black Food Geographies: Race, Self-Reliance, and Food Access in Washington D.C.* Chapel Hill: University of North Carolina Press.

———. 2018. "'We Will Not Perish; We're Going to Keep Flourishing': Race, Food Ac-cess, and Geographies of Self-Reliance." *Antipode* 50, no. 2: 407–24.

Reiley, Laura. 2021. "Agriculture Secretary Tom Vilsack Says Only 0.1 Percent of Trump Administration's Covid Farm Relief Went to Black Farmers." *Washington Post*, March 25, 2021. https://www.washingtonpost.com/business/2021/03/25/vilsack-interview -usda-rescue-plan/.

Ruben, Mathew. 2001. "Suburbanization and Urban Poverty under Neoliberalism." In *The New Poverty Studies: The Ethnography of Power, Politics, and the Impoverished People in the United States*, edited by Judith Goode and Jeff Maskovsky, 435-69. New York: New York University Press.

Reynolds, Kristin. 2014. "Disparity Despite Diversity: Social in Justice in New York City's Urban Agriculture System." *Antipode* 47, no. 1: 240–259.

Reynolds, Kristin, and Nevin Cohen. 2016. *Beyond the Kale: Urban Agriculture and So-cial Justice Activism in New York City*. Athens: University of Georgia Press.

Reynolds, Kristin, Block, Daniel R., Hammelman, Colleen, Jones, Brittany D., Gilbert, Jessica L., and Henry Herrera. 2020. "Envisioning Radical Food Geographies: Shared Learning and Praxis through the Food Justice Scholar-Activist/Activist Scholar Community of Practice." *Human Geography*: 1–16.

Robinson, Cedric J. 1983. *Black Marxism*. Chapel Hill: The University of North Carolina Press.

Rose, Daniel J. 2014. "Women's Knowledge and Experiences Obtaining Food in Low-Income Detroit Neighborhoods." In *Women Redefining the Experience of Food Insecurity: Life Off the Edge of the Table*, edited by Janet Page-Reeves. London: Lexington.

Rosol, Marit. 2012. "Community Volunteering as Neoliberal Strategy? Green Space Production in Berlin." *Antipode* 44, no. 1: 239–57.

Russell, Andrew, and Iain R. Edgar. 1998. "Research and Practice in the Anthropology of Welfare." In *The Anthropology of Welfare*, edited by Iain R. Edgar and Andrew Russell, 1–15. London: Routledge.

Rutland, Ted. 2018. *Displacing Blackness: Planning, Power, and Race in Twentieth-Century Halifax*. Toronto: University of Toronto Press.

Safransky, Sara. 2017a. "Land Justice as a Historical Diagnostic: Thinking with Detroit." *Annals of the American Association of Geographers*: 1–14.

———. 2017b. "Rethinking Land Struggle in the Postindustrial City." *Antipode* 49, no. 4: 1079–100.

———. 2014. "Greening the Urban Frontier: Race, Property, and Resettlement in Detroit." *Geoforum* 56: 37–48.

Sanchez-Otero, Gernan. 1993. "Neoliberalism and Its Discontents." *NACLA Report on the Americas* 26, no. 4: 18–21.

Sassen, Saskia. 2004. "The Global City." In *A Companion to the Anthropology of Politics*, edited by David Nugent and Joan Vincent. Oxford: Blackwell.

———. 2004b. "Going beyond the National State in the USA: The Politics of Minoritized Groups in Global Cities." *Diogenes* 203: 59–65.

Sbicca, Joshua. 2018. *Food Justice Now! Deepening the Roots of Social Struggle*. Minneapolis: University of Minnesota Press.

———. 2015a. "Food Labor, Economic Inequality, and the Imperfect Politics of Process in the Alternative Food Movement." *Agriculture and Human Values* 32, no. 4: 675–87.

———. 2015b. "Farming While Confronting the Other: The Production and Maintenance of Boundaries in the Borderlands." *Journal of Rural Studies* 39: 1–10.

———. 2012. "Growing Food Justice by Planting an Anti-Oppression Foundation: Opportunities and Obstacles for a Budding Social Movement." *Agriculture and Human Values* 29, no. 4: 455–66.

Sbicca, Joshua, and Justin Sean Myers. 2017. "Food Justice Racial Projects: Fighting Racial Neoliberalism from the Bay to the Big Apple." *Environmental Sociology* 3, no. 1: 30–41.

Sbicca, Joshua, Minkoff-Zern, Laura-Anne, And Shelby Coopwood. 2020. "'Because They Are Connected': Linking Structural Inequities in Farmworker Organizing." *Human Geography* 13, no. 3: 263–276.

Scanlon, Heather. 2015. "The Country Club Plaza, Our Retail Claim to Fame." *Squeezebox*, July 14, 2015.

Schein, Richard H. 2012. "Urban Form and Racial Order." *Urban Geography* 33, no. 7: 942–60.

———. 2006. *Landscape and Race in the United States*. New York: Routledge.

Schensul, Jean, Margaret LeCompte, Bonnie K. Nastasi, and Stephen P. Borgatti. 1999. *Enhanced Ethnographic Methods: Audiovisual Techniques, Focused Group Interviews, and Elicitation (Ethnographer's Toolkit)*. Lanham, Md.: AltaMira.

Schuller, Mark. 2012. *Killing with Kindness: Haiti, International Aid, and NGOs*. New Brunswick, N. J.: Rutgers University Press.

Schirmer, Sherry Lamb. 2002. *A City Divided: The Racial Landscape of Kansas City, 1900–1960*. Columbia: University of Missouri Press.

Schneider, Susan. 2013. "Discrimination at USDA: Response to New York Times." *Agricultural Law*, May 1, 2013.

Seamster, Louise, and Danielle Purifoy. 2020. "What Is Environmental Racism For? Place Based Harm and Relational Development." *Environmental Sociology* 22: 1–12.

Shannon, Jerry. 2014. "Food Deserts: Governing Obesity in the Neoliberal City." *Progress in Human Geography* 38, no. 2: 248–66.

Shaw, Wendy S. 2007. *Cities of Whiteness*. London: Wiley-Blackwell.

Sheller, Mimi. 2015. "Racialized Mobility Transitions in Philadelphia: Connecting Urban Sustainability and Transport Justice." *City & Society* 27, no. 1: 70–91.

Shortridge, James R. 2012. *Kansas City and How it Grew, 1822–2011*. Lawrence: University of Kansas Press.

Simpson, Michael, and Jen Bagelman. 2018. "Decolonizing Urban Political Ecologies: The Production of Nature in Settler Colonial Cities." Annals of the American Association of Geographers 108, no. 2 (2018): 1–11.

Singer, Merrill. 1994. "AIDS and the Health Crisis of the U.S. Urban Poor: The Perspective of Critical Medical Anthropology." *Social Science and Medicine* 39 no. 7: 931–48.

Slocum, Rachel. 2010. "Race in the Study of Food." *Progress in Human Geography* 35, no. 3: 303–27.

———. 2008. "Thinking Race through Corporeal Feminist Theory: Divisions and Intimacies at the Minneapolis Farmers' Market." *Social & Cultural Geography* 9 no. 8: 849–69.

———. 2007. "Whiteness, Space and Alternative Food Practice." *Geoforum* 38 no. 3: 520–33.

———. "Anti-Racist Practice and the Work of Community Food Organizations." *Antipode* 38, no. 2 (2006): 327–49.

Smith, Neil. 1996. *The New Urban Frontier: Gentrification and the Revanchist City*. London: Routledge.

Stanford, Lois. 2014. "Negotiating Food Security along the U.S.-Mexican Border: Social Strategies, Practice, and Networks among Mexican American Women." In *Women Redefining the Experience of Food Insecurity: Life off the Edge of the Table*, edited by Janet Page Reeves, 105–26. Lanham, Md.: Lexington Books.

Stovall, Maya, and Alex B. Hill. 2016. "Blackness in Post-Bankruptcy Detroit: Racial Politics and Public Discourse." *North American Dialogue* 19, no. 2: 117–27.

Stryker, Rachael, and González, Roberto J., eds. *Up, Down and Sideways: Anthropologists Trace the Pathways of Power*. New York: Berghahn.

Sugrue, Thomas J. 1996. *The Origins of the Urban Crisis: Race and Inequality in Postwar Detroit*. Princeton: Princeton University Press.

Susser, I. 1996. "The Construction of Poverty and Homelessness in US Cities." *Annual Review of Anthropology* 25: 411–35.

Suzuki, Yuka. 2017. *The Nature of Whiteness: Race, Animals, and Nation in Zimbabwe*. Seattle: University of Washington Press.

Tepper, Beverly J., Young-Suk Choi, and Rodolpho M. Nayga Jr. 1997. "Understanding Food Choice in Adult Men: Influence of Nutrition Knowledge, Food Beliefs and Dietary Restraint." *Food Quality and Preference* 8, no. 4: 307–17.

Thomas-Houston, Marilyn M. 2005. *"Stony the Road" to Change: Black Mississippians and the Culture of Social Relations*. Cambridge, U.K.: Cambridge University Press.

Thurow, Roger. 2013. "Soiled Legacy: Black Farmers Hit the Road to Confront a 'Cycle of Racism'—Many Lost Lands, Dignity, as USDA Denied Loans Whites Routinely Got." *Wall Street Journal*, May 28, 2013.

Trudeau, Dan. "Patient Capital and Reframing Value: Making New Urbanism Just Green Enough." 2018. In *Just Green Enough: Urban Development and Environmental Gentrification*, edited by Curran, Winifred, and Trina Hamilton, 227–38. New York: Routledge.

Turner, Margery Austin, Rob Santos, Diane K. Levy, Doug Wissoker, Claudia Aranda, Rob Pitingolo, and the Urban Institute. 2013. "Housing Discrimination Against Racial and Ethnic Minorities 2012." *Report prepared for U.S. Department of Housing and Urban Development*. Washington, D.C.: 1–77.

Twitty, Michael W. 2015. "Barbecue Is an American tradition—Of Enslaved Africans and Native Americans." *Guardian*, July 4, 2015.

U.S. Census Bureau; Quick Facts 2017. Table PST045216. https://www.census.gov/quickfacts/fact/table/US/PST045216. (4 September).

Van Sant, Levi. 2016. "When Local Comes to Town: Governing Local Agriculture in the South Carolina Lowcountry." *Capitalism Nature Socialism* 28, no. 2: 64–83.

Vasudevan, Pavithra. 2021. "Brown Scholar, Black Studies: On Suffering, Witness, and Materialist Relationality." In *Feminist Geography Unbound: Discomfort, Bodies, and Prefigured Futures*, edited by Banu Gokariksel, Michael Hawkins, Christopher Neubert, and Sara Smith. Morgantown: West Virginia University Press.

Wacquant, Loic. 2008. *Urban Outcasts: A Comparative Sociology of Advanced Marginality*. Cambridge: Polity.

Walker, Juliet, E. K. 1986. "Racism, Slavery, and Free Enterprise: Black Entrepreneurship in the United States before the Civil War." *Business History Review* 60, no. 3: 343–82.

Ware, Vron. 2015. *Beyond the Pale: White Women, Racism and History*. London: Verso.

Wedel, Janine R. 2004. "Blurring the State-Private Divide: Flex Organisations and the Decline of Accountability." In *Globalisation, Poverty and Conflict: A "Critical Development" Reader*, edited by Max Spoor, 217–38. Netherlands: Kluwer Academic.

Weiss, Brad. 2011. "Making Pigs Local: Discerning the Sensory Character of Place." *Cultural Anthropology* 26, no. 3: 438–61.

White, Monica. 2018. *Freedom Farmers: Agricultural Resistance and the Black Freedom Movement*. Chapel Hill: University of North Carolina Press.

———. 2017. "'A Pig and a Garden': Fannie Lou Hamer and the Freedom Farms Cooperative." *Food and Foodways* 25, no. 1: 20–39.

———. 2011a. "D-Town Farm: African American Resistance to Food Insecurity and the Transformation of Detroit." *Environmental Practice* 13, no. 4: 406–17.

———. 2011b. "Sisters of the Soil: Urban Gardening as Resistance in Detroit." *Race/Ethnicity: Multidisciplinary Global Contexts* 5, no. 1: 13–28.

Williams, Brett. 1996. "Babies and Banks: The "Reproductive Underclass" and the Raced, Gendered Masking of Debt." In *Race*, edited by Steven Gregory and Roger Sanjek, 348–65. New Brunswick, N.J.: Rutgers University Press.

Wilson, David. 2012. "Introduction—Racialization and the U.S. City." *Urban Geography* 33, no. 7: 940–41.

Wilson, David, and Roger Keil. 2008. "The Real Creative Class." *Social and Cultural Geography* 9, no. 8: 841–47.

Wilson, Topher. 2016. "Toad-a-Loop: A West Bottoms Mystery." *Squeezebox*, October 25, 2016.

Witt, Doris. 2004. *Black Hunger: Soul Food and America*. Minneapolis: University of Minnesota Press.

Young, William H., and Young, Nathan B. 1950. *Your Kansas City and Mine*. Kansas City, Mo.: Midwest Afro-American Genealogy Interest Coalition.

Zhang, Li. 2008. "Private Homes, Distinct Lifestyles: Performing a New Middle-Class." In *Privatizing China, Socialism from Afar*, edited by Li Zhang and Aihwa Ong, 23–40. Ithaca: Cornell University Press.

INDEX

apprenticeships, 132–33, 144

Black communities, 29, 47, 67, 86, 173, 177
Black diets, 26, 97, 105–7, 122
Black geographies, 13, 29, 140, 172, 185
Black land ownership, 130, 176–177, 178
Black neighborhoods, 46, 113, 154, 186, 198
blight, 1–17, passim; 68, 74, 85–91 passim;
   combat, 90–91; designations, 12, 85, 91;
   divergent understandings of, 183; and food
   insecurity, 82, 91; and vacancy, 62, 74;
   mentioned, 114, 188, 193
Brookside Market, 83–84, 137

certification, 83, 135–37; costs, 136, 143; organic,
   137
certified kitchen, 83, 136–37; market, 84
chefs, 76, 125–126, 142–46; local, 59, 138
City Beautiful, 39, 54, 153
City Market, 38, 55, 57, 59, 135
community gardens, 63, 65–70, 149–51, 159–60,
   195
community land trusts, 198–99
Community Supported Agriculture. *See* CSAs
Country Club Plaza, 28, 49, 58, 143. *See also*
   Nichols, J. C.
covenants, restrictive, 5, 12, 20, 131
CSAs (Community Supported Agriculture),
   138–39, 142–43

Daily Bread. *See* Our Daily Bread
diets, 63–65, 74, 96, 104–8, 121, 197; Black, 26,
   97, 105–7; Black, regulation of, 105; healthy,
   107; mentioned, 17, 185–90 passim

discrimination, 198; geographic evidence of, 60;
   in policy, 68, 127–28, 130, 141–42; by white
   homeowners, 20, 43, 48
disinvestment, 3, 14, 29, 55, 69–70, 73–74; East
   Side neighborhoods, 60; vacancy as driver
   of, 66–67; mentioned, 58, 86, 122
displacement, 8, 14, 28–29, 47, 51, 57; denial of,
   58; mentioned, 39, 45, 151, 153, 156–57
diversity work, 191, 194

East Side, Kansas City: Black residents,
   perspectives of, 14, 90–91, 112–15, 116,
   181–82, 185; entrepreneurship, 126;
   foodie, perspectives of, 60, 67–68, 73–75;
   gentrification of, 182–83; history of, 31,
   44–51;
economic development, 1, 53, 84, 91, 93; City's
   growth and, 28
Economic Development Corporation. *See* EDC
EDC (Economic Development Corporation),
   53, 55
enslaved people, 31, 33, 105
erasure, 13–14, 57, 74, 128, 181, 193; discursive,
   107–8, sociocultural, 28–29

Farmers and Friends, 71, 138, 141, 180, 190. *See
   also* Grow KC
farmers markets, 92–93, 95–97, 135–36, 160–62,
   165; sales, 142–43; vendors, 82–85, 135, 137,
   161
farm-to-table restaurants. *See* restaurants
Feast, 109–11, 113–23, 195, 204n4.2; food-
   insecure, 117–18, 192. *See also* The Pantry
Federal Housing Administration. *See* FHA

GEOGRAPHIES OF JUSTICE AND SOCIAL TRANSFORMATION

www.ingramcontent.com/pod-product-compliance
Lightning Source LLC
Chambersburg PA
CBHW010139270326
41926CB00022B/4501

* 9 7 8 0 8 2 0 3 6 4 0 9 4 *